Commodity Options

Commodity Options

Trading and Hedging Volatility in the World's Most Lucrative Market

Carley Garner and Paul Brittain

Vice President, Publisher: Tim Moore
Associate Publisher and Director of Marketing: Amy Neidlinger
Executive Editor: Jim Boyd
Editorial Assistant: Myesha Graham
Operations Manager: Gina Kanouse
Digital Marketing Manager: Julie Phifer
Publicity Manager: Laura Czaja
Assistant Marketing Manager: Megan Colvin
Cover Designer: Alan Clements
Managing Editor: Kristy Hart
Project Editor: Chelsey Marti
Copy Editor: Geneil Breeze
Proofreader: Kathy Ruiz
Indexer: Lisa Stumpf
Senior Compositor: Gloria Schurick
Manufacturing Buyer: Dan Uhrig

©2009 by Pearson Education, Inc.
Publishing as FT Press
Upper Saddle River, New Jersey 07458

FT Press offers excellent discounts on this book when ordered in quantity for bulk purchases or special sales. For more information, please contact U.S. Corporate and Government Sales, 1-800-382-3419, corpsales@pearsontechgroup.com. For sales outside the U.S., please contact International Sales at international@pearson.com.

Company and product names mentioned herein are the trademarks or registered trademarks of their respective owners.

Printed in the United States of America

First Printing January 2009

ISBN-10: 0-13-714286-2
ISBN-13: 978-0-13-714286-6

Pearson Education LTD.
Pearson Education Australia PTY, Limited.
Pearson Education Singapore, Pte. Ltd.
Pearson Education North Asia, Ltd.
Pearson Education Canada, Ltd.
Pearson Educación de Mexico, S.A. de C.V.
Pearson Education—Japan
Pearson Education Malaysia, Pte. Ltd.

Library of Congress Cataloging-in-Publication Data

Garner, Carley, 1977-
  Commodity options : trading and hedging volatility in the world's most lucrative market / Carley Garner and Paul Brittain.
     p. cm.
  Includes index.
  ISBN 0-13-714286-2 (hardback : alk. paper) 1. Commodity options. I. Brittain, Paul. II. Title.
  HG6046.G37 2009
  332.63'28—dc22
                                       2008026048

This book is dedicated to women in commodities

Contents

Acknowledgments

I would like to thank my friends and family for their undying support and believing in me in all that I do. More importantly, I am grateful to all those who doubted for giving me the motivation to keep going forward.

I am forever in debt to my parents (David, Robin and my uncle Ron) for being the examples I needed to develop the work ethic and integrity necessary to survive in the "real world."

Thanks to my brother Doug for being himself and for giving me the courage to do the same.

Thanks to Tracy for being there in both good times and bad, but most of all for having strong opinions and always standing up for what she believes in even if it wasn't convenient.

Thanks to Jim Boyd and FT Press for taking a chance on a first time author and being very supportive throughout the process.

All my clients are greatly appreciated not only for doing business with me but for teaching me along the way. If it weren't for their love of the markets and constant line of questioning none of this would have been possible. Specifically, I am grateful for the way they keep me on my toes and make me realize that there is life beyond the markets.
—Carley Garner

I would like to thank my wife Susan and my daughters Ashley, Sarah, and Angela for giving me the push I need to get out there in the markets everyday and my partner Carley Garner whose dedication, hard work, and overall greatness made this book happen. It's the people around you who truly define what you are.
—Paul Brittain

About the Author

Carley Garner—Senior Market Analyst and Broker, *Stocks & Commodities Magazine* Columnist and Industry Educator

Carley Garner is a Magna Cum Laude graduate of the University of Nevada, Las Vegas, from which she earned dual bachelor's degrees in both Finance and Accounting.

Upon completion of her education, Carley jumped into the options and futures industry with both feet and quickly became one of the most recognized names in the business. Within months in the business, she had published her first article in a nationally distributed periodical. She has been featured in the likes of *Stocks and Commodities*, *Futures*, *Active Trader*, *Option Trader*, *Your Trading Edge*, and *Pitnews Magazine*. Carley is often interviewed by news services such as Reuters and Dow Jones Newswire, and has been quoted by the *Investor's Business Daily* and *The Wall Street Journal*. She has also been known to participate in radio interviews. Her newsletters are widely distributed and focus on stock index and Treasury bond futures. She has worked hard to "garner" a loyal following and has become proactive in providing free trading education, for details visit www.CarleyGarnerTrading.com.

Paul Brittain—Commodity Broker and Trading Veteran

Paul Brittain entered the futures industry in 1983 and has experience in all aspects of the business. He has spent many years working with other market professionals to develop options and futures trading techniques suitable for almost every type of trader, individual, and commercial alike. He has been trading options on U.S. Exchanges since their inception, and is considered an options expert within the field.

Based on his belief that a knowledgeable trader is a happy and more successful trader, he began to focus on customer education. He shares his experience as well as the trading methods he's developed through his dealings in the business throughout his lengthy career. Mr. Brittain has made a name for himself on the seminar circuit and is often invited to speak on expert panels sponsored by national publications. His writing has been featured in several industry publications including *Futures* and *PitNews Magazine* and he has had his trading experiences profiled in *Trader Monthly* (June/July 2005 issue). Additionally, he has dedicated himself to free online trader education.

Currently he produces and publishes three newsletters, The Beast, The Big MacDaddy, and The Optionologist.

Visit www.CommodityOptionstheBook.com for additional information on the authors.

Introduction: An Unconventional but Effective Approach to Option Trading

Many books have been written about options on futures, unfortunately we believe that many of them are either contradictory or just a meandering compilation of exchange-generated research and material. In our opinion, much of the available literature leaves you even more confused than you were before you opened the book. With this book we hope that we have taken a step toward changing what has been the norm in this genre.

The biggest mistake that some authors make is to apply stock option theory to options on futures. It is a misguided perception to believe that an "option is an option." Although they are spelled the same, they aren't comparable. The nature of the underlying vehicle differs greatly, causing the options to take on completely different characteristics. After all, everybody agrees that trading stocks is different from trading futures, so why would anybody assume that trading options on stocks is synonymous with trading options on futures? It is our observation that authors of such material may simply be looking to capitalize on book and course sales through the recycling of stock option theory.

In the early 1980s the industry was dominated by operations that would now be referred to as a "long option only" houses. At the time, options on futures were not readily available in the United States. The instruments that were being sold were "dealer granted" precious metal options, which were based on actual metal holdings of the option writer at the time of the contract origination.

In the mid-1980s, the various exchanges started introducing options on futures known as *Exchange Traded Options* or *ETO*s. The explosion in this new trading vehicle was nothing short of breathtaking. Based on experience and speaking with others in the industry, during this time many retail customers were still limited to trading long option strategies. What we found is that they were either dissuaded by the brokerage firm or flatly refused permission to employ short option strategies. Several excuses were given, but the arguments were in our opinion one sided and weak. It has been said that the most common basis for keeping the public away from short options is the perceived risk. However, we believe that in most cases this view holds no merit mathematically or practically. Surely option selling is no more risky than trading futures contracts; after all you get the money up front. Nonetheless, insiders were making a lot of money selling options to individual traders, and they likely wanted to keep it that way.

In fact, much like the world of finance coined the term "cash cow" to describe a business with healthy income but requiring little maintenance, insiders have dubbed option selling the "cash cow" of the futures markets. However, we must point out that in business and trading alike, there are inherent risks, and the risks can be substantial, especially when trading commodities.

Fortunately, things have changed over the years. Option selling is now conveniently available to all traders who want to partake. The result appears to be a more level playing field for market participants.

Years of following the trading strategies and recommendations of the popular option trading gurus forced us to witness the disappointment of strictly long option strategies. Due to time decay and the tendency of markets to stay range bound, the strategy only delivered minimal random profits. Even those recommended by the so-called experts in the field didn't yield better results, at least as far as we could see.

Frustrated by the situation, we chose to take control of our and our clients' destinies by researching, developing, and implementing an option trading method that had the potential to capitalize on both the advantages and disadvantages of long option trading. To do so, we had to disregard the long option strategies instilled into many of us and take into consideration only what was real.

The descriptions of the trading methods used in this book were meant to be easily understood and, even more important, easy to employ. The strategies outlined throughout this book can be effective and efficient option plays; accordingly we and our clients use many of them on a daily basis. In fact, we are so comfortable that our approach to the markets is viable in the long run that we choose to publish our trades on the Internet and distribute them by e-mail *before* we execute them in the marketplace. We like to call this "The Good, the Bad, and the Ugly" because we show it to you without filters. We stand by a simple statement "Seeing is Believing"!!

Open Your Eyes to the Potential of Both Long and Short Option Trading

Commodity futures and options traders can buy or sell in any order without the additional burdens that stock option traders may face.

If you were buying soybean options throughout the spring and summer of 2003 or the summer of 2005 you may have experienced the hazards of a long option strategy. Once a market begins to "run," the extrinsic value of the options written against it explodes exponentially. This makes long option plays expensive. Along with the price tag, options buyers should be aware of the difficulties of turning a long option into a profit. If you are unfortunate enough to be a buyer after a sudden increase in volatility, you will begin losing money quickly if the volatility dies. It is common for long option traders to lose money as volatility decreases regardless of the direction of the market. Imagine the frustration of being right about the direction of the market and still not make money. Unfortunately, this is a common occurrence.

It has been said that trading futures is a zero sum game. In other words, there will be only one winner and one loser. This is not entirely correct given that the brokerage house always wins due to the transaction costs collected, unless of course there is an error in executing the trade. Essentially, a brokerage firm is paid a commission to ensure that your trade is effectively and efficiently executed. The amount of commission paid is determined by several factors such as the firm you have chosen, the level of service that you require, the funding in your account, and often the volume of trades that you execute. Regardless of whether your trades are winners or losers, the brokerage firm still gets to keep the commission earned by completing the transaction on your behalf.

Of course, a brokerage firm is not without risk. Not only are traders paying commission for the execution of the trade but they are also shifting the risk of error involved in placing the trade. Brokers are human too; errors are possible and in the long run probable. If your broker makes an error during the execution, she is liable for the damages and must make your account "right" again. Those paying online discount commission rates are charged less money per round turn in exchange for assuming the responsibility of their own trade placement and potential self-inflicted error.

However, for our purposes, we can assume a zero sum payout. Given this assumption, it should be clear to you that trading is a game of odds and probabilities.

If trading were easy, we would all quit our jobs and move to the Caribbean.

Simply conducting research, looking at a commodity chart, and picking the right market direction isn't enough to become a profitable trader. Instead, you will have to work hard at putting the odds in your favor. One way this can be done is by using a combination of long and short options to obtain an objective. Keep in mind that in trading simply putting the odds in your favor doesn't ensure success in the short term, but long-term success definitely wouldn't be possible without it.

Think about it this way, after you enter a trade the market will either go up, down, or sideways. The way that we see it, this gives you a 33% chance of picking the right direction, and if you are trading long options this probability goes down dramatically because you are working against a strict time frame. Wouldn't it be great if you could make money in two of these instances? Better yet; what if you could profit from a market regardless of the direction, or lack of for that matter? With a comprehensive understanding of options and how they work in conjunction with each other, it can be done. This is not to say that there are arbitrage opportunities, or that it will be easy; it won't. Wherever there is potential reward, you will find risk alongside. With the right techniques, however, you can considerably improve your odds of profitable trading.

"You win some, you lose some. And then there's that little-known category."
Al Gore

We hope that you walk away from this with a better understanding of how to use long and short options collectively to increase your likelihood of triumph in these treacherous markets. Throughout this book we will go into much more detail on how this can be done; but more important, we hope that you can apply the tools that we give you to the commodity markets in a profitable way.

Carley Garner and Paul Brittain

chapter 1

Option Basics: A Crash Course in Option Mechanics

The concept of options has been around for a long time. Ancient Romans, Greeks, and Phoenicians traded options based on outgoing cargoes from their local seaports. When used as a derivative of a financial instrument, an *option* is generally defined as a contract between two parties, a buyer and a seller, in which the buyer has the right but not the obligation to buy or sell the underlying asset at the denoted strike price. In the world of finance and trading, a *derivative* is defined as any asset in which its value is derived, or resulting, from the value of another asset. Likewise, the *underlying asset* is an asset on which the value of the derivative is dependent.

What Is an Option?

There are two types of options, a *call* option and a *put* option. Understanding what each of these is and how they work will help you determine when and how to use them. The buyer of an option pays a premium (payment) to the seller of an option for the right, not the obligation, to take delivery of the underlying futures contract (exercise). This financial value is treated as an asset, although eroding, to the option buyer and a liability to the seller.

There are two sides to every option trade, a buyer and a seller. Traders willing to accept considerable amounts of risk can write (or sell) options, collecting the premium and taking advantage of the well-known belief that more options than not expire worthless. The premium collected by a seller is seen as a liability until the option either is offset (by buying it back) or expires.

- **Call options**—Give the buyer the right, but not the obligation, to buy the underlying at the stated strike price within a specific period of time. Conversely, the seller of a call option is obligated to deliver a long position in the underlying futures contract from the strike price should the buyer choose to exercise the option. Essentially, this means that the seller would be forced to take a short position in the market upon expiration.

- **Put options**—Give the buyer the right, but not the obligation, to sell the underlying at the stated strike price within a specific period of time. The seller of a put option is obligated to deliver a short position from the strike price (accept a long futures position) in the case that the buyer chooses to exercise the option. Keep in mind that delivering a short futures contract simply means being long from the strike price.

	Call	Put	
Buy			Limited Risk
Sell			Unlimited Risk

To understand what an option is, you need to know the various components that comprise it. This next section explains the following:

- Strike price
- Intrinsic and extrinsic value
- Time value, volatility, and demand

Strike Price

Most literature doesn't include strike price as a factor of determining the extrinsic value of an option. It is assumed that the strike price is built into the supply and demand equation of the option. Naturally, a strike price closer-to-the-money will be in higher demand.

The *strike price* is the price at which the buyer of a call option has the right to purchase the futures contract, or the buyer of a put option has the right to sell a futures contract. This is also referred to as the *exercise price*.

The strike price is one of the biggest factors in determining both the extrinsic and intrinsic value of an option. Obviously, the closer the strike price is to the underlying futures contract the more valuable the option will be, even if there is no intrinsic value. This makes sense, because the closer the strike price is to the underlying market the better the odds are that the option will expire in-the-money and the higher the demand will be for the contract.

Intrinsic and Extrinsic Value: Components of an Option Price

The value of any given option is composed of two components:

● Intrinsic value
● Extrinsic value

Option Price=Intrinsic Value+Extrinsic Value

Intrinsic Value

Intrinsic value is what you would have if the option expiration was today.

The intrinsic value of an option is the amount that the market price is higher than the strike price for a call and lower than the strike for a put. In other words, the intrinsic value is the amount of money that the option would be worth if it expired today. For the option to have intrinsic value, the option must be in-the-money.

In-the-money and *out-of-the-money* are often falsely used by beginning traders. Many traders refer to a profitable option trade as being in-the-money. However, this is not the case. An option can be in-the-money and not profitable. Likewise it can be out-of-the-money and be a profitable trade.

Call options are described in the following way (see Figure 1.1):

● **In-the-money**—The futures price is above the strike price.

● **At-the-money**—The futures price is at the strike price.

● **Out-of-the-money**—The futures price is below the strike price.

It is important to know and understand the terminology involved in commodity trading; this could help to avoid costly mistakes stemming from miscommunication between you and your broker. In-the-money is a commonly misused term. Many beginning traders use this phrase to refer to a profitable trade rather than the intrinsic value of the position.

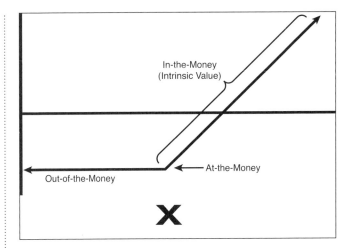

Figure 1.1 The intrinsic value of a call option

Put options are described in the following way (see Figure 1.2):

● **In-the-money**—The futures price is below the strike price.

● **At-the-money**—The futures price equals the strike price.

● **Out-of-the-money**—The futures price is above the strike price.

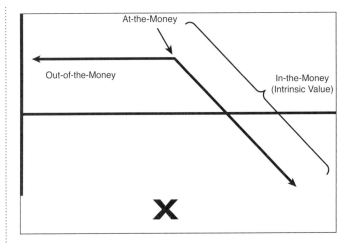

Figure 1.2 The intrinsic value of a put option

As shown in the Figure 1.3, the intrinsic value increases tick for tick as the market moves beyond the strike price of the option. In this case, it is a corn call option with a strike price of $2.70. With the market at $2.80 the option has an intrinsic value of 10 cents; with the market at $2.90 the option has an intrinsic value of 20 cents, and so on. It is important to realize that before expiration the option value will not be equal to the intrinsic value because it will also have extrinsic, or time, value.

The intrinsic value of an option can easily be calculated, but the extrinsic value of an option is impossible to estimate at any given time in the future other than expiration. This is because the extrinsic value is made of a combination of time, volatility, and demand.

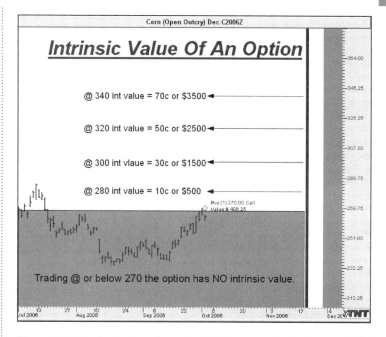

Figure 1.3 The intrinsic value of a $2.70 corn call with the market at various prices

Extrinsic Value

Extrinsic value is based on a combination of the strike price, time, volatility, and demand. We like to think of extrinsic value as the "icing on the cake." Due to the nature of its components, it is impossible to estimate extrinsic value. Beginning traders often ask questions such as, "If I buy a call and the market goes up *x* number of points, what will it be worth?" Unfortunately, the answer depends on factors that can't necessarily be measured quantitatively.

Extrinsic value is like "icing on the cake."

Example

If a trader buys a September $6.00 soybean call option for 10 cents in June with the underlying futures price at $5.80 and the market rallies to $6.00 by the beginning of July, the option will likely be worth much more than the original premium paid. After all, there will still be a lot of time value left on the option and the option is now at-the-money.

Example II

If a trader buys the same option, in the same circumstances, but it takes the underlying futures until August to reach $6.00, the trade will likely be a loser. More time premium would have eroded from the option value than it would have benefitted from the market being closer to the strike price.

As you can see, it is possible to be right in the direction of the market and still lose money on a long option trade. This is exactly why it is so difficult to make money as an option buyer. It is hard enough to be right, but direction is only the first obstacle.

The *extrinsic value* of an option is based on a combination of the following factors:

● Time

● Volatility

● Demand

Of these factors, time is the only predictable element. You know what they say, "Time waits for no man."

Throughout this book we will cover several hands-on examples to illustrate the risks and potential rewards involved with each strategy and scenario. It is important to realize that all calculations are based on the assumption that the trade is held until expiration. This is because at expiration the options will have no extrinsic value, which is nearly impossible to predict at any given point. At any time prior to expiration, the profit or loss experienced on the trade may be outside the original profit and loss parameters based on the price of the underlying contract at option expiration. This is especially true in the case of option spreads.

Time Value

The longer the amount of time until an option's expiration, the greater the time value of a particular option will be. This makes sense, because the longer the buyer possesses the right to exercise the option the more valuable that right is. Remember, in commodity trading anything can happen. It is not out of the question for a relatively worthless option to come to life and post abnormal gains (or losses for the seller) by expiration. Keep in mind that this is the exception rather than the rule, but it can and does happen.

Time value works against the buyer of an option, but works for the seller. This is because the time value portion of the option is constantly eroding until reaching zero at the time of expiration.

Volatility

If the price of the underlying futures contract is fluctuating considerably, there is both a greater profit and a greater loss potential. Thus options tend to be more expensive to buy when volatility is high. Likewise, sellers will collect more premium for a short option during times of inflated volatility. Of course, premiums are high for a reason—the risk and reward are equally magnified.

Volatility can be a double-edged sword. It can be lucrative if you are in a favorable position, but losses may be substantial if you happen to be on the opposite side. This is the case whether you are holding long or short options.

Trading Volatility

Because of the effect volatility has on option premium, it is a good idea to buy options when the market is quiet and sell them in times of high volatility. Those holding long options during an explosion in volatility have been known to enjoy impressive profits. On the other hand, short option traders may find themselves in a less than desirable position should they be in a market that experiences significant increases in volatility after they have entered a position.

Demand

If the number of traders willing to buy an option at a given price is greater than the number of traders willing to sell the same option, the value of that option appreciates. It is the nature of the option markets to experience high demand of call options in a market that is in an uptrend and high demand of put options in a downtrend. Thus, it is not uncommon to see overpriced options in such scenarios. An interesting phenomenon in the equity indices, put options are almost always priced high to comparative calls. This

Some traders look to be the contrarians of the masses. If everyone else seems to be buying the option, it may be time to sell it.

is partly due to equity holders hedging their portfolios along with the expectation that markets drop faster than they go up. You may have heard the concept of higher put valuation referred to in the context of a "volatility smile" or "skewed volatility." In the case of equity indices the implied volatility of an at-the-money option is often less than that of an out-of-the-money option, or negatively skewed. This is especially true in the case of distant strike priced puts; interestingly, this didn't seem to be the case until after the crash of 1987.

If you are unfamiliar with the term *implied volatility*, it is important to note that the term differs greatly from *market volatility* (often referred to as *historical volatility*). Historical or market volatility is a direct measure of price movement, while implied volatility is a function of the derivative value (option premium) itself rather than the underlier. Therefore, options with differing strike prices or expiration dates but based on the same underlier may have differing levels of implied volatility. The formal definition of implied volatility is, in its simplest form, the volatility implied by the market price of the option

Another component of demand is strike price.

Strike price is obviously one of the biggest factors in the market's determination of option value. The closer to the money an option is, the more valuable it is to the buyer and the riskier it is to the seller. This makes sense; people are willing to pay more for an option that seems to have a better chance of paying out than they would for an option that will most likely expire worthless. As we cover in great detail throughout this book, the delta value of an at-the-money option is 50 and has roughly 50 percent odds of expiring in-the-money.

The Art of Option Trading

It doesn't matter how you trade, or which indicators you use. The only thing that matters is whether you make money.

In options trading the infamous adage "There is more than one way to skin a cat" holds true. Many traders choose to ignore technical or charting tools and focus on market fundamentals. Yet others look strictly at chart formations to construct trades. Regardless of the market analysis tools used, we have found that traders can increase their odds of success by becoming familiar with option strategies other than buying outright calls or puts.

Over the next several chapters we outline and analyze many of the commonly used option strategies. We offer our opinion on when each strategy should be used and the manner in which we recommend using them. Additionally, we cover the associated risks and rewards of each of the differing approaches. As you will find, our interpretation of risk may be different than what you might find in alternative literature. For instance, in our opinion limited risk is not necessarily synonymous with less risk. In fact, in most cases limited risk, although it provides a cap to potential losses, may create a scenario in which your probability of loss is extremely great.

Although there are only four basic instruments in trading (long, short, call, put), there is a seemingly unlimited number of combinations of these components resulting in various levels of risk and reward. Throughout this book, we highlight some of the most common forms.

Each of the option trading styles mentioned throughout this text may or may not be appropriate for your risk tolerance. It is our goal to provide you with the information that you need to skew the odds away from the market insiders and toward you as a retail trader. Remember, roughly three out of four independent speculators walk away from the futures and options market with less money than he came with. However, only you can decide whether any of these trading methods are suitable for you and your piece of mind.

chapter 2

An Option Is an Option Is an Option…Think Again

After a trip to the local bookstore, it becomes quickly apparent that an abundance of stock option theory literature is available to those willing to invest the time. As the popularity of futures and options on futures trading has exploded, many of these writings have been renamed, repackaged, and reprinted by the authors in an attempt to transpose them into futures option theory. However, the assumption that trading options on futures and trading options on stocks can be synonymous is a gross misconception.

There is no argument that the characteristics and mechanics of the options themselves are identical. The definition of a call or put option doesn't change relative to the underlying asset. The payoff diagram, risk and reward calculations, and overall concept of trading them will always be the same, regardless of whether the options were written on stocks or commodities. Likewise, all options are derivatives (meaning that their value is derived from the value of something else), and they all have strike prices, expiration dates, and a standardized delivery process at expiration.

Despite all these similarities, a few glaring differences cannot be overlooked. Primary distinctions include the nature of the underlying medium and the logistics of market execution. There are also some peripheral disparities that you should be aware of such as tax treatment, regulators, and trading tools. This isn't to say that the strategies outlined in this book can't be used in the world of stocks, because they certainly can and are used by traders everyday. Even so, it is imperative that traders be aware of the characteristics of equities and futures and accordingly the mechanics involved in implementing these strategies.

Throughout this book we take what you thought you knew about option trading and challenge it, or at least offer an alternative perspective. For example, one of the most commonly touted concepts in option theory is the Greeks. As we discuss later, the Greeks are a set of mathematical equations developed to measure things such as volatility and time decay relative to option premium. While the fluidity of stock options aids in the accuracy of these calculations, we believe that differences such as liquidity mitigate the validity of concepts such as the Greeks in the world of trading options on futures.

Just as many lessons learned in grammar school aren't necessarily applied in the real world, a lot of option theory is just that—theory. It looks good on paper, but may not be effective in practice. Nonetheless, these are the opinions that we have developed based on observations that we have made, and we invite you to challenge our perception.

Options on Futures, aka Options on Commodities

As you have probably already realized, commodity options are written with a particular futures contract as the underlying. If you recall, the underlying asset is one on which the value of the option is dependent. Thus, just as a futures contract is a derivative (the value is derived from) of a physical commodity, an option is a derivative of a specific futures contract. As you have probably inferred, the price of an option is dependent on the price of, or fluctuation thereof, the futures contract that it is written against.

As the commodity markets become more and more popular, stock option traders are migrating to options on futures in droves. We have determined four primary distinctions between options on stocks and options on commodities that we strongly believe stock option traders must be aware of before attempting to make the transition. These distinguishing factors include differences in the underlying asset, the mechanics of the option markets, tax treatment of gains and losses, regulating bodies, and trading tools.

Differences in Underlying

The biggest distinguishing factor between options on futures contracts and options on stocks doesn't lie in the option itself but in the underlying asset that it is written against. Thus, instead of focusing on the difference in the option markets, first we are going to explore discrepancies regarding the underlying assets themselves. Some of the key disparities are leverage, expiration of the underlying, dividends, and liquidity, but before we explore some of these issues let's take a look into what a futures contract really is.

A futures contract is just what its name implies. It represents the *future* obligation to either accept or provide delivery of the underlying commodity. Specifically, it is a legally binding commitment to deliver or take delivery of a specified quantity and quality of a commodity at a price agreed on in the trading pit of an exchange. Contrary to what many assume, a commodity doesn't have to be grown or mined. Financial products such as currencies, bonds, and stock indices are also considered commodities because their futures contracts are standardized, thus they are considered fungible products. A *fungible product* is one in which the user wouldn't have a preference for one unit over the other.

Most futures market participants never come in contact with the underlying commodity.

Despite the fact that futures exchanges were developed to facilitate the delivery of actual commodities, less than 3% of market participants today ever see the underlying commodity that they are trading. Most market participants opt to offset their holdings prior to expiration, specifically the first notice day, to avoid delivery of the underlying commodity.

Although you will often hear negative banter regarding the risk of having 5,000 bushels of corn delivered to your doorstep, this is more hype than reality. In fact, even if you accidentally hold a contract beyond the first notice day and the exchange gives you notification of intent to deliver the underlying there is still a way out of it. Should this happen to you, your brokerage firm will retender the delivery.

The right to *retender* is the ability of a holder of a certain futures contract, who has received a notice of intention to deliver from the clearinghouse, to offer the notice for sale on the open market, thus offsetting the obligation to take delivery under the contract.

However, as a trader all you really need to know about retendering is that it will cost you a few hundred dollars in processing fees, but alleviates any obligation to accept delivery of the underlying commodity.

Most commodity traders never even see the underlying product. Rather than taking delivery of the commodity, they offset their position with the exchange.

As previously mentioned the key difference between equities and futures, in terms of an underlying asset to an option, lies in leverage, expiration of the underlying, dividends, and liquidity; let's take a closer look.

Leverage

Options of all types provide leverage to the buyer; however, futures contracts themselves are leveraged. Futures exchanges provide traders with the opportunity to buy or sell a contract (in any order) without being required to have the entire value of the contract on deposit.

In other words, an option on a stock provides traders with a leveraged trading vehicle; an option on a futures contract provides leverage to an already leveraged vehicle. As you can imagine, the combination of the two can be magnificent (if you are on the right side of the trade of course). Unfortunately, leverage is a double-edged sword and can work against the trader just as it works for them at times.

Should there be an explosion in volatility, we argue that the profit potential may be greater on commodity options. In the case of a powerful market move we believe that the explosion in premium may be magnified when the option is a derivative of a leveraged asset in relation to a nonleveraged asset. For a reasonably small amount of money you could potentially be holding a very leveraged position should the option become in-the-money.

With that said, it is important to realize that the overall effect of an option on a leveraged contract is mitigated a bit by the premium of the option. Assuming that the market is efficient, theory suggests that options are fairly priced to account for the probability that they will pay off at expiration. Consequently, traders bid the price of an option on a futures contract with the knowledge that the underlying is leveraged. Thus, an option on a futures contract with similar positioning and circumstances as an option on a stock will likely be comparatively more expensive. Note that this is based on our personal familiarity and interpretation and would be difficult to prove mathematically. This is because we are, in essence, trying to compare apples to oranges. In fact, many out there may not agree with our conclusions, but you are free to form your own opinion.

Let's take a look at a simplified example; a typical stock option has the potential to command 100 shares of stock should the option become in-the-money. If a share price is trading at $100, which is relatively high (ignoring the effects of the premium paid), the option has the potential to mimic the profit and loss diagram of holding approximately $10,000 of the underlying equity should the option become in-the-money.

In the same way, an option on a futures contract has the potential to fluctuate in price similar to that of the underlying futures contract itself should it become deeply in-the-money, or of course it becomes in-the-money and the buyer opts to exercise. By the way, it is almost never in the best interest of the option buyer to request that his long option be exercised. Doing so simply forfeits any time value still left in the premium.

Each commodity is different in terms of contract size and required margin, and thus the amount of leverage; but to give you an idea of how it works let's take a look at corn.

The value of a corn option, if in-the-money, would oscillate similarly to the underlying futures contract that represents the future delivery of 5,000 bushels of corn. Note that the deeper in-the-money that an option is, the higher the delta value will be or the more responsive it will be to the ebb and flow of the market. On the other hand, an option that is out-of-the-money will have a smaller delta value. We will go over this concept in more detail later in the chapter. Delta is an important concept to understand because it is one way of measuring the potential risk and reward of a given option trade.

With corn trading at $2.50, which is relatively low, the buyer of a futures contract is in essence trading about $12,500 of the underlying commodity. This is calculated by taking the price of the commodity and multiplying it by the dollar value per penny of the futures price ($50 x $2.50). In this case, and for most of the grain contracts, a corn futures contract makes or loses $50 per penny of price movement. At the time of this writing, corn was trading closer to $4.00 per bushel. This is a little out of the ordinary, but at that moment an in-the-money option contained the ability to take delivery of a futures contract from the strike price. That futures contract represented approximately $20,000 of the underlying commodity—now that is leverage. It is important to note that the margin for corn futures has been fluctuating between approximately $500 and $1,100. Thus, a trader buying or selling a futures contract is actually profiting or losing on the price fluctuation of about $20,000 worth of corn with a deposit of just over $1,000.

While the corn example was eye opening in terms of leverage, in reality it is a relatively lightly leveraged contract in comparison to others. To illustrate, an S&P futures contract represents over $350,000 with the S&P at 1430 and a margin requirement of about $20,000. An even more extreme example would be a bond future that represents the future delivery of $100,000 of the underlying and at the time of this writing was margined at about $1,800.

If all this talk about leverage has gotten you excited, that is our cue. It is our responsibility to jog your memory on the benefits and consequences of leveraged speculation. Leverage is a double-edged sword; it can work for you, and at times can be extremely enjoyable and even better, profitable. Unfortunately, leverage can also work against you. Try to imagine being long (you bought) a crude oil contract on a day in which OPEC announces an increase in output. A $1 move in the price of crude oil equates to a $1,000 profit or loss on a futures contract. A sharp reversal in prices against your position is anything but fun. In fact, if you were overleveraged it may leave you financially impaired and potentially out of the trading game forever.

As already mentioned, we argue that (likely because of the leverage involved) commodity options tend to be a little more expensive relative to similarly positioned stock options. This makes sense in that in the long run all options are priced fairly according to the information available to all market participants. It is no secret that a commodity option is written on a leveraged futures contract, thus the premium of the option is adjusted accordingly. Therefore, long option plays in the futures markets *may* be a little more challenging, but in line with the risk reward characteristics of markets and finance, the winners have the potential to be very large. We also remind you that this is our interpretation, and due to the sharp differences in stock and futures options characteristics these two instruments are difficult to compare in terms of which is the "better" leveraged.

Expiration

As brokers we have noted that the concept of expiration is one of the biggest hurdles that stock traders must overcome in their switch to options on futures. Of course, by definition options have an expiration date regardless of the underlying asset. However, unlike a stock, which has no finite life span, a futures contract does. Depending on the futures contract that you are trading, the contract may expire on the same date as the option, or it may be at a relatively proximate, but distant date.

As an option trader, the expiration or delivery date of the underlying futures contract is important in two major ways, but neither of them will ultimately play a role unless the option is held until expiration. For starters, a stock option trader will be assigned a stock position from the stated strike price if the trader's long option expires in-the-money. Once this occurs the trader is free to hold the newly acquired security indefinitely (unless of course the underlying is an index that is cash settled).

In the case of options on futures, the trader may or may not be free to take delivery of the underlying contract depending on the contract being traded and the corresponding expiration date. Remember, most commodities and options are traded on four major U.S. futures exchanges and until recently each of these was doing business completely exclusively of the others. Thus, there were, and still are, differing rules and procedures for option expiration. To add additional complexity, contracts traded on the same exchange may also have different specifications when it comes to option expiration due to the nature of the underlying futures contract.

For example, in the case of the Chicago Board of Trade's (CBOT) grain contracts, an option trader can be assigned the futures contract, but will then be forced to get out of the market in a matter of days to avoid either taking or making delivery of the actual commodity.

For those trading S&P options on the Chicago Mercantile Exchange (CME), option expiration means taking delivery of the underlying futures contract if your long option position is in-the-money, but not all months are treated the same.

Serial options are those that expire in months other than that of the futures contract. S&P futures are quarterly meaning that they expire in the months of March, June, September, and December. Accordingly, any options that expire in months other than the quarterlies—including January, February, April, and so on—are categorized as serial options. This is important because those long options that are exercised into futures contracts in a serial month will result in a futures position that can be held up to the expiration of the futures contract, which may be as distant as about two months away. Those exercised into a futures contract on a quarterly option will be subject to cash adjustment. This is because the quarterly option and the futures contract expire on the same day. We strongly believe that traders should avoid being subject to cash settlement in any of the stock index futures. It is difficult enough to trade a market in which you have at least some control over when and where you get out; imagine being "stuck" in a trade in which your profits or losses are partly dependent on a seemingly arbitrary calculation made by a third party—in other words, the cash settlement of the exchange.

While the notion of expiration is relatively simple, it seems to be often overlooked and can be extremely complicated at times, leaving traders vulnerable to costly mistakes. Traders who are in the habit of letting their options go into expiration and holding the underlying seem to have trouble getting out of the contract in time to avoid some type of inconvenience and monetary loss at the direct hand of a lack of understanding of the futures contract expiration procedures.

On the expiration date of the futures contract (not the option) the exchange matches all those that have held their contracts, either long (bought) or short (sold), and are looking to either take delivery of the commodity or deliver the underlying commodity. Those holding long positions are expected to take delivery, and those with short positions are expected to make delivery. At this point, the futures contract becomes completely untradable, often referred to by insiders as being "off the board." Prior to the expiration day, the exchange states a first notice day. On the first notice day, all market participants that are not intending to take part in the delivery process are encouraged to exit their positions. Those long futures beyond this date run the risk of being given a "delivery notice" by the exchange; those short futures aren't at risk of being forced to deliver the underlying until contract expiration but do face an increasingly illiquid market beyond the first notice day and should exit accordingly.

Too many beginning traders make the mistake of overlooking first notice day and end up receiving a delivery notice. Should you make this mistake, it is no reason to panic. Assuming that you don't want 5,000 bushels of corn delivered to you, you must notify your brokerage firm. The broker will then "retender" the delivery on your behalf. This involves some paperwork to be completed by your broker and a fee of about $300, paid by you of course, but avoids you being required to accept the actual underlying commodity.

Knowing and understanding the mechanics of the commodity may be the difference between profits and losses. If you are a beginning trader, you would most likely want to trade with a full service broker until you become familiar enough with the markets to avoid unnecessary and compromising situations over options or futures expiration. Stock traders don't have to worry about delivery, but if you are a responsible and organized commodity options trader neither will you.

Dividends

This appears obvious, but it seems to be disregarded by many. Unlike stocks, commodities pay no dividends. The only cash flow that occurs in commodity trading is upon exit of the trade, and hopefully the cash flow is positive. This concept becomes more critical when delving into option theory. Some of the most popular option models account for stock dividends, additionally most of them do not account for leverage.

Dividends, along with earnings growth, also play a role in the nature of the stock market. In theory, a share of stock is simply the expected value of future cash flows in the form of dividends or the expected sale price of a share at some point in the future. It is assumed that in the long run, the combined corporate earnings and thus dividends will grow exponentially. Accordingly, the stock market has a strong tendency to forge gains on a long-term basis, and this is one of the many reasons that commodities do not.

Liquidity

Whether it is through mutual fund investments or aggressive equity trading, it is probable that a majority of the people that you know are already holding some type of exposure in the stock market. On the other hand, if you are like most households it is likely that you haven't participated in the options and futures markets.

Although the popularity of futures, and options on futures, trading is growing exponentially, the overall involvement is still paltry in comparison to that of equities. Due to this lack of familiarity among the retail public, it is logical that the commodity markets in general do not experience the same level of trading volume that many stocks enjoy. Nonetheless, many futures and options contracts are extremely liquid. Knowing which contracts are and are not adequately liquid is key.

For reasons uncertain, beginning traders tend to be drawn to many of the markets that really shouldn't be traded by speculators (at least those without deep pockets). Conceivably this is because of movies such as *Trading Places*, or the tendency of the media to focus on these particular markets. Regardless of the source of the attraction, we believe that in many cases they are better off being avoided. Some of the commodities that we are referring to are lumber, rough rice, the CRB Index, and pork bellies. Other option markets such as orange juice, cocoa, and soybean oil are relatively thin but certainly tradable as long as proper care and caution are practiced. It is important that you work with an experienced broker. That person would ideally be able to steer you clear of potentially dangerously illiquid markets, or at least bring it to your attention before the lesson is learned the hard way.

Another important realization that should be made is in regard to newly developed markets. Exchanges are constantly adding new products to trade, and it often takes several years for the liquidity to pick up to a respectable level. Thus, be leery of participating in trading newer products.

A good example of this is housing index futures; on paper the idea seems ingenious but has yet to live up to expectations. The market was built on the premise that people could hedge the value of their homes, or participate in speculative real estate plays using the futures market. Unfortunately, most found that a lack of liquidity created extremely high transaction costs through widened bid/ask spreads. The *bid/ask spread* is simply the amount of compensation that the executing market maker requires for taking the other side of your trade. Remember, there are always going to be two price quotes, the one that you can buy (ask) at and the one that you can sell at (bid); the difference is the bid/ask spread.

Nature of Market and Price Movement

Many beginning futures traders are hesitant to consider selling a contract short, or betting on the downside of a commodity. This phenomenon is likely due to the fact that by nature the stock market tends to gain in value over time (see Figure 2.1). Sure, there will be ups and downs, but the overall direction is ultimately higher. As a result, we have been conditioned to believe that being long in a market (buying) is the natural position and is most comfortable for many. Wise stock traders realize that in a market that goes up more than it goes down, the odds are in favor of speculating on positive price movement, as opposed to betting on the downside. Additionally, those wanting to take bearish (short) positions in equities must borrow shares of stock from their brokerage firm to make the transaction and are faced with interest charges on the marginable balance. Of course, being responsible for interest charges creates yet another obstacle between the short seller and a profitable trade. Not only does the trader have to be accurate in the direction of the stock and the timing of the move, but the trader also must be so enough to overcome the interest charges incurred.

Unlike stocks, commodities tend to trade in a price envelope or trading range, as seen in the soybean chart shown in Figure 2.2. In the case of agricultural commodities, supply and demand work together to find an equilibrium price; despite how it sounds the equilibrium price is constantly changing with the supply and demand of the underlying commodity. There will be long-term price swings resulting in moves toward the upper range of the envelope, and subsequently toward the lower end. A cycle such as this may take several months, or even years, to develop; nonetheless, in theory the price action will be relatively sideways. With that said, the range of a particular commodity sometimes shifts higher to bring both the ceiling and the floor of the market to relatively higher levels. An example of this can be seen in the soybean market in the 1970s, and it may be possible that the 2007/2008 soybean rally may have been the market's way of shifting the trading range higher.

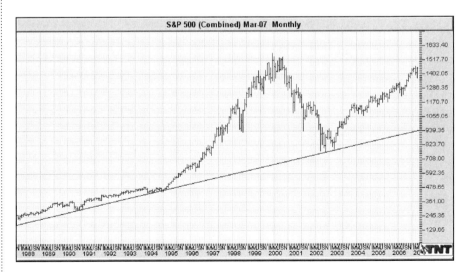

Figure 2.1   Long-term S&P futures chart

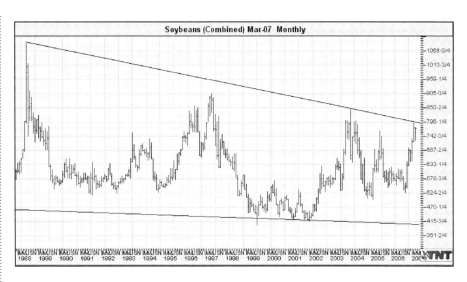

Figure 2.2 Commodities such as soybeans tend to trade in "envelopes" rather than a continuous uptrend as stocks have in the long-run.

Standardized Point Value

One of the most challenging aspects of trading commodity options is becoming familiar with how each contract is quoted. Stock and stock option prices are conveniently standardized, yet each commodity contract has a differing multiplier and format. This includes the number of digits in the strike price as well as the number of digits used to depict the premium paid or collected and the multiplier. In fact, in the case of treasuries, the futures and the options are quoted differently. Bond futures are quoted in terms of 32nds of a full handle or point, while the options are quoted in 64ths. This can be confusing for those in the industry, let alone a beginning trader. Keep in mind that all other commodity markets use the same multiplier for both the futures contract and option premium.

The most valuable commodity is knowledge.

Before you can understand the potential profit and loss on any given trade you must understand the rudiments. As you work your way through this book, you will become more comfortable with the pricing structure.

In the case of most commodity options or futures contracts, you simply multiply each tick by the assigned point value to determine the actual dollar amount of each contract, or more important the profit or loss on a given trade. To demonstrate, the multiplier in cotton is $5. If you go long December cotton from 57 cents, or 57.00, and are able to liquidate the position at 57.50 you would be profitable by $250 ($5 x 50).

Perhaps one of the most commonly traded complexes for traders migrating from stock options to options on futures is the grains. The grain complex is also one of the most confusing in terms of how they are quoted. The primary grain futures such as corn, soybeans, and wheat are quoted in cents per bushel with a minimum tick of a quarter of a cent. Each tick is denoted in fractions with 8 as the denominator. Thus, a quarter of a cent would be 2/8ths, a half of a cent would be 4/8ths, and three quarters of a cent would be 6/8ths. When looking at a quote screen, you never see the denominator, but it is assumed. If corn is trading at two dollars fifty-three and a quarter cents, it would be shown as 253'2. The multiplier for these contracts is $50, so for each penny that the market goes up or down, a futures position will make or lose $50.

Grain options are quoted in identical terms to the futures, but this isn't always the case. If you recall from the previous discussion, bond futures are quoted in 32nds while bond options are quoted in 64ths. In both cases, a full point value is equal to $1,000. From this you can see that one tick in the futures market is equal to $31.25 ($1000/32) and one tick in the options market is equal to $15.625 ($1000/64). On a quote screen 100 and 12 full points and 25/32nds would look something like this, 112'25. This can be interpreted as one hundred and twelve full handles and twenty-five thirty-seconds, making the total value of this contract $112,781.25.

We don't expect you to walk away from this explanation feeling confident in your ability to calculate profit and loss. We do, however, want to illustrate the complexities of commodities and point out that perhaps working with a full service broker until these concepts are second nature is an optimal solution.

Stock Splits

Corporations that issue stocks subsequently have the ability to issue stock splits, or reverse splits, to keep their share prices near what they believe to be an attractive level. This is important should they need to use the equity markets as a source of raising additional capital as an alternative to the debt market. Simply put, if a firm wanted to slash its share price in half, it could issue another share for each outstanding share. This doesn't decrease the value of the firm, but it does dilute the worth of each individual share. In *theory*, this could be done with commodities. For example, you could cut the contract size of corn to 2,500 bushels from 5,000, but in the eyes of the futures exchange it isn't worth the headache because doing so takes away from the standardization of contracts that has allowed the futures market to flourish. Instead of changing the parameters of a contract, most exchanges have begun offering "mini" sized versions of their most popular products. Contrasting from a stock split, the new mini contract doesn't replace the old one; instead they both trade side by side.

Difference in Option Markets

Along with differences in the underlying contracts, there are several important variations between the nature of, and logistics of execution in, the option markets themselves. Becoming familiar with these differences can be a primary factor in determining whether you trade profitably. Some of the discrepancies between the stock option market and the commodity options market are the number of listed products, technology, independent futures exchanges, liquidity, market participants, LEAPS, and getting accurate quotes.

Number of Products

The Chicago Board Options Exchange (CBOE) alone lists several hundred, if not thousands, stock options, and options on over 40 indices. Far fewer commodity options are offered (less than one hundred), and even fewer have enough liquidity to be efficiently traded based on our experience.

Technology: Electronic Versus Open Outcry

A majority of the daily stock option volume is executed electronically. In view of that, trade execution occurs without much human intervention. It is literally a matter of seconds between the time an order is placed online, executed by the exchange, and then confirmed to the customer.

Some futures exchanges, namely the CBOT and the CME, have made valiant efforts to provide electronic option markets. Volume on these electronic options is increasingly becoming popular, but more often than not when we execute options on futures we do so in an open outcry environment for reasons explained later. Trading open outcry options in some markets means that an order placed online will result in a ticket being printed at a trade desk located on the floor of the exchange; a runner then runs the order to a filling broker standing in the pit. Once the order is filled, a runner physically carries the fill back to the trade desk to be "key punched" into a computer to finally be reported to the customer. In our case, we often actually call directly to the trading floor and place our order with an executing firm. From there, the logistics are the same as an online order as outlined previously.

We typically prefer using the open outcry means of executing options simply because the futures exchanges haven't found a way to make multileg spreads work in an electronic environment. For example, if you wanted to bundle a combination of calls, puts, longs, and shorts together as a spread (or package deal), it wouldn't be possible via the electronic option exchange. However, when placing orders for individual options the electronic market is a convenient choice for commodity traders.

To an outsider, it may look disorganized and even a bit archaic; however, industry insiders like to refer to the trading pit as "organized chaos." Errors do occur, but believe it or not they are somewhat rare. Luckily, even for options traded in an open outcry pit modern technology has begun to take some of the steps out of execution. In some cases a runner has been replaced with computerized handheld trading "decks" similar to a PDA. Despite improvements, it is easy to see how cumbersome the process can be.

Independent Futures Exchanges

Almost all equity options are listed on more than one exchange. In the world of stocks, it is possible to buy an option on the CBOE and then offset it on a different exchange such as the PHLX.

Although some futures exchanges provide similar products, they are not interchangeable. The metals markets are a good example. The CBOT has listed gold and silver contracts identical to that traded on COMEX in terms of size and point value. However, the products trade exclusively on their corresponding exchanges. If you buy a gold option through COMEX, you wouldn't be able to offset it through the ECBOT metals market and vice versa.

Liquidity

More than four and a half million options contracts are traded daily on the CBOE alone, totaling a value in the billions in each trading session. The liquidity of some commodity options can be relatively spotty, making it crucial that you know which markets have enough participants to actively trade and which should be traded sparingly or avoided all together.

Nearly everybody you know likely owns stock or has interest in a mutual fund, but as pointed out before, not many people are aware of, let alone trading in, the futures markets. By osmosis, equity options tend to lure more participants than options on futures. Some option markets that we have found not to be liquid enough to effectively trade are lumber, pork bellies, rice, oats, and copper. There are many others, but these are among the illiquid option markets that tend to attract the most interest.

While option market liquidity can be determined by looking at the daily volume and open interest statistics, this information may not be enough. Through our experience, we have found that despite impressive open interest activity in option contracts such as natural gas and unleaded gasoline, they aren't necessarily convenient for small traders. Much of the open interest in these options is through bulk execution (hundreds or thousands of lots), but the day-to-day volume really isn't enough to provide the fluidity needed to keep the bid/ask spreads manageable and allow traders to easily enter and exit their positions. A full-service broker should be able to provide the appropriate guidance to avoid trading markets such as these without the proper disclosures of potential consequences.

Different Participants

As a trader, it can be helpful to understand who you are competing with. It has been said that the average investor spends 8 to 10 years trading stocks before she becomes comfortable enough to step into equity options. Those delving into trading options on futures tend to be considerably less experienced. In fact, through our observations as brokers we believe that many beginning commodity traders try their hand at options before ever executing a futures trade. Perhaps beginning futures traders are more susceptible to the "get rich quick" mentality and are lured by the perception of options having mitigated risks. Regardless, on the surface it appears as though commodity option traders as a whole may be less familiar over all with the markets that they are trading relative to stock option traders. This doesn't necessarily mean that the arena is less competitive, just different.

LEAPS

In the world of equities, there are contracts known as *LEAPS*, or *Long-Term Equity Anticipation Securities*. They trade like any other equity option, but they have an expiration date nine months or more into the future. In commodities, there are options trading with such maturities, but the industry has yet to distinctly label them.

Once again, liquidity becomes an important issue. Most stock investors, and even the IRS, consider holding a position for less than one year a short-term trade; conversely, a majority of futures traders refer to a two-month trade as long term. These differences in perception have an effect on the comparative liquidity of options with distant expiration dates. Hence, the liquidity in the distant option months tend to be relatively thin in the futures markets while equity options maintain their volume over longer time periods. We believe that an experienced broker will be able to tell you which contracts, and contract months, are safe to actively trade and which should be treated with caution.

Quote Availability

Because most stock options are traded electronically, quote vending is also electronic. The result is readily available quotes, including bid/ask spreads, at little or no cost. As previously discussed, although the futures industry is working diligently to increase the number of electronic options and their liquidity, commodity options are primarily traded in an open outcry environment. Thus, for live bid/ask quotes to be dispersed the exchange would need to have someone standing near the pit constantly entering bids and offers for each strike price. Logistically, this just isn't economically feasible.

With the exception of a *few* electronically traded markets, the exchanges don't provide real-time bid/ask quotes leaving retail commodity traders to rely on their broker to get accurate option pricing. Accordingly, those looking to trade options will likely have a more positive experience trading with a broker that has the ability to access the trading floor of the exchange to better service their clients.

Difference in Tax Treatment

The tax code can be extremely complicated, especially when it comes to paying taxes on investment income. We are merely going to mention some of the key differences in tax considerations between equity option trading and options on futures trading. You should consult with a tax professional for details and guidance.

Long-Term Versus Short-Term

Realized gains and losses for security traders are categorized as short-term capital gains, unless they are held for longer than 12 months. This is important because short-term gains are taxed at a higher rate than long-term and are treated differently in terms of carry over gains and losses, or those that are postponed to be claimed in future tax years.

Futures traders are allowed to blend their gains between the categories of long-term (60%) and short-term (40%). Thus, assuming that you traded profitably, you would be subject to a lesser tax liability as a futures trader than you would as an equity trader on positions held for less than a year. Consequently, you would be potentially subject to a higher tax liability as a futures trader than you would a stock trader in the case of positions held longer than a year. This is because commodity trades aren't categorized as long-term and short-term capital gains. Accordingly they wouldn't benefit from the lower tax rate that long-term capital gains normally enjoy; instead the trade would be taxed at the 60/40% blend between long-term and short-term gains. However, it is rare for commodity traders to hold a position for such a time period, and this likely wouldn't be much of a negative consequence of commodity trading.

Reporting Tax

Primarily due to the categorization of long-term gains versus short-term gains, stock traders must report a detailed trade-by-trade account of the activity in their accounts. For active traders this could be cumbersome. Additionally, for those who are speculating in the markets as opposed to investing, the tax burden tends to be heavier. After all, a majority of speculative positions likely span over a relatively short time period.

Futures traders enjoy the simplicity of reporting a lump sum profit or loss on their Schedule D as opposed to listing a trade-by-trade account of the year's activity. At the end of the year, the primary commodity account holder will receive a 1099 reporting his net profit or loss for the year. This number represents the bottom line of trading activity post all commissions and fees and is reported to the IRS for tax purposes.

Difference in Regulators

We all agree that regulation is a must in the financial markets. Without rules, chaos and manipulation would be rampant. The early stage of Forex is an example of what a lack of regulation could breed (false claims, misleading advertising, trading against the house, and so on).

As industry insiders, we are grateful for the protection and guidance regulatory bodies provide to investors as well as brokers and brokerage firms. As a market participant, it is important to realize which agency is overseeing the markets you are trading should an issue arise.

SEC

The equity markets, and thus equity options, are regulated by the Securities Exchange Commission (SEC), along with the NASD (formerly known as the National Association of Security Dealers). The NASD is a self-regulatory body responsible for regulation with oversight of the SEC. Both have a relatively tight hold in the industry and work diligently to ensure that proper protocol is being exercised by market participants.

NFA/CFTC

All domestic futures exchanges are regulated by the Commodity Futures Trading Commission (CFTC), along with the self-regulatory arm of the industry, the National Futures Association (NFA). Like the SEC and equities, these two agencies work together to ensure proper conduct in the futures industry. However, there is one key difference. The CFTC requires that Futures Commission Merchants (FCM) firms hold customer funds in an account segregated from their own. In other words, a futures brokerage firm is not allowed to co-mingle customer funds with its own. This stipulation was created in an attempt to prevent bankrupt FCMs from taking customer money down with them. It isn't foolproof, but it is a great safety measure and provides a sense of comfort to commodity traders.

Difference in Trading Tools

It is true that trading is trading regardless of the arena; however it might be necessary to adjust techniques and indicators to conform to differences in option markets. Thus, it might not be wise to assume stock trading gospel can be applied directly to commodity options. Instead, commodity option traders should gain a full understanding of the mechanics of the market at hand and act accordingly. This is not to imply that stock option tools are useless in commodities because that simply isn't the case. Nonetheless, we would like to point out to those looking to make the transition from stocks to commodities that caution is warranted and ignorance will not be blissful. Here are a few of the primary differences of which we believe you should be aware.

The Greeks

Many stock option traders swear by a group of mathematical equations known simply as the "Greeks"; included are the delta, gamma, theta, vega, and rho. The Greeks are used to mathematically estimate things such as the sensitivity in option value relative to price changes in the underlying, or the how the price of the option erodes over time.

In our opinion, experienced commodity option traders will likely agree, the Greeks are less reliable in the arena of options on futures. There is no harm in looking at the figures in your analysis, in fact we use delta values on a daily basis, but we believe that trading solely on your findings may lead to financial destruction.

Commodity options have a few characteristics that prevent the Greeks from offering traders the same insight that the equations may provide stock option traders. Through experience, we have come to believe that the primary short-coming to the theory of the Greeks is a lack of liquidity in many of the commodity options.

Options on futures are not always fluidly traded; this can cause intraday calculations of the Greeks to be nearly impossible. We argue that without a trade price of a specific option contract, the true value of the Greeks isn't attainable. In theory, you could determine the theoretical value using the Black and Scholes model, and then input that price into the Greek formulas, but you know what they say about functions.... You get out, what you put into them. The results are prone to being a useful estimate, but putting fictitious prices into a formula is ultimately going to give you a fabricated result.

As you will see from Figure 2.3, the liquidity of commodity options differs greatly between contracts. The example in Figure 2.3 illustrates an option chain for the June Australian dollar, which we believe to be relatively thin in volume. Later we will compare a stock option that we believe to also have relatively light volume. We are specifically choosing these market conditions to clearly make our point.

Looking at the option chain, the Last column denotes the last trade. This screen shot was taken within the last hour of the trading day, and only a handful of options had actually traded. Or perhaps more accurately, only a handful of fills had been reported. These particular options are traded in an open outcry environment; for a fill to show up on the quote screen, a runner on the floor would have had to deliver the fill to a floor clerk who would have had to type in the fill electronically. Knowing that these options have not traded during the session, it is obvious that the Greeks in this chain are based on theory and are not necessarily reality. The Th Value column denotes the theoretical value based on Black and Scholes. Aside from calling the floor for a bid/ask spread, this is the most accurate quote available for those trading open outcry options. As you will see in Figure 2.4, trading stock options can be a little more convenient when it comes to market information.

Also note the Open Int column in the Australian dollar options; this column represents the open interest for each strike price. As you can see, there is some action in each of the strike prices, but trading is relatively sparse. Such liquidity will work against the trader during both entry and exit of the trade. This doesn't mean that markets such as the Australian dollar are off limits; it simply means that traders should look to this market only if there is believed to be an attractive opportunity and if they are willing to accept the additional risk and responsibility that comes with participating in a thinner market.

Underlier			Last		Change		%Change		Last
AD M7			0.8345		0.0040		0.4816		

| DTE | Calls | | | | | | | | | Strike |
	Delta	Th Value	Old Set	Last	Gamma	Theta	Vega	Rho	Open Int	
52	0.9461	0.0497	0.0459		3.1153	0.0000	0.0003	0.0011	3	0.7850
52	0.9363	0.0448	0.0411		3.8350	0.0000	0.0004	0.0010	44	0.7900
52	0.9170	0.0401	0.0365		4.9366	0.0000	0.0004	0.0010	25	0.7950
52	0.8968	0.0354	0.0319		6.1654	0.0000	0.0005	0.0010	148	0.8000
52	0.8638	0.0310	0.0276		7.7430	0.0000	0.0007	0.0010	24	0.8050
52	0.8200	0.0268	0.0236		9.4510	0.0001	0.0008	0.0009	133	0.8100
52	0.7695	0.0228	0.0198		11.1696	0.0001	0.0009	0.0009	1	0.8150
52	0.7105	0.0190	0.0163		12.7861	0.0001	0.0011	0.0008	760	0.8200
52	0.6399	0.0155	0.0130	0.0159	13.7844	0.0001	0.0012	0.0007	13	0.8250
52	0.5680	0.0126	0.0104	0.0130	14.4455	0.0001	0.0012	0.0007	19	0.8300
52	0.4942	0.0101	0.0082	0.0100	15.2740	0.0001	0.0012	0.0006	14	0.8350
52	0.4193	0.0079	0.0063		14.8696	0.0001	0.0012	0.0005	13	0.8400
52	0.2716	0.0047	0.0037	0.0041	13.2428	0.0001	0.0010	0.0003	8	0.8500
52	0.1812	0.0027	0.0020		9.6330	0.0001	0.0008	0.0002	2	0.8600
										850.0000

Figure 2.3 A commodity option chain calculates the Greeks based on theoretical value rather than a true market value. This is because some commodity options do not see a constant flow of orders, and an accurate bid/ask spread isn't available on most contracts due to the fact that they are traded in an open outcry environment rather than an electronic market.

As shown in Figure 2.4, stock option traders enjoy a readily available bid/ask spread regardless of the liquidity of the contract. Also note that the Opint column seems to have a little more trader interest than our comparable commodity option. Although the commodity option chain in Figure 2.3 doesn't show the bid/ask spread, it is probable that the spreads are wider on a percentage basis than those shown in the stock option chain. For these reasons, it can be helpful to work with an experienced full-service commodity broker.

Calls							Strike	Puts						
Symbol	Last	Chg	Bid	Ask	Vol	Opint		Symbol	Last	Chg	Bid	Ask	Vol	Opint
May 07 Calls			(31 days to expiration)					NMX @ 130.69						**May 07 Puts**
NMXED	13.00	0	11.80	12.40	0	71 Trade	120.00	NMXQD	1.05	+0.05	0.95	1.15	2	629 Trade
NMXEE	8.60	0	8.00	8.50	0	392 Trade	125.00	NMXQE	2.15	0	2.05	2.25	0	1,032 Trade
NMXEF	5.50	+0.03	4.90	5.40	35	854 Trade	130.00	NMXQF	3.90	-0.10	4.00	4.20	2	525 Trade
NMXEG	3.40	0	2.75	3.10	0	374 Trade	135.00	NMXQG	6.60	0	6.80	7.10	0	263 Trade
NMXEH	1.60	-0.25	1.55	1.65	12	1,249 Trade	140.00	NMXQH	10.60	+1.20	10.50	10.70	80	244 Trade

Figure 2.4 Although the daily volume on this particular stock option isn't great, the transparency allows for more informed decisions. This is available to traders because stock options are primarily traded on an electronic exchange as opposed to open outcry.

This brings up another downfall in regard to Greeks on commodity options: the bid/ask spread. This problem doesn't necessarily occur in option contracts that are heavily traded, such as the S&P, grains, and interest rate products. However, if you are interested in buying or selling options in markets that don't have a lot of speculators, such as copper, lumber, or rough rice, we believe the Greeks to be less than dependable. We have found that the bid/ask spread on these options can be extremely wide and may result in completely unreliable calculations in the Greeks. Once again, this is our opinion and can be argued from many angles.

Similar to measures of standard deviation, a higher delta is equivalent to higher risk.

With that said, in our opinion, the delta value is the most useful of the Greeks when trading commodity options. An option's delta represents the change of an option price relative to the change in the underlying futures contract. This is the most commonly used option calculation, and for the purposes of commodity option trading, we find it to be the most useful. Delta values range between 0 and 1 when referring to a call option, or 0 and -1 in reference to a put option, with 1 being the most correlated to the underlying futures contract and 0 being least correlated.

$$\text{Delta} = \frac{\text{Change in Option Price}}{\text{Change in Underlying Futures}}$$

The delta of a call option has a positive value, while the delta of a put option has a negative value. This is because the value of a call option increases in value as the market goes up (positive correlation), while the value of a put option decreases as the market goes up (negative correlation). Once again, the delta measures the magnitude of this correlation.

For example, if an option has a delta value of .50, then for every point of movement in the underlying futures price the option will appreciate or depreciate by one-half of a point. The farther in-the-money the option becomes, the closer the delta will be to 1 (or -1 in the case of puts); the farther out-of-the-money an option is, the closer the delta will be to 0.

For instance, if July soybeans are trading at $6.00 per bushel, and a trader purchases a $6.00 July soybean call (an at-the-money call option) for a cost of 20 cents or $1,000, the option will immediately lose one-half of a cent in value if the futures market drops one full cent. Likewise, if the market jumps up a cent to $6.01 the option will gain one-half of a cent in value. This is a simplistic example in that it ignores the bid/ask spread paid to the floor broker, but gives you the basic idea of delta value and how an at-the-money option typically fluctuates with price movement.

Keep in mind that the delta value is sometimes thought of as an approximation of the probability that that particular option will expire in-the-money. Therefore, an at-the-money option typically has a delta of .50 or 50%. This means that at any given time there is about a fifty/fifty chance that the market will be higher or lower at sometime in the future, so it seems logical that an at-the-money option faces the same odds. The farther out-of-the-money the strike price of an option is, the smaller the reaction the option price will have to movement in the underlying futures contract, and the lower the probability that that option will expire in-the-money. Keep in mind, however, that this is a rough estimation and should be used only as a guideline. In other words, pay attention to this interpretation but don't rely on it.

Black and Scholes Option Models

The commonly used Black and Scholes model is based on six assumptions:

● The stock pays no dividend during the life of the option.

● European exercise terms are used.

- Markets are efficient.

- No commissions are charged.

- Interest rates remain constant and known.

- Returns are lognormally distributed.

Because of these assumptions, there are obvious downfalls in the model's ability to determine the fair value of a stock option, let alone a commodity option. Yet, the results tend to be close enough to the actual market price to be useful in both trading arenas, although, if you are trading an electronic option, having the theoretical value isn't really a necessity—after all you likely have access to a real-time quote feed. For those trading open outcry options, it is a must.

Perhaps the most prominent flaw in the Black and Scholes model is that it provides a single price that doesn't account for the bid/ask spread. In the case of stock options, the bid/ask spread may be minimal, but in certain commodity options the discrepancy may be magnified.

Those that have been involved with the futures markets for quite some time understand the approximate range of the spread and can determine an accurate option quote based on the value derived from the Black and Scholes model. This process likely seems cumbersome to those spoiled by the luxury of trading electronic stock options, but for those trading open outcry options it is a necessary step.

In our opinion, a good commodity broker will not only be able to give you an estimated bid/ask quote based on the hypothetical value but will also have contacts on the floor who will provide accurate option pricing. In effect, based on our experience, if a broker does a lot of business with a trading desk, the filling broker may be a little more "friendly," and this *may* translate into more efficient execution and possibly even tighter bid/ask spreads. As in life in general, when it comes to order execution it sometimes comes down to whom you know not what you know. Once again, these assumptions are based on firsthand observation and interpretation, but may or may not be seen in the same light by other industry insiders.

Conclusion

The goal of this chapter was to point out the key differences between trading options in the commodity markets as opposed to trading options on equities. Although, a call and a put have the same general function, it is imprudent to assume that differences in the underlying asset are irrelevant. Additionally, being familiar with the differences in logistics and market characteristics are necessary, especially for stock traders looking to migrate into the commodities markets.

With that said, the strategies outlined in this book can be used in all option trading environments. Whether you are trading stocks, futures, or even Forex, a call and a put have the same definition and can be used to form spreads in the same manner. Consequently, the success of the trading strategy is largely dependent on the trader's knowledge and understanding of the underlying asset and market characteristics.

When it comes to stock options comparative to futures options, one isn't necessarily better than the other; they are simply different. Most important, they should be approached and traded according to these differences and with the recognition that option trading, like any investing, involves risk. We will provide you with the option trading tools to trade in any arena, but it is up to you to apply them appropriately to the marketplace at hand.

chapter 3

Long Option Strategies

A long option strategy is just as the name implies. It might include the purchase of a single option or it might be the purchase of an option spread in the form of a strangle or a straddle. In any of these long option strategies, the risk is limited but the reward is theoretically unlimited. This chapter will focus on the mechanics of the strategy as well as the limitations. In our opinion, long option traders are forfeiting some of the probability of profit potential for a piece of mind. As a long option trader the absolute worst case scenario for a particular trade is to lose all the money spent on the option or option spread. This is true regardless of how wrong the original speculation turned out to be. As you will soon be aware, limited risk isn't necessarily synonymous with less risk.

Why Long Options Aren't Always a Great "Option"

Although many beginning traders are lured into buying options due to the fact that they involve limited risk, in many cases this may be the least desirable way to trade commodities. Despite the obvious benefit of limited risk, other factors work against the odds of success: primarily, time decay, the 80/20 rule, time limit, and market direction.

● **Time decay**—An option is an eroding asset. Every minute that passes has a negative effect on the value of any given option. Many people are under the assumption that if you buy a call option and the market goes up you will make money. This cannot be further from the truth. While it is possible for the value of an option to go up in a rising market, it is also possible for a call option to lose value in an ascending market.

> **Example**
>
> July corn is trading at $2.20 and a trader buys a $2.40 call for 5 cents or $250 with 2 months of time left. For the option to be profitable the market will have to climb enough to outpace time decay. If on the day of expiration the market is trading at $2.38, even though the market has rallied 18 cents from the day of purchase the option will expire worthless to result in the maximum loss of $250 plus commission and fees for the buyer. Depressing isn't it? The trader's speculation was correct, but the market didn't go far enough in the allotted time frame to return a profit at expiration. At any time prior to expiration, it is possible that the position would have been profitable, but that would depend on the extrinsic value. In other words, had the market rallied to $2.38 immediately after the option was purchased the trader likely could have sold the option for more than was originally paid because it would have had a significant amount of time value left in the price and the demand for that option would be high considering it would only be a few cents out-of-the-money.

> **Example**
>
> Let's use a variation of the preceding example. If the market was at $2.43 at the time of expiration, the trader would have incurred a loss of 2 cents or $100. Although the market climbed above the strike price of the call option, it didn't climb enough to overcome the premium paid for the option. We cover this in more detail as we go, but the break-even point of a long call option is equal to the strike price plus the premium paid. For this trader to have made his money back, without regard to transaction costs, the market would have had to be at $2.45 ($2.40+.05) at expiration.

- **80/20 rule**—The 80/20 rule has been used to describe several relationships in the world of finance, and commodities are no different. While we haven't done the math, it has been said that markets spend roughly 80% of the time trading within a defined range and 20% of the time changing that range. If this is true, it makes sense to apply this rule to long options. After all, it takes a substantial price move for a trader to be profitable on a long option at expiration. Many believe that as many as 80% of all options expire worthless. Several studies have been conducted on this theory, and the actual number seems to be closer 70% based on data provided by the CME. It is important to note that the CME's calculations were based on options held to expiration—of course many traders, whether long or short, don't hold their position until expiration. There are inherent flaws with the method of coming to this conclusion, but the idea is firm. More options than not expire worthless.

As outlined previously, even those options that expire in-the-money may not be worth enough to pay back the premium paid by the purchaser. This reason alone should be enough to deter you from being an option buyer. The only way to make money in the futures market is to put the odds in your favor. More often than not, simply buying options works against the goal of putting the probabilities to work for you instead of against you.

- **Time limit**—As we all know, options have an expiration date. This is an obvious disadvantage for long option traders. To be profitable, not only does the market have to go in the right direction to a minimum magnitude, but it has to do so within a specified time limit. Once again, this obstacle often means the difference between a trader that is right in the direction of the market winning or losing any given trade.

- **Market direction**— Upon entry there is approximately a 33% chance of the market going in the direction of a long option speculator. This makes perfect sense. After all, the market is either going to go up, down, or sideways. A call option buyer can *potentially* make money if the market goes up. However, in a directionless or bearish market climate, a long call option will quickly erode in value. This leaves a long option player with a 66% chance of loss immediately after entering the trade.

When to Use Long Options

Where some may see garbage, others see opportunity.

While we have attempted to show you the downfalls of long option strategies we don't recommend avoiding them at all times. Sometimes simply buying a call or put option is the advantageous thing to do. There are a few instances in which an experienced trader realizes that the potential reward outweighs the negative factors:

- **Low volatility**—During times of low market volatility, option premium can become extremely cheap. Additionally, markets tend to move in cycles. Periods of low volatility are often followed by periods of high volatility. If you are holding a long option during an explosion in volatility, the payoff could be tremendous. In fact, it is possible for the value of an option to increase even if the market isn't necessarily going in the direction that favors valuation. This may occur as the result of an increase in volatility.

- **Extreme prices**—If a market is trading near all-time highs or lows and you are predicting a violent reversal, an outright call or put option might be the best strategy. Option premium in the opposite direction of a strong trend tend to trade at a discount. Thus buying counter-trend options might be affordable and wise. After all, a long option play provides traders with unlimited profit potential and allows a potential trend reversal and a possible explosion in volatility pays off nicely if circumstances are favorable.

- **Quiet markets**—Certain markets tend to involve low levels of volatility or a decreased amount of leverage, which often keep option prices relatively low. Markets fitting this description often include corn, sugar, orange juice, and cocoa. It is important to remember, though, that markets are dynamic, and just because a particular market fits into this category today, doesn't necessarily mean that it has always been or always will be.

Alternative Uses of Long Option Strategies

The futures and options markets were originally derived to provide commercial firms a forum to hedge price risk; however, speculators often use the arena to hedge portfolio risk. For example, purchasing a long S&P put option can be compared to buying insurance against your stock portfolio. Just as car and life insurance can be expensive when compared to the monetary benefits reaped over the life of a policy, put buyers are often left with worthless protection. Nonetheless, should a catastrophic event occur the purchase of a put as a form of insurance may save a retirement portfolio from ruin.

Additionally, commodity futures traders may opt for long options as a method of limiting the risk of loss on a particular position or a portfolio of futures positions. For example, a commodity futures trader who has established a position and expects to hold it for the "long haul" may purchase out-of-the-money options to hedge the risk of an explosion in volatility in the opposite direction of the original trade. Once again, this is a form of insurance, and it can be costly. In some circumstances this may be a justifiable strategy, but we argue that, assuming you are financially capable, in many cases it pays to be the insurer not the insured. Justifiable circumstances may include low market volatility, extreme prices, quiet markets, or to protect profits on a futures position.

Use long option strategies sparingly, but remember that there are times in which buying options may be the most rational approach to trading a market.

Factoring in Commission

Transaction costs can vary widely depending on factors such as the chosen brokerage firm, the level of service requested, trading volume, and account size. Because there is such a large range in the level of commission paid, and for the sake of simplicity, we have opted to leave commission out of the calculations throughout this book. Of course, in the real world there are costs to executing trades.

On top of commission charged, the exchange also requires that a fee be paid on every option or futures contract executed. These are known as *exchange fees* and are nonnegotiable. However, if you are a sizable player, your brokerage firm may absorb the fee for you. This doesn't mean that the fees don't have to be paid; it simply means that your broker is using part of the commission charged to you to pay the exchange fee. Each exchange, in fact each market, has a different fee structure. Typically contracts executed electronically carry a lower fee than those executed in an open outcry environment. Likewise, the New York exchanges (New York Board of Trade, New York Mercantile Exchange, and Commodity Exchange or COMEX) tend to have higher exchange fees than those located in Chicago (CBOT, CME).

Some firms, not necessarily ethical albeit, charge clients $100 or more for a round turn commission. If you are unfamiliar with the term, *round turn* refers to both getting in and out of a position. In some instances you will hear it called a *round trip*, because it covers a trip around the market.

On the other hand, certain markets have inherently lower expenses and can be traded at a deep discount commission rate. Rates as low as $2 per round turn plus exchange fees are possible in some electronic markets.

As you can see, it would be nearly impossible to pick a commission rate to use in the calculations that encompasses the masses because the scale of commission rates is so large. However, we are going to show you how you can figure your individual commission rate into any of the calculations that we cover later in the book.

For every option purchased the commission and fees add to the cost; for every option sold the commission and fees subtract from the amount collected. While the examples contained in this text do not include transaction costs in the calculations due to the diverse nature of available rates, we will remind you throughout the book to include commission and fees into your figures.

Long Call Option

When to Use

- When you are very bullish.
- The more bullish you are the further out-of-the-money (higher strike price) you can buy.
- No other position can give you as much leverage with unlimited profit potential and limited downside risk.

Profit Profile

- Theoretically unlimited profit potential.
- The break-even at expiration is equal to the strike price plus the premium paid plus commission and fees

BE = Strike Price + Premium Paid + Transaction Costs

- For each point the market goes above break-even, the profit at expiration increases by one point.

Risk

- Buying an option involves limited risk.
- Losses are limited to the amount paid for the option plus the total transaction costs.
- Maximum loss is realized if the market is below strike price at expiration.

Example

In early 2004, sugar was one commodity that lured beginning traders into the futures markets (see Figure 3.1). At the time, the volatility was low enough that new traders could participate in the markets and experience the emotions of fear and greed without being exposed to unmanageable risk. In 2006, market conditions were drastically different. However, those traders savvy enough to take note of the low levels of volatility and react by buying call options prior to the price explosion would have faired extremely well. To illustrate, in May 2004, a trader could have purchased a March 2006 10 cent sugar call option for about $300. In January 2006, the value of that option would have peaked at nearly $11,000 based on theoretic value (see Figure 3.2). Naturally, it would have been unlikely that a trader liquidated the options at the peak; but as you can see the potential profits might have been substantial regardless of the exact exit point.

As an option buyer, your risk is limited, but it may be very high in terms of dollar amount and probability if you are buying the wrong options at the wrong time.

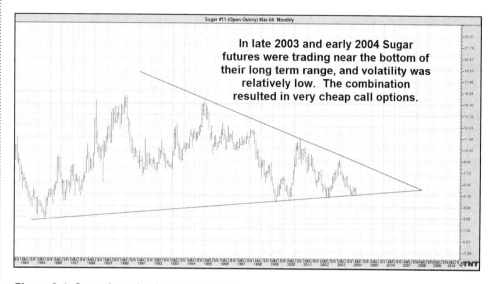

Figure 3.1 Sometimes buying options makes sense.

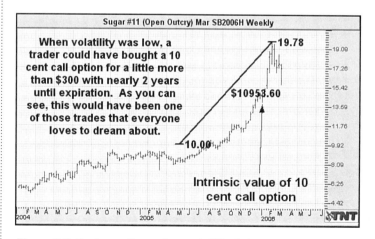

Figure 3.2 Buying options when volatility is low can sometimes pay off handsomely.

Long Put Option

When to Use

- When you are very bearish.
- The more bearish you are the further out-of-the-money (lower strike price) you can buy.
- No other position can give you as much leverage with unlimited profit potential and limited risk.

Profit Profile

- Theoretically unlimited profit potential.
- The break-even at expiration is equal to the strike price minus the premium paid minus the commission and fees

BE=Strike Price-Premium Paid-Transaction Costs

- For each point the market goes below break-even, the profit at expiration increases by one point.

Although buying options involves limited risk, depending on market conditions, the odds of profitability may be relatively low. For this reason, we don't advocate buying expensive options. The line in the sand that we have drawn to determine what is potentially too much to risk on a single long option is $500.

Risk

- Buying options involves limited risk.
- Losses are limited to the amount paid for the option plus the total transaction costs.
- Maximum loss is realized if the market is above the strike price at expiration.

Neutral Long Option Plays

Sometimes the best trades are the ones that you don't make.

Just as we are not big advocates of buying outright calls or puts we are typically not fans of straddling or strangling a market using long options. Such strategies involve buying both a call and a put in search of a substantial price move in either direction. These trades are inherently neutral, but in our opinion are most often losing propositions.

In fact, in many cases a long strangle or straddle play may offer worse odds than a directional long option play such as simply purchasing an outright call or put. This is because with a straddle or strangle, the underlying futures contract will have to move enough to make up for the premium spent on both the call *and* the put. By nature of the position, a trader can make money on only one side of the trade, either the call or the put. This means that the market will have to make a substantial move in one direction or the other to produce a profitable position.

Additionally, unlike a spread that involves short options, option strangle and straddle buyers must overcome the fact that time erosion is working against them on *both* legs of the trade. As you can imagine, this strategy requires exceptional market conditions in order to turn a profit. Simply put, under most circumstances there are far more efficient ways to trade the futures markets.

Simultaneously buying a call and buying a put seems to be a good idea on the surface, but once you start looking at the math you will find that more often than not, it is a difficult way to make money. While it is true that the trade can make money if the market goes up or down, it is also true that the market would have to make a tremendous move to return anything to the trader.

In the case of a long straddle or strangle, the break-even point is figured based on the premium paid for both options. Thus, as described previously, the trade makes money only if the market moves enough to make up twice the premium that would be needed if only one side of the strangle or straddle was purchased. As you can see in Figure 3.3, the market has to move substantially just to break even.

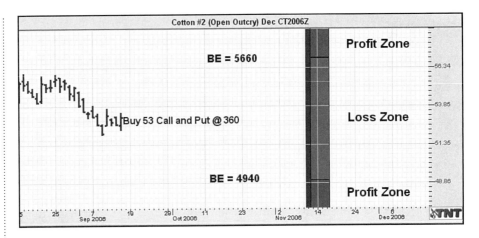

Figure 3.3 The break-even point of a long option straddle play can put the odds of success grossly against the trader.

In this case, the premium required to purchase the two options would be 360 points or $1,800. The exposure on this trade is limited to the premium paid, but who wants to risk $1,800 on one trade—especially one in which the odds of success are grossly against you? In this example, December cotton would have to rally above 56.60 or drop below 49.40 by expiration for this trade to be intrinsically profitable. Keep in mind that these figures don't include transaction costs, which act as another obstacle that may prevent the trade from making money.

Long Straddle

Buy an at-the-money put and call (same strike price).

When to Use

- You think the market will move sharply but don't know which direction to expect.
- A good position to use when the market has been flat or trading in a narrow range and a breakout is expected.

Profit Profile

- Profit potential is unlimited in either direction.
- At expiration the break-even is equal to the strike price plus or minus the *net* amount paid for the spread plus or minus the transaction costs

BE on Call Side=Strike Price+Premium Paid+Transaction Costs

BE on Put Side=Strike Price-Premium Paid-Transaction Costs

Risk

- Risk is limited to the amount paid for the spread plus commission and exchange fees.
- The maximum loss is reached if at expiration the market is at the strike price of the purchased options.

A trader that straddles the market is indifferent to the direction, but is anticipating a large move and a corresponding increase in volatility. The idea of making money whether the market goes up or down is desirable for many beginning traders. In their minds there is a fifty/fifty chance of the market going either up or down. If you have both a call and a put, how could you lose?

Well, there is a reason why people don't simply buy straddles and wait for the market to go either up or down. It is not that easy; the odds are stacked grossly against the position. While it is true that the trade is directionless and has the potential to make money regardless of the path that the market takes, it is highly unlikely that the underlying futures contract will move enough to cover the original cost of the trade.

For a straddle to be profitable at option expiration, the corresponding futures market would have to move enough to overcome the premium paid for both the put and the call (don't forget about commissions) in the time period allotted. A market's tendency to stay range-bound makes a move of this magnitude difficult to attain. Figure 3.4 illustrates the type of move necessary to return a profit to a straddle buyer.

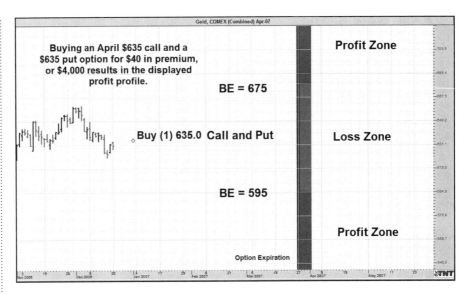

Figure 3.4 Long straddles can be very expensive. This creates a scenario in which it takes a considerable market move to return a profit to the straddle holder.

Similar to a simple long option, the break-even point of a long straddle is equal to the strike price of the long options plus or minus the premium paid. In the case of an upward bound market, the break-even point on the trade would be the long call option strike price plus the premium paid for both the long call and the long put along with transaction costs. In the case of a falling market, the straddle breaks-even at expiration if the market is trading below the strike price of the long put minus the premium paid for both the long call and the put minus commissions and fees. Simply put, for profit and loss purposes, the straddle should be treated as a single trade. Any profits sustained on one side of the trade must overcome losses suffered on the other side of the trade.

Example

Straddles are often used in a market that has been trading in a range for a prolonged period of time. Accordingly, market volatility is low, and the corresponding option premium should be relatively affordable.

Throughout mid-2006 the price of soybeans traded sideways. The market seemingly ignored the "spring rally" that typically occurs based on the planting and harvesting cycle of bean crops. Due to high levels of demand and other fundamental factors supporting prices, many speculators found themselves disappointed in the lack of volatility.

In August a trader may have assumed that the sideways market couldn't last forever. Unsure of the direction, and with November soybean futures trading near $6 per bushel, a trader could have purchased a November $6 straddle for 48 cents, or $2,400 (48 x $50).

Doing so would create a trade that will be profitable at expiration above $6.48 and below $5.52 ignoring transaction costs (see Figure 3.5). It is important to reiterate that this is only the case at expiration; anytime before expiration the profit or loss is dependent on the extrinsic value of the option which is based on time, volatility, and demand. These things cannot be predicted and therefore it is impossible to define a profit and loss zone for options that have not yet expired.

Figure 3.5 Straddles offer unlimited profit potential and limited risk, but a high probability of loss.

Simply put, unless the market rallies or drops 48 cents, the trader will experience a loss of up to the entire premium paid. The maximum loss occurs at the strike price of the call and put at expiration and is reduced by every tick that the market moves above or below that strike price, as illustrated in Figure 3.6.

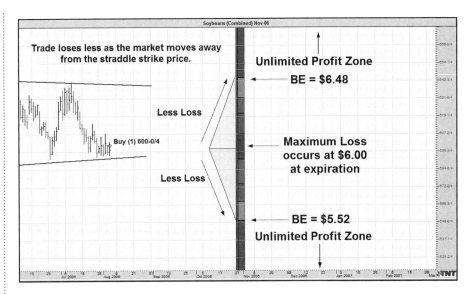

Figure 3.6 Losses are mitigated as the market moves away from the strike price of the straddle.

Should the market be trading in either of the profit zones at expiration, above $6.48 or below $5.52, the profit on the trade will be the magnitude in which the market is beyond the stated break-even points. In the case of a rally, if November soybeans are trading at $7.00 at expiration the profit on the trade would be $2,600 ((7.00-6.48) x $50).

If the market rallies, but not enough to reach the break-even point, the trader's loss is reduced by the distance that the market is above the strike price of the option. To illustrate, if November soybeans are trading at $6.15 per bushel at option expiration the option would be worth 15 cents. Thus, the trader would only lose 33 cents ($6.48-$6.15) or $1,650.

Likewise, if the market drops but is trading above the break-even point of $5.52 at expiration, the trader's loss is reduced by the distance that the market is below the strike price of the put. For example, if at option expiration November soy beans are trading at $5.75 the $6.00 put is intrinsically worth 25 cents, but the trade would be a loser in the amount of 23 cents or $1,150. This figure is derived by taking the total premium paid minus the intrinsic value of the option at expiration (48-25=23, 23 x $50=$1,150).

An alternative version of the straddle, and perhaps a trade with a slightly better probability of profit, is the long option strangle. The primary difference between a straddle and a strangle is the spacing of the strike prices. As you have learned, a *straddle* involves a long put and a long call with (ideally) the same strike price. A *strangle* entails the purchase of an out-of-the-money call and an out-of-the-money put.

Long Strangle

Buy out-of-the-money call.
Buy out-of-the-money put.

When to Use

● When the market is range bound and you expect it to break out by making a large move, but the direction is difficult to predict.

● Similar to a straddle but a generally less expensive strategy to implement; however, it should also be done during times of relatively low volatility and premium.

Profit Profile

● The profit potential is unlimited in either direction.

● The break-even point at expiration is equal to the strike price plus or minus the net cost of the spread plus or minus the transaction costs.

BE on Call Side=Strike Price+Premium Paid +Transaction Costs

BE on Put Side=Strike Price-Premium Paid-Transaction Costs

Risk

● Risk is limited to the amount paid for the position plus the transaction costs.

● Maximum loss is realized if at expiration the market is trading between the strike price of the put and the call.

Similar to a straddle, a trader who buys a strangle isn't attempting to pick a direction, the trader is simply looking for a sharp change in the price of the underlying futures contract. The odds of a strangle being profitable are nearly as dismal as that of a straddle; however the out of pocket expense, and thus the risk, are considerably lower. This is because instead of buying two at-the-money options, the trader is buying two out-of-the-money options. Once again, the market will have to move enough to cover the cost of both the call and the put, which would take a violent market move. In fact, the magnitude of the price movement in many cases would likely be similar to that of a straddle. Therefore, we believe that there really isn't much of a benefit to buying a straddle over a strangle other than the delta value. In other words, a straddle position will gain or lose value with more immediate market moves, while a long option strangle will have a positive change in value only after a fierce move in the market.

Figuring the break-even point of a long strangle is identical to that of a long straddle. You simply take the strike price and add or subtract the total premium paid. Once again, if the market rallies, your break-even on the strangle will be the strike price of the call option plus the premium paid for both the call and the put options plus commissions and fees paid. If the market is heading lower, the break-even is the strike price of the long put minus the premium paid for both the long call and the long put minus the transaction costs.

Also similar to the straddle, a strangle holder will lose less for every tick the market makes beyond the strike price but before the break-even point. If you recall, in a long option strategy your maximum risk is what you pay for the options. As illustrated in Figure 3.7, if the price of May corn was at $4.00 at the time of expiration, the trader would be in a losing trade, but it wouldn't be the maximum loss of 25 cents, the amount of premium paid for both the call and the put. Instead, the trader would lose the amount of total premium paid minus the intrinsic value (how far in-the-money the option is). In this case it would be 15 cents, or $750 (25 cents paid-10 cents intrinsic value=15 cents * $50=$750).

In its simplest form, the trade results in the maximum loss unless the market is above or below the strike price of the long options. As illustrated in Figure 3.8, the trader loses less as the market approaches the break-even point. Beyond the break-even point, the trader is profitable.

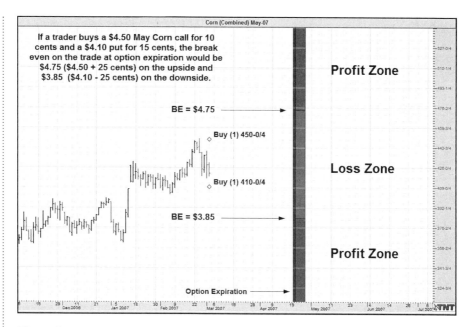

Figure 3.7 Like straddles, long strangles require a substantial market move just to break even. This leaves the odds of success on this type of strategy less than desirable in most instances.

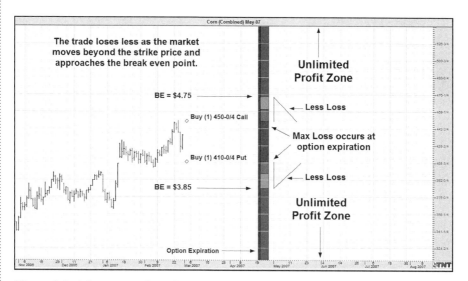

Figure 3.8 A long strangle suffers in a quiet market. Thus, a trader who simultaneously buys an out-of-the-money call and put is looking for an explosion in volatility and price.

Strangles require a substantial market move in order to return a profit at expiration, however in a quiet market or prior to an expected event this may be an optimal strategy.

Under normal circumstances we are not advocates of either an option straddle or an option strangle. However, there will always be exceptions. For instance, if a market has been experiencing very low levels of volatility for a prolonged period of time there may be an opportunity to buy an option straddle or strangle in anticipation of an increase in volatility.

Conclusion of Long Option Strategies

Buy it when you hate it and sell it when you love it!

In our opinion, it is wiser to buy an option when premium is discounted and sell it when premium is overpriced, or in equilibrium. It is as simple as stocking up on groceries when there is a big sale; during times of high or average prices you wish that you were the one selling the groceries rather than buying them.

Next time you read of the riches made by those who bought an option and cashed out with ten times their money or even more, sit back and think about the majority who paid their hard-earned money for an option that expired worthless. The frustration and helplessness of watching hundreds, or even thousands, of dollars evaporate is not an enviable experience.

Later in the book, we offer a few alternative ways to get involved with the commodity markets with what we believe to be better stacked odds.

chapter 4

Short Option Strategies

The concept of short option trading is typically not well received by beginning traders. Aside from the horror stories often highlighted in the media and trading literature, short option traders face limited profit potential and unlimited risk. From a logical standpoint, the idea of such a trading endeavor seems unattractive. However, it isn't a coincidence that the practice was once protected by industry insiders and retail accounts were discouraged to participate. If proper risk management techniques are defined and followed (this is much easier said than done), we believe that option selling delivers optimal odds of success for traders.

A premium collection strategy can be compared to a base-hit in baseball; while homeruns typically attract all the attention it is often the base-hits that win the game. If you are trading for the sake of ego, you likely won't be an effective option seller because you will constantly be searching for the "big one" and this is directly related to accepting unnecessary risks. If you are happy with simply "getting on base" and making money one trade at a time, this approach might fit your personality.

Why Sell Options?

Casinos bring in gaming revenue confident that over time they will collect more than they pay out in winnings. Similarly, insurance companies collect premiums in anticipation of the probability of future payouts. Option traders may benefit from the same logic by selling premium, thus capitalizing on probabilities as opposed to entering a position hoping to profit on a "long shot."

On the surface, selling options for the sole purpose of premium collection appears irrational. After all, the strategy involves unlimited risk and limited reward. However, a closer look into the reality of the options market reveals a side of short option trading that even the cynics cannot ignore. While many traders boast of huge profits attained from a single long option play, these stories are rare in comparison to those in which traders have lost some, or all, of the premium paid for an option.

In a sense, option buyers are throwing good money after bad in hunt of that one big market move that could return extraordinary profits. Given the fact that markets spend most of their time trading in a range, it is easy to see why few traders experience the abnormal returns that drew them to commodities in the first place.

A less exciting, but more fundamentally sound approach would be to attempt to profit from markets that are trading in a range. The most efficient means of taking advantage of a "quiet" market is to strangle the current range by selling calls above technical resistance and puts beneath support levels. With that said, just as insurance companies sometimes have to pay large claims and casinos have to honor jackpots, short option traders may find themselves on the wrong side of a runaway market. Such moves are moderately uncommon, but can be lucrative to option buyers and devastating to sellers. However, if you were an option seller during the 2007 commodity boom and stock market turbulence, it may have been a disappointing year. While on a long-term basis dramatic price moves are considered to be the exception, sometimes when it rains it pours.

The logic of a short option strategy such as a strangle, is similar to that of insurance companies. Insurers collect premiums on policies with the expectation of future payouts. By knowing the probability of a claim, they can calculate their expected return for assuming the risk of the policyholder. They are confident that overtime they will profit despite their obligation to pay claims from time to time.

By nature, options are a depreciating asset. Just as a new car buyer will find that the value of her purchase diminishes once the automobile is driven off of the seller's lot, an option buyer will find that the time value of a long option erodes with every passing minute.

It should be obvious by now that selling options provides traders with a long-term advantage over buyers. After all, the seller of a call option can profit in a declining market environment as well as a market that is trading sideways. In fact, it is possible for a seller of a call to also profit during times of increasing prices given that the market does so at a slow enough pace. A buyer can profit on a call option only if a market rallies over a specific price in a specific time limit.

Nonetheless, traders continue to be lured into long option strategies. This is likely due to the fact that purchasing an option provides traders with unlimited profit potential and the risk is limited to the premium paid. The peril in this type of approach, as mentioned before, lies in the fact that although one's losses are limited, it is highly likely that an option buyer will lose some or all of the value of the option.

Theoretically Unlimited Risk: Option Selling Can Be Hazardous to Your Wealth!

The exposure to unlimited losses faced by option writers is merely theoretical. In theory a market could go up forever, but it isn't likely, and if it does...hopefully you will get out of harm's way beforehand. Additionally, commodities can't go to zero, but they can drop significantly. However, due to the leverage and risk involved it is imperative to have adjustment strategies in place before a position is executed. While unlimited risk is technically impossible, it may *seem* unlimited during times of high market volatility, and the damage can be great.

"We are all just one trade away from humility." Marv, from the movie *Wall Street*

If there is one thing that we hope you walk away from this book with, it is the realization that trading commodities through options or futures, long or short, involves a considerable amount of risk exposure. Thus, it isn't necessarily suitable for everyone. Reading books day and night, relentlessly watching business news, and even years of paper-trading may not be enough to ensure profits. It is often said that trading is 95% mental and 5% mechanical, and we believe this to be true. Without the ability to control the powerful emotions, fear and greed, it is likely that you will become one of the "statistics."

Perhaps this is especially true with short option trading. While we argue that the probability of success in short option trading is higher than that of option buying or outright futures in the long run, in the short run short danger is imminent. Various studies (one being by the CME) suggest that the probability

of an option expiring worthless is in the neighborhood of 75%. As a short
option trader, this is key; with all else being equal this assumes a three in four
chance of success on any given trade. However, there are a lot of factors not
considered in this assumption that mitigate the odds of success greatly such as
transaction costs, explosions in volatility prior to expiration (these can cause
massive losses even if the option never becomes in-the-money), and margin
issues. These outside factors make it difficult to measure the probability of
options in general expiring worthless, but our experience leads us to believe that
sellers are still ahead of the game if they have the capital, knowledge, instinct,
and fortitude to survive the losing trades.

Short Option Fundamentals

An *option premium* is the actual market price of a particular option at a
particular time. It is necessary to understand the fundamentals of option pricing
before implementing a short option strategy. The exact price that buyers and
sellers are willing to accept at any given time is based on two major factors:
intrinsic and extrinsic value.

As mentioned in previous chapters, intrinsic value refers to whether an
option is in-the-money, and to what degree. For example, the intrinsic value of
a call is the amount of premium by which the futures price is above the strike
price (also known as *exercise price*). Accordingly, a put option is said to have
intrinsic value when the futures price dips below the strike price. An option with
intrinsic value is ideal for an option holder but creates an undesirable situation
for an option writer. If a short option expires in-the-money, the writer will be
assigned a corresponding position in the futures market from the strike price. In
the case of a short call, the seller will be short the futures from the stated strike
price. Conversely, a trader with a short put will be assigned a long futures
position from the strike price. It is often in the best interest of the option writer
to offset a position prior to expiration in the case of an in-the-money option.
Only those with extremely strong convictions about market direction should be
willing to hold an option to expiration with the expectation of being assigned a
futures position, although, in a thinly traded option market this may be more
desirable than trying to offset the option and being subject to significant bid/ask
spreads.

The Premise Behind Option Selling

Once again, the extrinsic value of an option is a combination of several factors, including the strike price relative to the futures price, market volatility, time to expiration, and demand for that particular option. The goal of an option seller is to profit from the erosion of extrinsic value. Times of increased volatility provide ideal circumstances for option sellers because option premiums are inflated. Similarly, it is helpful to understand that the depreciation of extrinsic value tends to accelerate during the last 30 days of an option's life creating an ideal scenario for option selling.

"Be fearful when others are greedy and greedy when others are fearful."
Warren Buffet

Preparing to Sell Options

Before executing short option trades, it is imperative that traders analyze the "climate" of the market. The three primary aspects of a market that should be considered are volatility, liquidity, and technical indicators.

Perhaps the most important factor to be considered is the liquidity of the market. With the possibility of unlimited risk, traders must be able to easily liquidate an unfavorable position. Options in thinly traded markets tend to have relatively wide bid/ask spreads, which will exaggerate losses and reduce profits. Markets that offer traders ample amounts of liquidity include stock indices such as the S&P 500, the Treasuries, and the grains such as corn and soybeans.

Volatility is an important component of extrinsic value. Naturally, during times of increased market volatility option premium tends to be inflated. This provides an advantage to sellers. Volatility can be determined by looking at indicators such as the historic volatility of the underlying futures contract or implied volatility of the option. Both of these are available on most charting software applications, but a simpler way is to view volatility visually is by overlaying Bollinger Bands on a price chart. Wider bands signal higher levels of volatility while narrow bands suggest a "tamer" market.

Technical Analysis and Option Selling

It doesn't matter how you trade, or which indicators you use. The only thing that matters is whether or not you make money.

Once a market is deemed suitable for option selling, a trader should scrutinize the technical condition to determine appropriate contract months and strike prices. Trading ranges as well as support and resistance levels should play a big part in short option placement.

The premise is logical: sell call options above significant technical resistance and sell puts below known support levels. Even if a market succeeds in penetrating known support and resistance, it will likely stall before doing so. To a short option trader, time is money. As mentioned before, every minute that passes diminishes the time value of an option.

Option Selling Isn't Always Appropriate

Depending on market conditions, it may not be appropriate to write strangles. The purpose of selling options is to increase the probability of success, thus attempts at picking tops and bottoms may be counterproductive depending on the level of market volatility. If a market is entrenched in a definitive uptrend, it may not make sense to sell calls. Doing so could lead to an unfavorable scenario but isn't necessarily off limits. On the other hand, selling puts on a downturn in a bull market can be extremely attractive. Even if the market does reverse and go against the short put position it probably won't do so immediately. Remember, as time goes by the extrinsic value of an option erodes providing profits to the seller and losses to the buyer. Keep in mind that each and every trade is situational and factors such as volatility and time can justify bending the rules.

Reverse Break-Even

Too many short option traders focus on their strike price relative to the underlying futures price, when in reality they should pay more attention to the intrinsic break-even point of the trade. Although it becomes an uncomfortable position, options that are in-the-money experience accelerated time value erosion. As long as the market stays within the intrinsic break-even it will be a profitable trade at expiration. Patience, combined with humility, is a virtue in short option trading. Even markets that are trending typically do not go straight up or straight down, providing opportunities for exiting uncomfortable short option positions. Traders will find that liquidation out of panic is often not the best remedy to the situation.

As with any trading method or system, losing trades are inevitable when trading short option strategies. Consequently it is important to point out that substantial risk is involved. Many option sellers fall victim to greed. Failure to cut losses short can put traders at the mercy of the market. While the odds of a profitable trade are in the favor of a premium seller, unlimited losses leave the seller extremely vulnerable. For this reason, adjustments and trading plans are crucial to maximizing the results and minimizing losses. Even the best traders and best-planned-out short option trades can find themselves in a compromising situation from time to time.

RBE Call Option=Strike Price+Premium Collected-Transaction Costs

RBE Put Option=Strike Price-Premium Collected+Transaction Costs

The Execution of Option Selling

Selling something before you own it can sometimes be a difficult concept to grasp, but it shouldn't be made any more difficult than it is. In essence, the exchange matches buyers and sellers of options just as they do buyers and sellers of futures contracts. Because the exchange involves an agreement rather than an actual good, there is no need to own anything. You simply must be willing to live up to your end of the agreement. Thus, a premium collector enters the trade by selling an option. To get out of the trade, or to offset the position, she plainly buys it back.

The premium collected by the seller of a call option is credited to the account up front. From there, the buyer of the option has to rely on the underlying futures market to rally enough to cover the cost of the option and then some to make it a profitable trade. If the market is trading below the strike price of the short call, the seller gets to keep the entire amount of cash that was credited when the option was sold. This is of course assuming that the position was held until expiration.

Again, when a trader sells an option, the cash value of the trader's trading account will increase by the amount of premium collected. This can sometimes mislead newer traders who are inexperienced when it comes to deciphering brokerage statements. For example, if a trader begins with a balance of $10,000 and sells an option worth $1,000, the cash balance in the account will increase to $11,000 (without regard to transaction costs). While the net liquidation value, or what would be left if all the trades in the account were offset, would stay the same ($10,000) until the option either changed in value or was bought back. In other words, even though the cash balance shows an increase in the account, the trader hasn't made any money.

It is important to pay close attention to the net liquidation value of your account; it is sometimes denoted as market value on a brokerage statement. Too often, option sellers incorrectly hone in on their cash position, which can be looked at as what the value of the account would be if all the short option positions that are currently open expire worthless. In this case, the cash value is a big "if" and shouldn't be assumed or expected.

A common mistake that traders make is to behave as though the cash credited to the account from the sale of an option is already theirs; this couldn't be further from the truth. The cash collected from the sale of an option is a liability, until the option either expires worthless or is offset.

As the option value erodes, it will take less of the cash originally collected to buy it back. The difference between the amount that it was sold for and the current price is the "paper" profit of the trade. However, until the option is actually bought back, or offset, there is still risk in the trade and should be considered a liability rather than an asset.

Exercise Me!

Beginning traders often express concern about the possibility of being exercised on a short option position. For those who are somewhat new to trading, the fear of being assigned a position in the futures market often overcomes rational thinking.

As an option seller, you would prefer to never have an option come into the money. Life would be much easier if you could sell premium, wait for expiration, and never have to make another decision. However, even though more options than not expire worthless, there will come a time in which your short option position becomes a loser, or even an extremely large loser. This may be in the form of a temporary penetration of your short option strike price, or it may be the big market move that tends to occur from time to time. These moves may not only threaten your trade but possibly even your entire account if the proper risk management techniques aren't employed—even then the markets show no mercy.

During these times of duress, you would be "lucky" to get a call from your broker informing you that the buyer of your short option is opting to exercise his holding. Even though being assigned a futures contract from your short option strike price may increase the delta (volatility) of your position, you will be better off than you would be if you chose to buy back the option to get out of the trade.

As we covered previously, the value of an option is made up of both intrinsic and extrinsic value. An option buyer could sell an option for the premium equivalent to the intrinsic *and* extrinsic value. Should he choose to exercise, he is giving up the extrinsic value of the option to take delivery of the underlying futures contract. As a long option holder, it would be a better (more lucrative) idea to simply sell the option, which would yield both the intrinsic and extrinsic value.

Despite common belief, being exercised as a short option trader isn't a burden, it is a benefit. Unfortunately for the short option trader, most long option traders understand this concept and simply sell their holding rather than exercise.

Knowing this, you can see that if the seller of an option receives an exercise notice she should be grateful. It is almost as if the buyer of the option has given the seller a gift...out of pity perhaps.

The Art of Adjustment

The vulnerability of short option positions requires traders to have keen instinct and adjustment abilities. There are a few basic ways to adjust, or protect, short options. Without knowledge and a great understanding of when to use, or better yet when not to use, these damage control techniques, traders will eventually be left in an account draining predicament. In fact, speculation in the futures markets can be treacherous. Even experienced short option traders with seemingly unlimited knowledge can find themselves at the mercy of the market.

Trading success or failure all comes down to a few decisions.

The Double-Out Rule

Before entering a short option trade, a trader should have already set her risk tolerance. In our opinion, this risk threshold should be double the amount of premium collected. For example, if you sell an option for $500 you would be looking to buy it back if the value of the option increased to $1,000 to realize a $500 loss on the trade. In other words, the trader would be risking a total of $500 in this example.

Identifying your tolerance for loss prior to entering provides a concrete mental stop loss intended to prompt traders to exit the trade before things get out of hand. This concept is based on the simple assumption that if an option doubles in value from the time that you originally sold it, it is time to admit that you were wrong by cutting your losses short and move on.

The double-out rule is simply a rule of thumb. In certain circumstances, it doesn't make sense to get out of a trade despite the fact that the premium has doubled. For instance, if a market appears to be near support or resistance and may quickly reverse, it might be in the best interest of the trader to continue along with the trade. Remember, there is a fine line between being a player and a prayer. You don't want to let losses get out of control . It is also important to realize that the markets can move extremely quickly, and there may be times in which the double-out point of your short option trade comes and goes much quicker than anyone could possibly react to.

Sell More Premium

An alternative to the double-out rule is to sell more premium. This is based on the premise that if you can "buy enough time" the market will eventually bounce in your favor. In essence, collecting more premium will allow the trader to move the break-even point to a more comfortable level. However, this can be risky because you are putting yourself in a position in which you will be playing catch up until the market finally moves in the desired direction or you run out of money.

Example

If a trader sold a 10,500 Dow put option for 50 points, or $500, the break-even at expiration on the trade would be 10,450 intrinsically. In other words, as long as the market is above 10,450 when the option expires the trade will be profitable. If the market drops against the position, but the trader still feels strongly that the market will eventually turn around the trader can sell more premium. If he sells the 10,400 put for 30 points, or $300, the reverse break-even point on the 10,500 put becomes 10,420 rather than the original 10,450.

There is a catch; doing this doubles the risk of the trade below 10,400 in the preceding example. Keep in mind, if the market continues to sink, this could mean excessive losses for the trader. This is similar to "doubling down" at a black jack table in Vegas.

Should the trader have deep enough pockets, it is theoretically possible to continue selling premium until the market finally turns around. After all, markets don't go straight up or straight down. However, doing so not only takes a sizable account, it also takes nerves of steel—but a little luck doesn't hurt.

Cover with a Futures Position

It is possible to hedge the risk on a short option by buying or selling a futures contract at or near the strike price of the short option to compensate for adverse price moves. In theory, this will protect your position tick for tick at expiration and allow the option seller to retain the entire premium collected should the option expire in-the-money. If this happens, the exchange will automatically assign a futures position, which will in turn offset the futures position that was executed to compensate for the troubled short option.

Example

If a trader is short a 9,500 Dow put, and the market drops to the strike price but looks to be heading even lower, it is possible to sell a futures contract to offset losses on the short put with gains on the short futures. In a perfect world, a trader could place a sell stop at 9,500, get filled at that price (no slippage), and the market would continue lower. Should the market stay below 9,500, at expiration the trader would have lost the exact number of points intrinsically on the short put than was made on the short futures contract. As a result of the market being below 9,500 at expiration, the trader would be assigned a long futures position from 9,500. At this point, the long futures and the short futures would offset each other. The trader would be left with the original premium collected minus commission as his reward.

As we all know, trades don't always go as planned. In fact, they almost never do. Let's take a closer look at an example in which the circumstances weren't so favorable.

Example

Imagine that the same trader short the same 9,500 put sold a futures contract at 9,500, but instead of the market continuing to descend it found a bottom and forged a rally. In this instance, it is possible for the trader to be losing on both the short option as well as the short futures. In fact, the short futures position would likely be losing more than the short put would be gaining back. Talk about frustrating.

Ratio Writes

This concept is covered in more detail later in the book, but it is important that you understand that this is a viable alternative to protecting a short option position. In its simplest form, a ratio spread involves one long option and two short options farther out-of-the-money. If your goal is to protect a short option trade, a one by two may often be the answer. It is highly possible that this trade can be executed at even money or a small credit. In the case of a small credit, the trader's reverse break-even would be pushed outward to a more favorable position. With that said, a ratio write may actually add risk should the market continue to go against the position. (See Chapter 7, "Synthetic Swing Trading," for additional details on ratio spreads.)

Short Call Option

When to Use

- When you believe the market is *not* going up (bearish).
- The strength of your belief determines what strike prices you should sell.
- Sell out-of-the-money options (higher strike prices) if you believe prices are not going up.
- Sell at-the-money options (at current price) if you strongly believe prices are not going up. *This is typically not a recommended strategy.*
- Sell in-the-money options (below current price) if you strongly believe market prices will fall. *This is not a recommended strategy.*

Profit Profile

- The potential profit is limited to the premium collected minus the transaction costs.
- Your reverse break-even point at expiration equals strike price plus the premium collected minus the transaction costs.

RBE=Strike Price+Premium Collected-Transaction Costs

- Trade profit is maximized if market expires below strike price.

Risk

- Exposes trader to unlimited risk; thus, these positions need to be watched closely.

- Your losses increase if the market rises faster than the time decay erodes the option value.

- The market trading above the reverse break-even is equivalent to being short the futures contract.

- At expiration your losses increase by one point for each point the market moves above the reverse break-even point on top of your transaction costs.

The seller of a call option is bearish the market and expects that the underlying futures contract will be trading at or below the strike price of the short call at option expiration. The buyer of the option provides the seller with a premium in exchange for the "option" to buy the underlying futures contract at the strike price.

Due to the nature of the transaction, the option seller gets the money up front. It is the seller's money to lose and the buyer's money to make back. As long as the underlying futures contract is below the strike price at expiration, the seller gets to keep the entire amount collected. If the market is above the strike price at expiration, the seller begins giving up profits until running out of premium, at which point the seller is losing money. Exactly where the option seller stops simply giving up the amount of premium collected and then losing money is known as the *reverse break-even point*.

Just as the buyer of an option should know where the market must go for the trade to be profitable at expiration, the option seller should have pinpointed where the trade stops being profitable. As shown previously, the reverse break-even of a short call option is equal to the strike price plus the premium collected minus commissions and exchange fees.

Figure 4.1 visually expresses the reverse break-even, and the profit and loss potential relative to this point. The chart is based on selling a $6.60 wheat call for 21½ cents. Those familiar with commodities and commodity pricing, realize that this was historically an extremely high level for wheat but an unbelievable rally in 2007 brought the market to unfathomable heights. However, something similar to this trade would have been possible in the spring of 2007.

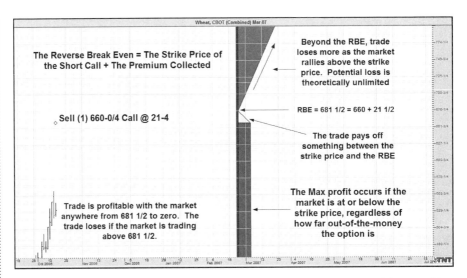

The Reverse Break Even = The Strike Price of the Short Call + The Premium Collected

Sell (1) 660-0/4 Call @ 21-4

Trade is profitable with the market anywhere from 681 1/2 to zero. The trade loses if the market is trading above 681 1/2.

Beyond the RBE, trade loses more as the market rallies above the strike price. Potential loss is theoretically unlimited

RBE = 681 1/2 = 660 + 21 1/2

The trade pays off something between the strike price and the RBE

The Max profit occurs if the market is at or below the strike price, regardless of how far out-of-the-money the option is

Figure 4.1 Although the profit potential is limited, a short option position provides healthy odds of success relative to long option plays but also involves unlimited risk.

The seller of a call option has the exact opposite intention of the buyer of that call option. The seller is expecting the market to either go down or at least not trade above the strike price of the short call. Of course, the long call trader expects the market to go up or be above the strike price of the short call option.

Notice that Figure 4.1 denotes the premium collected of 21 1/2 as 21-4. In the case of corn, soybeans, and wheat they are quoted in terms of cents per dollar. The minimum tick or the smallest increment of price movement in the futures market is a quarter of a cent—options can be traded in eighths (1/8), but are most often quoted in quarters. Each quarter is designated by eighths of a cent. Thus, if the price of the option was 21 1/4 it would be quoted as 21-2, which stands for 21 cents and 2/8ths. 21½ is shown as 21-4, and 21 3/4 is expressed as 21-6 for 6/8ths. Each cent in wheat is $50, so in the example in Figure 4.1 the option seller would have received $1,075, or (21½ x $50).

Example

As illustrated in Figure 4.2 if a trader sold a 1400 call in the S&P for $5 in premium, which is equivalent to $1250 (5 x 250), the reverse break-even at expiration would occur at 1405. Above this level the trader is exposed to unlimited risk. At this point it is similar to being short a futures contract in that the risk is theoretically unlimited and the delta value of the option increases to a level near that of a futures contract. Below 1405 and between 1400, the trader is profitable by the difference between the futures price and the reverse break even point. Thus, if the market is trading at 1403, the intrinsic profit on the trade would be $2 (1405-1403) in premium.

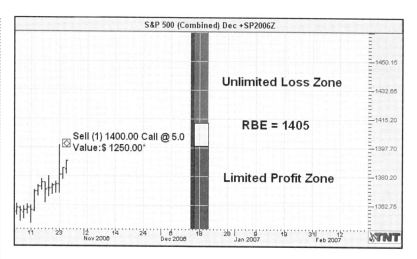

Figure 4.2 As you can see, selling a call creates a scenario in which limited profit potential is available below the RBE, but the loss is theoretically unlimited above the RBE.

If the market is trading below the strike price, 1400, at expiration the trader would keep the entire premium collected. The profit on the trade would be $5 in premium, or $1250 ($250 x 5), before commissions and fees. On the contrary, if the futures price at expiration is higher than the RBE of the call option, the loss is equivalent to the current market price minus the calculated RBE. For instance, if the S&P was trading at 1415 at expiration, the trader would have lost 10 handles (1415-1405), or $2,500 ($250 x 10).

This example illustrates the fact that although selling a single option is a directional trade, there is room for the trader to be "wrong" without the trade ending up in a losing proposition. Selling an out-of-the-money option may allow the market to go up, down, or sideways without endangering the profitability of the trade. Of course there is a catch; the market can't move too swiftly against the short option. In this case, the market can be about 8 points higher at expiration than it was when the trade was executed before it becomes a loser. Once again, beyond this point (the reverse-break-even) the risk is unlimited to the upside.

As witnessed in the preceding example, if positioned correctly, the seller of a call can be profitable at expiration whether the market goes up, down, or sideways subsequent to entering the trade. The risk lies in the potential for the market to go up too much, or beyond the reverse break-even point.

The benefit of selling options as opposed to buying them, or even trading futures contracts, is that there is some room for error. The amount of room is determined by the placement of the strike prices and the premium collected.

Short Put Option

When to Use

- If you believe the market is *not* going down (bullish).
- The strength of your belief determines what strike prices you look to sell.
- Sell out-of-the-money options (lower strike prices) if you believe prices are not going down.
- Sell at-the-money options (at current price) if you strongly believe prices are not going down. *This is typically not a recommended strategy.*
- Sell in-the-money options (above current price) if you strongly believe the price will rise. *This is not a recommended strategy.*

Profit Profile

- Your profit is limited to the premium collected.
- The reverse break-even at expiration is equal to the strike price minus the premium collected plus the transaction costs.

RBE = Strike Price − Premium Collected + Transaction Costs

- The profit is maximized if market expires above strike price.

Risk

- Exposes trader to unlimited risk; these positions need to be watched closely.
- Your losses increase if the market drops faster than the time decay erodes the option value.
- The market trading below the reverse break-even point is equal to being long a futures contract.
- At expiration your losses increase by one point for each point the market is below the reverse break-even.

Mechanically, selling a put option is much like selling a call option. The difference lies in the anticipated direction of the underlying futures contract. While the seller of a call option is bearish and hopes that the market is trading at or below the strike price at expiration, the seller of a put option is bullish. A put seller hopes that the market is trading at or above the strike price of the put at expiration.

Put sellers are anticipating that the market will travel higher, or at least won't drop below the strike price of the short put. As in the case of the short call, a short put will have some room for error assuming that the strike price is out-of-the-money.

The reverse break-even calculation of a short put option is ideally similar to that of the short call. However, instead of adding the premium collected to the strike price you will subtract it from the put strike price as shown in Figure 4.3. In this case, selling a Dow 10,500 put for 150 points, the trade would have an RBE of 10,350 or (10,500-150).

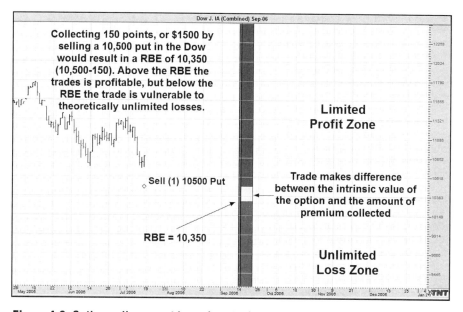

Figure 4.3 Option sellers must know how to determine their RBE to fully understand their risk.

As the market approaches and penetrates the strike price of a short option, the delta value of the option increases. An in-the-money option behaves similarly to that of a futures contract. The deeper in-the-money the option gets, the higher the delta value is. Remember, the delta value of a futures contract is 1, because for every point the underlying market moves the futures position provides an equal profit or loss. Therefore, the max delta of a short option is 1.

As mentioned previously, the risk of loss to an option seller is theoretically unlimited. In the case of a short put, the loss at expiration is equivalent to the RBE minus the futures price assuming that the market is in fact below the RBE. In this example, with the RBE at 10,350 the trade will lose 100 points (100 x $10=$1,000) if the futures price is 10,250 at expiration. Likewise, if the market is priced at 10,150 at expiration the loss to the trader would be 200 points or $2,000.

Option Selling Versus Trading Futures

Understanding that the max delta of a short option is 1 and more often than not the delta will be lower than that of a futures contract, it is easy to see that selling options is a less volatile proposition than trading outright futures contracts.

After all, your profit or loss will, under most circumstances, respond less to fluctuations in the underlying market, *and* you get the money up front.

Markets tend to go down faster than they go up; for this reason put sellers must be additionally cautious.

The premium collected for a short option can be considered "cushion" for adverse price movements in the underlying. This is because an in-the-money short option is similar to being in the futures market, but the original extrinsic premium received by the seller effectively offsets intrinsic losses on the option at expiration. Also supporting our assumption that selling options is less risky than trading futures, options do not have limits. While a futures contract may be locked limit, option traders are free to enter and exit as they want, given that they are willing to accept the market prices. With that said, the bid/ask spreads and corresponding option pricing can be somewhat irrational during times of locked limit futures markets. This is because future traders are buying and selling options to offset their risk of another limit move.

This contradicts many of the myths circulating in regards to short option horror stories. The idea of limited profit and unlimited loss is constantly being argued by option selling opponents. However, futures traders are subject to the same unlimited loss potential, but because the position also involves unlimited (but also unlikely) profit potential, futures trading has managed to gain a wider acceptance.

While there are distinctive advantages to selling options, a few drawbacks also must be understood prior to participating in such a strategy. For one, it normally isn't a great idea to place stop orders on options as a means of limiting losses. Unlike most futures markets, which are fluidly traded, option contracts are traded sporadically and tend to have much wider bid/ask spreads. The breadth of these spreads allows for stop orders to be filled in circumstances in which the trader may not be ready to cut losses. For this reason we tend to place mental stops; of course doing so means that the trader will have to be psychologically capable of pulling the plug on the trade before losses get out of hand. I think we have mentioned before, that this is much easier said than done.

Additionally; prior to expiration, the extrinsic value of any given option can explode exponentially with an increase in volatility. As the option premium blows up, the risk of the market-maker taking the other side of the trade increases making the bid/ask spread wider than it may otherwise be. The combination of these events can sometimes make short option positions extremely costly to liquidate. Positions can go from being profitable or slightly underwater to completely devastating in the blink of an eye. However, this is the risk that option writers take. If you recall, short option traders understand that in the long-run the strategy has a good chance of being profitable, but from time to time there will be compromising situations. This concept can be compared to the practice of insurance companies collecting premium for years but being caught off guard by hurricane Katrina. Even after such a devastating financial blow, insurance companies found a way to stay solvent and eventually profitable. Naturally, to do so they had to have deep pockets and accurate ways to calculate and mitigate risk.

Don't Underestimate the Risk of Illiquid Markets

Keep in mind that one disadvantage of selling options over buying or selling futures contracts is the fact that option markets tend to be much less liquid; some option markets shouldn't even be considered candidates for option sellers. Examples of these markets are pork bellies, lumber, and rough rice.

He who knows nothing, is confident in everything.

Be sure to pay close attention to the daily volume and open interest of the option market overall, including the month and strike price that you are interested in trading. Illiquid markets can lead to wider bid/ask spreads, which can become a significant obstacle in buying back a short option in a volatile or runaway market.

A story that we sometimes tell refers to an instance in which a client sold a lumber call option and after a few days of limit down trading sessions he still couldn't buy the option back at a profit due to the wide bid/ask spread and a highly illiquid market. To clarify, the bid/ask spread that the floor broker required to take the other side of the trade was enough to cover a big move in the underlying futures market. On a side note, if you have ever been to the CME you may have been shocked by the action, or lack of, in the lumber pit. It wouldn't be totally out of character for the two or three executing brokers standing in the trading pit to be reading a paper or playing solitaire; and yes this is during market hours.

Short Straddle

Sell an at-the-money put and call (same strike price).

When to Use

- You think the market will *not* move sharply in either direction.
- You are looking to profit from a flat market.

Profit Profile

- Profit potential is limited to the premium collected minus the transaction costs.
- At expiration the reverse break-even is equal to the strike price plus or minus the net amount collected for the spread, plus or minus the transaction costs.

RBE on Call Side=Strike Price+Premium Collected-Transaction Costs

RBE on Put Side=Strike Price-Premium Collected+Transaction Costs

- Maximum profit is achieved at expiration if the market is at the strike price.

Risk

- Risk is unlimited in either direction.
- Having unlimited risk on both sides, this position needs to be watched very closely.

A short option straddle contains the same risk and reward as an outright short call or short put position, but the trade is inherently directionless. Unlike being short a call or a put, a short straddle holder doesn't necessarily care whether the market goes up or down. The concern is with how far it goes either up or down. A short option straddle is designed to be profitable in a market that is experiencing either low volatility or decreasing volatility relative to the point at which the straddle was sold.

Because a straddle involves an at-the-money call and an at-the-money put it is almost certain that one side of the trade will be in-the-money at expiration. The only instance in which neither options would expire in-the-money would be if the futures price settled exactly at the strike price of the straddle on the day of expiration.

In our opinion, under most circumstances, this is an aggressive trade for an option seller to make due to the delta value of the position. Because there is risk of either the call or the put coming into the money immediately, the position may be subject to massive and immediate swings in value.

Another disadvantage in selling a straddle is that the trader will more than likely find himself with a deep in-the-money option and facing a potentially massive bid/ask spread. As previously mentioned, the spread between the bid and the ask is what the floor broker requires in compensation for accepting the risk of executing the trade. Because in-the-money options tend to have less daily volume than do out-of-the-money options, the floor broker is exposed to a higher level of risk. Once a floor broker takes the other side of your trade, the broker would quickly have to find a way to "dump" the position to mitigate the risk. If there aren't a lot of traders in that particular option contract, it is much harder to find someone to offset the trade. As you can imagine, this makes the risk of execution higher as well as the bid/ask spread.

Of course, any time that you sell an option there is risk that it may become in-the-money or even deep in-the-money, but the odds of this happening are much greater if you are selling at-the-money options or an option straddle.

The Reverse Break-Even Point

The reverse break-even point of a short straddle is identical to the break-even point of a long straddle. The difference is simply the seller of a straddle makes money with the market *within* the reverse break-even point for both the put and the call while the buyer of the straddle doesn't begin to make money until the market is *beyond* the break-even (see Figure 4.4). Please note that the reverse break-even and the

Knowing your risk is even more important than knowing your profit potential.

break-even point will be at the same level; the difference is that the RBE relates to the position of the straddle seller, while the BE corresponds to the long straddle trader.

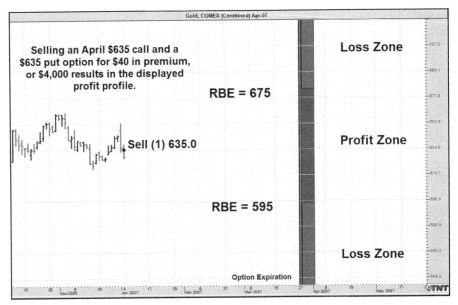

Figure 4.4 A short option straddle pays off if the market expires within the reverse break-even points of the call and the put. Beyond these points, the trader faces theoretically unlimited loss.

Example

To see the mechanics of a short straddle, we are going to revisit the example used in a previous chapter to explain a long straddle. Assuming that we took the side of the straddle seller, rather than the buyer, this trade makes money if the market remains in a sideways channel.

Unlike the long straddle, a short straddle makes more money with the market near the strike price of the straddle. As the market moves away from the strike prices, the profit diminishes where eventually (at the reverse break-even point) the trade intrinsically (at expiration) becomes a loser.

If you sold a $6.00 soybean call and a $6.00 soybean put for a combined premium of 48 cents, you would be left with a trade that makes money anywhere between $6.48 and $5.52, as illustrated in Figure 4.5. This can be calculated by adding the total premium collected to the strike price, 48 cents plus $6.00; and subtracting the total premium collected from the strike price of the straddle, $6.00 minus 48 cents. These two areas are referred to as the reverse break-even points of the straddle.

The maximum profit on the trade would occur at expiration if the underlying futures contract is exactly at $6.00, but that is a bit far fetched, although it is said that the market migrates toward the nearest strike price near the end of trade on option expiration. The most that this trade could possibly return to the executor is equal to the amount of premium collected. Beyond the reverse break-even points, $6.48 on the upside and $5.52 on the downside, the trade is exposed to theoretically unlimited risk.

Straddle writers are looking for the market to trade sideways; big moves in either direction result in exposure to theoretically unlimited risk. This type of trade has a much higher delta than a short strangle (discussed in the next section) or an outright short call or put.

The easiest way to interpret the risk and reward on this trade is to take into consideration that you are collecting money for the trade up front. In the best case scenario, you will get to keep the entire premium, but realistically the chances of the market settling at $6.00 on the day of expiration are slim. Thus, for every cent that the market is away from your strike price at expiration you will be giving back a cent of the premium collected. Simply put, you will profit less and less as the market moves away from the strike price of the straddle. Eventually, from an intrinsic standpoint you will run out of the money that was originally taken in. This is the reverse break-even point; beyond this level you begin to lose money as the market continues.

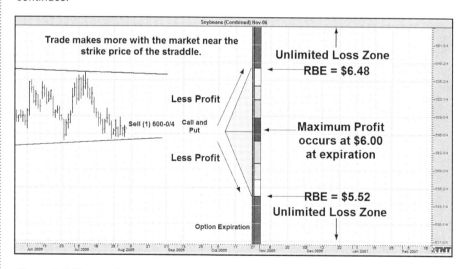

Figure 4.5 The maximum profit on a short straddle occurs if the market is at the strike price at expiration. As the market moves away from this point, the trader will have less and less profit. Beyond the RBEs of the straddle, the trader faces unlimited loss potential.

Short Strangle

Sell out-of-the-money call.
Sell out-of-the-money put.

When to Use

- When the market is range bound and you expect it to stay in the range or fail to make a large move before expiration.
- Similar to a straddle but you will collect less premium by selling out-of-the-money options. A short strangle offers a wider margin of error.

Profit Profile

- The profit potential is limited to the premium collected minus the transaction costs.
- The reverse break-even point at expiration is equal to the strike price plus or minus the premium collected for the spread plus or minus the transaction costs.

RBE on Call Side = Strike Price + Premium Collected - Transaction Costs

RBE on Put Side = Strike Price - Premium Collected + Transaction Costs

- Maximum profit is realized if the market at expiration is trading between the sold strike prices.

Risk

"Things may come to those who wait, but only the things left by those who hustle."
Abraham Lincoln

- Risk is unlimited in either direction.
- The market trading above the sold call or below the sold put is equivalent to being on the wrong side of the futures contract.
- Having unlimited risk on both sides, these positions need to be watched very carefully.

The short strangle is comparable to the short straddle. They are both directionless trades involving a short call and a short put option, limited profit potential, and theoretically unlimited risk. The primary difference is the distance between the strike prices. Unlike the straddle, which involves selling an at-the-money put and an at-the-money call, a strangle entails selling an out-of-the money put and an out-of-the money call. The result is a directionless trade with a lower delta value than the straddle. Remember, a lower delta value means that the options fluctuate less as the underlying futures market moves. In essence, this creates a lower volatility trade, and in our opinion a lower risk trade. After all, most measures of risk are based on standard deviations, and a trade that has a lower delta will by nature have a lower standard deviation.

The risk and reward profile of a short strangle is exactly opposite of the long strangle. Plainly put, if the buyer of the strangle is profitable, the seller is experiencing a loss, and vice versa. Accordingly, the break-even point of the long option straddle is calculated as the strike price plus or minus the premium *paid*; the seller calculates his reverse break-even by adding or subtracting the premium *collected*. In other words, the BE and the RBE will be the same figure for the buyer and the seller, but the profit zones will be opposite of each other. The buyer makes money if the market trades beyond the BE; the seller makes money if the market trades between the RBE.

Example

As mentioned previously, a short strangle is the opposite of a long strangle. The profit and loss zones will be the inverse of each other and so will the risk and reward.

In this case, we are selling a corn strangle (short call and short put) for a total premium of 25 cents. The $4.50 call has a premium of 10 cents, and the $4.10 put is going for 15 cents. Of course, for the sake of simplicity, this example is hypothetical and doesn't account for the bid/ask spread that the floor broker receives. A more realistic example would be a spread that can be bought for 25 cents could be sold for 24 cents.

To calculate the reverse break-even points for the trade, you simply add the total amount of premium collected (25 cents) to the strike price of the short call, and subtract the total amount of premium collected from the strike price of the short put. This creates a trade that is profitable anywhere between $4.75 ($4.50+.25) and $3.85 ($4.10-.25) before commissions and fees, as illustrated in Figure 4.6. Between these two points, the trader receives a limited profit. However the maximum profit in the amount of premium collected only occurs if the market is trading between the strike prices of the strangle at expiration.

"When I have to depend on hope in a trade, I get out of it."
Jesse Livermore

A short strangle typically has a lower delta than a short straddle. This simply means that the trade is slower paced. Each side of the spread will make, or lose, less money with movements in the futures market relative to an at-the-money straddle.

Beyond the RBEs of the trade, the position is exposed to theoretically unlimited losses. Thus, if the market drops below $3.85 before or at expiration, the position behaves similarly to a futures contract in that the risk is unlimited, and the delta value is increased. Once again, the delta value of an at-the-money option is .50; as the option becomes deeper in-the-money the delta value increases accordingly but will never surpass the delta value of a futures contract, 1. So a deep in-the-money option is similar to holding a futures position in terms of risk and price fluctuation.

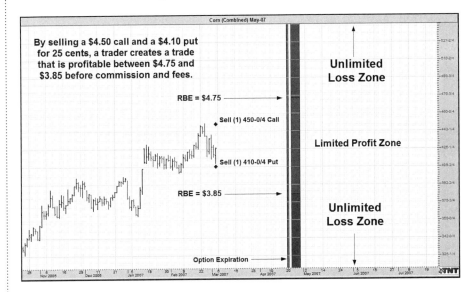

Figure 4.6 The reverse break-even is calculated by adding the total premium collected to the call strike price and subtracting the total premium from the put strike price before considering commissions and fees.

The maximum profit of 25 cents occurs if the underlying futures contract is trading between $4.50 and $4.10 at expiration. Beyond the strike prices at expiration, the trader is giving back "profits," or the premium collected, until the trader runs out of money 25 cents above or below the strike price at the corresponding RBE. Between the strike price and the RBE, the trader is profitable, but as the underlying futures contract gets farther beyond the strike price, the profit is decreased tick for tick (see Figure 4.7).

Correct speculation on the direction of a market can be difficult. The allure of a short strangle is the ability to profit from a market regardless of the direction. The risk of a short straddle is being caught in an exploding market. Beyond the RBEs of the trade, exposure to unlimited risk comes into play.

For example, if the underlying futures contract was at $4.60 at expiration, the trade would be profitable by 15 cents before commission and fees. This is calculated by taking the difference between the strike price and the market, 10 cents, and subtracting that from the total premium collected (($4.60-$4.50)-.25=.15). Likewise, if the contract was at $4.70 at expiration the trade would only be profitable by 5 cents before commission and fees.

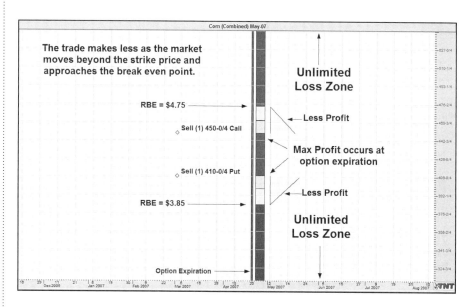

Figure 4.7 A strangle writer makes money anywhere between the RBEs, but makes less in between the strike price and the RBE.

chapter 5

Credit Spreads

Some traders are intrigued by the odds of success that short option traders enjoy, but are not willing to accept theoretically unlimited risk on a trade that provides limited profit potential. An alternative to selling naked options, the term "naked" referring to the fact that there is unlimited risk, is the credit spread. A *credit spread* involves the sale of an option with the purchase of a distant option of the same kind. In other words, if a trader sells a call option, a call option with a higher strike price can be purchased to limit the trader's risk.

Limited Risk Premium Collection

Essentially, when executing a credit spread a trader is giving up a portion of the collected premium for peace of mind. It is a clear advantage to have confidence in knowing that no matter what takes place throughout the life of the trade, at expiration the loss is limited. However, just as everything else in the world of trading, buying protection can act as a double-edged sword.

Although loss is limited, it has been suggested that the overall probability of a losing trade is greater with a credit spread relative to selling naked options. This theory lies in the fact that it is much more difficult to adjust a spread than it is a lone short option. Also, although losses can be defined, the dollar amount can be substantial, and losses are arguably more likely.

Bullish or Bearish?

Credit spreads can be directional or neutral. Those who are bullish in a particular market may want to simultaneously sell a put and purchase one at a lower strike price. This is referred to as a *bull put spread*. The premium collected represents the maximum profit, while the distance between the strike prices minus the premium received provides the maximum loss. A trader without a bullish or bearish bias may opt to sell credit spreads on both sides of the market; this is known as the *iron condor*.

Example

If a trader believes that the stock market will go higher over the next several weeks, he could look to capitalize on the move by selling puts in the S&P and purchasing a long option beyond the strike price of the short option to cap the risk. The multiplier in the S&P is $250 and to confuse the situation the premium is quoted in dollars; a trader sold a September S&P 500 1250 put for $2.80 in premium, or $700, expiring in less than a month. Uncomfortable with the potential catastrophic risk inherent in selling options, suppose a 1220 put could be purchased for about $0.20 in premium, or $50.

Maximum Profit $2.60 in premium ($650)=Premium Collected $2.80 ($700)–Premium Paid $0.20 ($50)

Maximum Loss $27.40 in premium ($6,850)=Difference in Strike Prices (1250–1220) x Contract Multiplier ($250)–Premium Collected $2.60 ($650)

These examples are without regard to transaction costs, but will provide you with an overall understanding of the mechanics of the trade. As you can see, the risk in such a trade is limited but it is limited to an unreasonable amount of risk.

Is Having Limited Risk Worth the Opportunity Cost?

Obviously, there is a trade-off between capping your risk and maximizing premium collected. Armed with the notion that most options will expire worthless, many traders are lured into selling naked options, but doing so results in a limited profit and unlimited loss. Even if an investor successfully collects premium eight out of ten times, the two inevitable losing trades have the potential to erase previous profits and then some.

"Good judgment is usually the result of experience, and experience frequently is the result of bad judgment."
Robert Hormats

Have you ever noticed that *all* insurance policies have a maximum benefit? This is not a coincidence. The insurance firm Lloyd's of London discovered the importance of limiting losses the hard way. They prided themselves on the sale of "no limit" policies, but in the early 1990s they were averaging close to $3 billion a year due to asbestos claims and quickly reconsidered their business model.

Reinsurance is another way in which insurers limit their risk. After collecting premium on a policy, firms allocate a portion of the proceeds to the purchase of insurance against the sold coverage. Credit spreads can be viewed in the same terms. Following the sale of an option, it might be beneficial to limit potential losses by purchasing a distant option for protection.

Another benefit of a credit spread is a reduction in required margin. Exchanges set the margin on limited risk spreads much lower than that of naked options. However, it is important to note that this also increases leverage, which may turn out to be unmanageable in highly volatile market conditions.

The Cons of Credit Spreads

As you can see in the previous example, a credit spread provides limited risk at a hefty price. Additionally, although limited the losses may be substantial relative to the amount of premium collected. In the previous example, a trader would have been risking $6,850 to make $650. Here are a few reasons that credit spreads may not be as profitable as they seem on the surface.

- Credit spreads are difficult to adjust or trade out of. Once you are in the trade, you may have to hold the entire position until expiration to avoid taking on unlimited risk by lifting a leg or to achieve an acceptable profit on the spread.

- The bid/ask spread plays a bigger part in credit spread trading than it does in a simple short option strategy. Unless a trader is willing to hold the trade beyond expiration, getting out of the spread may require a trader to give up much of the profit potential or take a bigger loss than previously anticipated.

- Exercise and assignments are even more intense in credit spreads than they are in outright option selling. This is because spread traders often have to sell options with closer to-the-money strike prices to collect enough premium to make the trade worthwhile. Additionally, due to the nature of a spread and the difficulty to get out

Credit spreads are a way to collect premium while still maintaining limited risk. It is important to realize that limited and minimal are not the same thing. Depending on the structure and positioning of the spread, the risk may be high.

before expiration, more traders hold the trade until the end. Complications also arise should the futures market be trading between the short option and the long option. If this is the case, the spread holder may have to buy or sell futures contracts against the spread at expiration to avoid being long or short the market in the following session. Times like this can be critical; you would likely need the help of a broker to avoid costly mistakes.

Bear Call Spread

Sell an out-of-the-money call.
Buy a further out-of-the-money call.

When to Use

- If you believe that the market is not going up (bearish).
- You are unwilling to accept unlimited loss potential.

Profit Profile

- Profit potential is limited to the premium collected minus transaction costs.
- At expiration the reverse break-even is equal to the short option strike price plus the net amount collected for the spread minus commission and fees.

RBE=Short Strike+Net Premium Collected–Transaction Costs

- Maximum profit is achieved at expiration if the market is at or below the strike price of the short call.
- The trade is profitable below the reverse break-even.

Risk

- Risk is limited by buying the distant option.
- Maximum loss is the difference between the short and long option strike prices less the premium collected plus transaction costs.
- Maximum loss occurs when the market is trading at or above the long call strike price at expiration.

Max Loss=Maximum Intrinsic Value of Spread–Total Premium
Collected+Transaction Costs

Similar to naked option selling strictly for premium collection, a credit spread trader is attempting to benefit from the probabilities that arguably suggest that option sellers will come out ahead in the long run. However, in the case of a credit spread, the trader is purchasing an option with a distant strike price to limit the risk of the trade.

In reference to a bear call spread, the trade would consist of selling a call option and buying a call option with a distant strike price. With this strategy the trader is bearish, or at least slightly bearish. Such a trade leaves some room for error, meaning that it is possible for a bearish trader to make money on this position even if the market goes up. If this trade is executed out-of-the-money, the trade can return a profit if the market trades sideways, goes down, *or* goes up but stays below the RBE of the trade.

The risk of a bear call spread is equal to the distance between the strike price of the long call and the strike price of the short call minus the total premium collected for the spread. The maximum loss occurs if the market is above the strike price of the insurance or long call.

The maximum profit potential on a bear call spread, without regard to transaction costs, is the amount of premium collected. Regardless of how right you are in the direction of the market, the absolute best-case scenario is keeping the amount of money received when the trade was executed. With that said, the odds of doing so may be better than they would be if you were trying to buy the spread. Buying the spread would simply be a bull call spread and would involve buying the call option closer to-the-money and selling at the distant strike price.

Example

Dow Jones futures have a multiplier of $10, so for every point of premium collected the true dollar amount is ten times that. In Figure 5.1, you can see that if a trader sells a 12,600 call for 135 points and buys a 12,800 for 55 points as insurance, she is collecting $800. The max profit zone at expiration occurs below 12,600, but the trade pays off a diminishing amount above 12,600 up to the reverse break-even point of 12,680. The RBE is calculated by adding the net premium collected to the short call strike price. Beyond 12,680 the trade loses more as the futures price moves toward 12,800, the strike price of the long call. At and above 12,800 the maximum loss is sustained at expiration; we will go over the mathematics shortly.

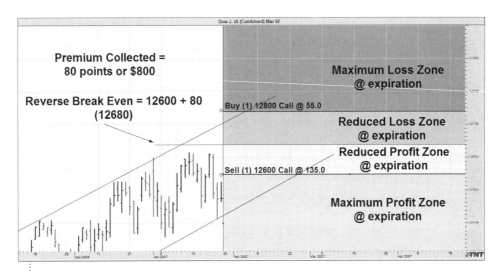

Dow J. IA (Combined) Mar 07

Premium Collected =
80 points or $800

Maximum Loss Zone
@ expiration

Reverse Break Even = 12600 + 80
(12680)

Buy (1) 12800 Call @ 55.0

Reduced Loss Zone
@ expiration

Reduced Profit Zone
@ expiration

Sell (1) 12600 Call @ 135.0

Maximum Profit Zone
@ expiration

Figure 5.1   The maximum loss at expiration occurs if the underlying futures contract is above the long call strike price. The maximum profit occurs if the market is below the short call strike price.

In Figure 5.1 a trader sold the 12,600 call for 135 points, or $1,350 (135 x $10) and bought the 12,800 call for 55 points or $550 (55 x $10). At these prices, the trade is a net credit of $800, or 80 points, but remember there would be two commission charges, and this reduces the premium collected.

The reverse break-even on the trade is calculated by adding the net credit to the strike price of the short call option. In this case it would be at 12,680 (12,600+80).

Credit spreads provide a limited risk method for premium collectors. However, credit spreads also subject traders to what we call the extrinsic handcuff. In essence, this term describes a scenario in which a credit spread trader may become seemingly trapped in a trade in which the market either went against the position or experienced an increase in volatility.

Looking at the big picture, excluding transaction costs, the profit zone at expiration begins at 12,679 and goes all the way down to zero. Likewise, the trade loses at 12,680 and above. Plainly put, this trade makes money as long as the futures market is trading under 12,680 at expiration.

The beauty of a trade like this is that if your interpretation of the market is wrong, your risk is limited. No matter what happens, your maximum loss on a bear call spread would be the distance between the strike prices minus the net credit collected at execution (don't forget to add transaction costs to the final number). In this case, the absolute risk of loss would be $1,200 before considering transaction costs. The risk on this trade can be calculated as follows, ((12,800-12,600)–80)=120); (120 x $10=$1,200). Once again, the maximum loss occurs if the market is trading at or above the strike price of the long call, 12,800, at expiration. Should the market be between the reverse break-even and the strike price of the long call, the trade will be a loser, but the magnitude will be reduced.

To illustrate if the market is trading at 12,700 at expiration, the trader will be at a loss of only $200 before commission. This is figured by subtracting the RBE from the price of the underlying, (12,700–12,680) x $10=$200.

Bull Put Spread

Sell an out-of-the-money put.
Buy a further out-of-the-money put.

When to Use

- If you think that the market is not going down (bullish).
- You are unwilling to accept unlimited loss potential.

Profit Profile

- Profit potential is limited to the premium collected minus transaction costs.
- At expiration the reverse break-even is equal to the short option strike price minus the net amount collected for the spread plus transaction costs.

RBE=Short Strike–Total Premium Collected+Transaction Costs

- Maximum profit is achieved at expiration if the market is at or above the short put strike price.

Risk

- Risk is limited by buying the distant option.
- Maximum loss is the difference between the strike prices of the short and long options less the premium collected plus the transaction costs.
- Maximum loss occurs when the market at expiration is trading at or below the strike price of the long put.

Max Loss=Maximum Intrinsic Value of Spread–Total Premium Collected+Transaction Costs

A bull put spread is the exact opposite of a bear put spread. While a bear put spread involves buying an at-the-money or out-of-the-money put option and selling a farther out-of-the-money put option, a bull put spread consists of a short put option placed at or out-of-the-money and a long put further out-of-the-money. A trader executing a bull put spread is anticipating that the market will either sustain current valuations enough to remain above the short put strike price or go higher.

Just as the bear call spread demonstrated in the previous example contains limited risk, the bull put spread offers traders the "comfort" in knowing the absolute worst-case scenario. In this case the risk is limited to the distance between the strike prices minus the amount of premium collected. However, just because the risk is limited doesn't mean that the trade is "safe" or even logical. Sometimes credit spreads contain excessive amounts of risk with little profit potential.

As a trader it is up to you to determine just how much risk you are willing to take for the corresponding reward. The risk tolerance and personality of the trader plays a big part in this. We have seen traders rationalize the execution of a bull put spread for a credit of $250 and a risk of nearly $5,000. In their point of view, they believe that the odds of sustaining a maximum loss are slim, and the probability of walking away from the trade with a profit is large.

Limited risk doesn't necessarily mean less risk.

We have a hard time justifying such a risk/reward ratio given the structure of the trade. While a naked short option trade faces theoretically unlimited risk, it may be a little "easier" to unwind the trade when compared to a two-legged credit spread. This is because the bid/ask spread may pose an additional hurdle for a spread trader. Additionally, depending on the delta value of the protective option, if the trade goes against you, the long option may not cushion the blow at all. If it is considerably out-of-the-money the premium erosion will likely outpace any benefits from the market moving in the direction of the option.

Example

Once again, the multiplier for the S&P futures and options is $250. If a trader executed the trade denoted in Figure 5.2 by selling a June S&P 1300 put for $16.50 in premium and buying the 1250 put in the same month for $9.80, the trader would collect a net premium of $6.70 ($16.50–$9.80), or $1,675 (6.70 x $250).

The risk on the trade is calculated by subtracting the amount of premium collected from the distance between the strike prices and multiplying it by $250. Thus, the max risk is equal to ((1300-1250)-6.70) x $250=$10,825. As you can see, the risk on the trade is limited, but the maximum loss is incredibly substantial. In such a case you would ask yourself whether buying the protection is even worth it. After all, would you be willing to risk nearly $11,000 on a trade if you were selling naked options. The answer is probably not (on purpose), so buying the protection isn't as comforting as one may think.

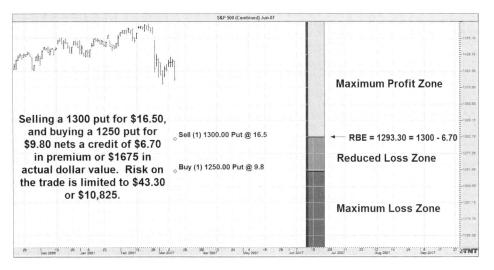

Figure 5.2 Credit spreads such as the bull put spread offer limited risk to the trader, but that risk can be quite large.

The maximum profit on this trade occurs if the underlying futures contract is trading above the strike price of the short put, 1300, at expiration, as illustrated in Figure 5.3. The maximum loss occurs at expiration if the market is trading at or below 1250, or the price of the long put. The reverse break-even of the spread is 1293.30. This is calculated by subtracting the net credit from the strike price of the short put before consideration of commissions, (1300–6.70)=1293.30.

The trade loses less than the maximum risk if the market is trading between the reverse break-even and the strike price of the long put at expiration. The farther the market moves beyond the RBE, the bigger the loss the trade becomes. Of course, the risk is capped at expiration once the market reaches the strike price of the long put option.

A bull put spread is used when a trader expects a market to head higher or at least be above the short put strike price at expiration. Just like a short put option provides the trader with some room for error, a bull put spread can be profitable to an extent whether the market goes up, down, or sideways. Of course, the risk lies in the potential for the market to drop beneath the RBE of the trade. Once again, limited risk is not synonymous with minimal risk.

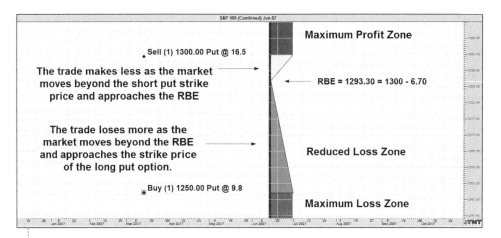

Figure 5.3 This trade pays off with the underlying futures trading above 1293.30 at expiration. The maximum profit occurs if the market is above 1300.

Iron Condor

Sell an out-of-the money call.
Buy a further out-of-the money call.
Sell an out-of-the money put.
Buy a further out-of-the money put.

When to Use

● In a range bound market and you think the market will not move sharply in either direction before expiration.

● This position is a limited risk short option strangle.

Profit Profile

● Profit potential is limited to the premium collected minus the transaction costs.

- At expiration the reverse break-even is equal to the short option strike price plus or minus the net amount collected for the spread plus or minus transaction costs.

RBE on Call Side=Short Strike+Total Premium Collected–Transaction Costs

RBE on Put Side=Short Strike–Total Premium Collected+Transaction Costs

- Maximum profit is achieved at expiration if the market is at or between the short call and short put strike prices.

Risk

- Risk is limited by the purchase of the distant strike priced options.
- Maximum loss is the difference between the short and long option strike prices less the premium collected, plus transaction costs (four commissions).
- Maximum loss occurs if the market is trading at or below the long put or at or above the long call at expiration. The amount is equivalent whether it is the call spread or the put spread that loses.

Max Loss =Intrinsic Value of Either Credit Spread–Total Premium Collected+Transaction Costs

An iron condor is simply the simultaneous execution of a bear call spread and a bull put spread. A trader who doesn't believe that a particular market is going to make a dramatic move in either direction may look to sell a credit spread above the market and below the market. The maximum profit is equal to the total premium collected for both the bear call spread and the bull put spread and occurs at expiration if the underlying futures contract is trading between the strike prices of the short options. The maximum loss occurs if the underlying futures contract is trading beyond either of the long option strike prices at expiration.

In regard to an iron condor, the reverse break-even, maximum risk, and maximum profit potential on the trade are calculated identically to that of the bull put spread and the bear call spread aside from the fact that the calculations involve the net credit for both the call spread and the put spread. In other words, the call spread and the put spread are treated as one trade in the calculations because it is only possible to lose on one side of the trade at expiration. For example, to figure the RBE of the trade you would add the premium collected for the bull put spread to the premium collected for the bear call spread and then add that number to the strike price of the call or subtract that number to the strike price of the put. Similarly, the maximum profit on an iron condor consists of the net credit collected for *both* the bull put spread and the bear call spread.

The attraction of an iron condor comes in the fact that it can make money whether the market goes up, down, or sideways, assuming that it doesn't move too far. The directionless structure of the trade means that at expiration you can lose on only one side of the spread. If the trade is a loser at expiration, the market must be above the reverse break-even of the bear call spread, or below the reverse break-even of the bull put spread; of course it cannot be both. Accordingly, only one side of the trade is margined, and the risk calculations involve the premium collected on both sides of the trade but only considers the potential of losing on one side or the other.

One important item to note is the transaction costs of such a trade. An iron condor involves four separate option contracts and thus four commission charges and four sets of exchange fees. Depending on the commission rate that you pay, this may or may not be substantial. However, it is important to be aware of. If your goal is to collect a credit of $300, but you are paying $100 to execute the trade, the risk may not be worth the reward.

An iron condor is simply a bear call spread and a bull put spread held simultaneously. The strategy is to exploit a market that is trading sideways. As with a short option strangle or a straddle, an iron condor can lose on only one side of the spread. The key difference is the characteristic of limited risk for the iron condor, and accordingly a reduced profit potential.

Keep in mind that if you are executing multileg option spreads, your broker will likely give you a lower commission rate—it never hurts to ask. Another point to note is that it is not possible to execute multiple leg option spreads using a single ticket in an electronically traded market; instead you would need to look to the open outcry option contracts for this. Naturally, it is feasible in the electronic options to place each leg on an individual ticket, but you wouldn't be able to place a limit order (name your price) on the package. Working with an experienced broker would likely be helpful in getting efficient execution of iron condors, after all slippage in the fill translates into less premium collected, which correspondingly increases the risk of the trade.

Example

The trade depicted in the Figure 5.4 portrays the profit and loss zones of an iron condor. As you can see in this example, the trade was executed at total credit of 17 1/2 cents. This was calculated by adding the net credit of the bear call spread of 9 1/2 cents to the net credit of the bull put spread, 8 cents. Keep in mind that the multiplier for soybeans is $50. Thus, this trade would have been a credit of $875 before commissions and fees (17 1/2 x $50).

Figure 5.4 An iron condor should be treated as one trade for purposes of risk and reward simply because it is possible to lose on only one side of the trade.

Because an iron condor consists of a call spread and a put spread, there is a reverse break-even on both sides. The RBE on the upside is simply the total amount of premium collected added to the strike price of the short call option. In this case it is $8.17 1/2 ($8.00+17 1/2 cents). Likewise, the RBE on the downside is the total amount of premium collected minus the strike price of the short put, $7.12 1/2, ($7.30–17 1/2 cents).

As illustrated in Figure 5.5, the trade is profitable at expiration if the underlying futures contract is trading between the RBEs, $8.17 1/2 and $7.12 1/2. The maximum profit of 17 1/2 cents occurs if the trade is within the strike prices of the short options, $8.00 and $7.30.

The maximum risk on the trade is equal to the distance between the strike price of the short and long options minus the total premium collected plus transaction costs. Looking at the call side, the maximum loss occurs if the underlying futures contract is trading above $8.30 at expiration. The risk on the trade is 12 1/2 (($8.30–$8.00)–17 1/2) cents at expiration. Because in this example, the strike prices of the put spread are equidistant to the call spread, the risk will be the same, but the calculation is slightly different, 12 1/2 cents (($7.30–$7.00)–17 1/2).

There seems to be a lot of confusion surrounding the difference between an iron butterfly and an iron condor. Although they are similar, the terms are not interchangeable. An iron condor involves two short options at differing strike prices, while an iron butterfly consists of two short options at identical strike prices (iron butterflies are covered later in the book).

Figure 5.5   An iron condor profits regardless of the market direction assuming that the underlying futures contract is within the RBEs at expiration.

chapter 6

Limited Risk Option Spreads

Options are versatile trading tools. As we learned in Chapter 5, "Credit Spreads," it is possible to combine long and short options with differing strike prices to accomplish a common goal. Long option traders can reduce their cost and risk by implementing a spread in which one option is purchased and one option is sold at a strike price distant to the original. This type of strategy is referred to as a bull call spread or a bear put spread depending on whether puts or calls are used.

> "If you don't profit from your investment mistakes, someone else will."
> Yale Hirsh

The primary benefit of using an option spread is the favorable break-even point. By selling premium further out-of-the-money, a trader is improving the odds of a successful trade by shifting the intrinsic break-even closer to the market. In the case of a bull call spread, the price at which the spread pays for itself is lower than it would be through the purchase of an outright call option. Similarly, the "scratch" level of a bear put spread will be higher than it would be had the trader simply purchased a put option. Keep in mind, even though this strategy involves a short option leg it is still considered to be a long option strategy. Any option or option spread that contains limited risk and is executed at a debit (or cost) is often referred to as a *long option play*.

BE Bull Call=Long Strike+Premium Paid+Transaction Costs

BE Bear Put=Long Strike–Premium Paid–Transaction Costs

Bull Call Spread

Buy an at-the-money or out-of-the-money call.

Sell a call with a higher strike price.

A bull call spread is just what the name implies. It is a bullish option strategy using the spread between a long call option and short call option with a distant strike price. The premise behind the strategy is simple; traders who execute a bull call spread are interested in limited risk and thus a marginless trade, but they would like to own a position relatively close to the market without having to pay an "arm and a leg."

In essence, the short call option acts as a type of *hedge* against the long option. As the market falls, the spread will be making money on the short option while losing on the long option. However, the aspect of the trade that is meant to be a hedge can become a problem if the market rallies. In an inclining market, the long option will be gaining value, but so will the short option, and this will cut into profits at any time prior to and at expiration.

In our opinion, the theory behind this trade is more logical than a simple long option play and is much sounder than a long straddle trade, but it isn't without flaws. First, while the trade is cheaper than a long call option of the same strike without an accompanying short call, it may still be above and beyond what we would normally spend on a long option play. Our line in the sand is $500; anything more than this is probably too much to risk on a long option trade. Keep in mind, that there may be certain circumstances in which spending more than the aforementioned amount is necessary and even prudent.

In most markets, a bull call spread cannot be executed at a cost of less than $500 without creating a trade in which the spread is too narrow to offer a profit potential worth your while. Even more important, at that price it is hard to execute a trade in which the long strike price and the short strike prices aren't too close together. A bull call spread constructed with the strike prices of the long and short call relatively close to each other creates a trade that is nearly impossible to liquidate at a profit before expiration. This is because, along with the strike prices, the delta value of the options will be similar.

"Ignorance is not knowing something: stupidity is not admitting your ignorance."
Daniel Turov

In the case of an incorrectly structured bull call spread, as the market moves up the trader loses almost as much on the short call as he is making on the long call. This can be frustrating. If the strike prices of the spread are too narrow, it is possible for a trade that is intrinsically profitable, or in-the-money, to not be profitable prior to expiration. In other words, if the options expired immediately the trade would return a profit to the trader assuming that the price of the underlying was beyond the break-even point; nonetheless if option expiration is sometime in the future the trader may have to wait to reap any of the reward. Once again, this is due to the similarity in the delta values of each of the options involved in the spread.

As we all know, markets are capable of sharp moves in any time frame. It is entirely possible that the market will fall below the profit zone prior to option expiration causing the incorrectly executed bull call spread to expire worthless despite being intrinsically profitable at some point prior to expiration. To reiterate, it is like having a profit "on paper" that you are unable to cash in until a date in the future and then watching those profits dwindle away to nothing, or even creating a loss, without any recourse. We often use the term *extrinsic handcuff* to describe this scenario. This is because in such a case the trader can feel trapped and at the mercy of the market. Being involved in a spread in which the delta values of each option are too similar multiplies the possibility of experiencing the extrinsic handcuff.

Keep in mind, it is possible to mitigate the extrinsic handcuff by ensuring that the strike prices of your bull call spread are sufficiently wide. For example, you wouldn't want to do a 100 point bull call spread in the Dow Jones futures market. Each point in the Dow Jones is equal to $10, thus the trade would offer a $1,000 payout potential and may be comparatively cheap, but the trade offers no flexibility. To see any profit at all, you would have to hold such a trade until expiration due to the fact that the strike prices of the spread are close together allowing the values of the long call and the short to move in similar fashion. Poor structuring of a bull call or bear put spread creates one more obstacle in an already difficult game.

When to Use

● You think the market will go up, but believe that the upside potential may be limited.

● You think the market will go up, but buying an outright call option near-the-money is too expensive.

Profit Profile

- Profit is limited to the difference between the strike prices minus the premium paid and the transaction costs.
- At expiration the break-even is equal to the long call strike price plus the net amount paid for the spread plus the transaction costs.

BE=Long Strike Price+Net Premium Paid+Transaction Costs

Risk

- Risk is limited to the amount paid for the spread plus transaction costs.
- The maximum loss is reached at expiration if the underlying futures market is below the strike price of the purchased call option.

Example

The premise behind a bull call spread is to enter the market with a lessened amount of out-of-pocket expense and limited risk. As illustrated in Figure 6.1, buying a soybean $7.60 call for 23 6/8 of a cent, which by the way is printed as 23'6 but called out as "twenty-three and three quarters," and selling a $7.90 call for 7 6/8 of a cent would result in a net premium paid of 16 cents. Because the multiplier in soybeans, and most of the grains, is $50 the total dollar cost of the trade is $800. The premium paid plus the transaction costs is the absolute risk on the trade. The maximum loss occurs if the market is trading below the strike price of the long call, $7.60, at expiration. In other words, even if soybeans drop to zero this trade only loses the initial outlay.

Bull call spreads offer limited risk as well as mitigated risk. On the other hand, it is important to realize that in many markets and scenarios an affordable bull call spread may only be possible by constructing a trade that is difficult to exit with a profit prior to expiration. This often happens when the strike prices of the long call and the short call are too close together causing the legs of the spread to have detrimentally similar delta values.

Then again, if the trade is spot on and soybean futures rally to new all-time highs, this trade only pays out the difference between the strike prices minus the premium paid for the trade. To illustrate, if the underlying futures contract is above $7.90 at expiration, the trade will make $700 (($7.90–$7.60)–16 cents x $50).

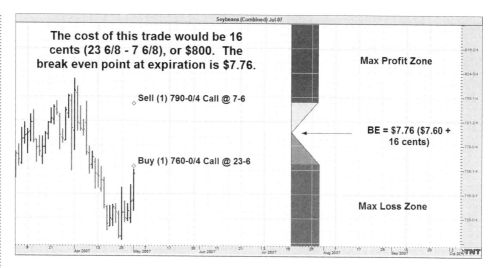

Figure 6.1 A bull call spread allows traders to enter the market with limited risk and less capital than may be required to buy a similarly placed option outright.

Simply by looking at the premium paid versus the maximum profit potential, you can see that it hardly seems worth the risk even before considering commissions and fees. Risking $800 to possibly make $700 doesn't seem to be putting the odds in your favor. In fact, it is doing just the opposite. In Chapter 7, "Synthetic Swing Trading," we demonstrate how to take a spread such as this and convert it into a trade that requires little or no out-of-pocket expense while increasing the odds of the trade. Naturally there are no guarantees in trading, but would you rather flip a coin or roll the dice?

To calculate the break-even on the trade, you simply add the premium paid to the strike price of the long call option; in this case it is $7.76 ($7.60+16 cents), as shown in Figure 6.2. Above the strike price of the long call and below the BE, the trade is a loser. The losses are mitigated by the amount that the market is trading above the long call strike price prior to reaching the BE. Beyond the BE the trade is increasingly profitable until it reaches the strike price of the short call option, $7.90, at which point the profits are maximized at expiration.

Beginning traders often wonder how they can have a bull call spread that is intrinsically in-the-money but not profitable. Before expiration, they may be making money on the long call but losing on the short call, or they may be the victim of premium erosion. Although erosion will benefit the secondary option in this spread, the primary option will suffer from the erosion of extrinsic value. This may leave the trader in a losing proposition despite correct speculation on the market.

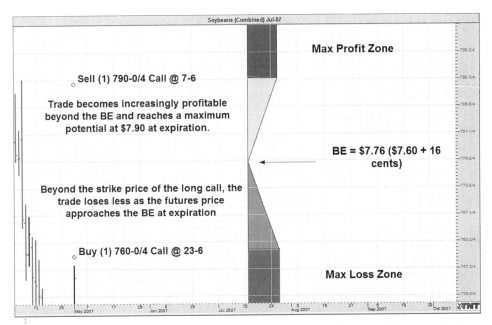

Soybeans (Combined) Jul-07

Sell (1) 790-0/4 Call @ 7-6

Trade becomes increasingly profitable
beyond the BE and reaches a maximum
potential at $7.90 at expiration.

Max Profit Zone

BE = $7.76 ($7.60 + 16
cents)

Beyond the strike price of the long call, the
trade loses less as the futures price
approaches the BE at expiration

Buy (1) 760-0/4 Call @ 23-6

Max Loss Zone

Figure 6.2 The maximum profit is only attainable at expiration. Prior to expiration
the time value, or extrinsic value, of the short option will reduce profits.

Bear Put Spread

Buy an at-the-money or out-of-the-money put option.
Sell a put option with a distant (lower) strike price.

A bear put spread is based on the same logic of a bull call spread; the sole
difference is the instrument used. As the name suggests, a bear put spread profits
in a declining market and consists of two put options, one long and one short.
The strike price of the long option will be closer to the underlying futures price
than the short option. As with the bull call spread, a trader who implements a
bear put spread is looking to get relatively close-to-the-money with little out-of-
pocket expense and limited risk.

The advantages and disadvantages of the bear put spread are identical to that
of a bull call spread. The opportunity cost of getting into the long option at a
discount is the possibility of the extrinsic handcuff. This should be somewhat
expected; there typically isn't such a thing as a deal without a catch. In the world
of option spread trading, this is the catch.

When to Use

● You think the market will go down, but believe that the downside potential may be limited.

● You think the market will go down, but buying an outright put option near the money is too expensive.

Profit Profile

● Profit is limited to the difference between the strike prices minus the cost of the spread and the transaction costs.

● At expiration the break-even is equal to the long put strike price minus the net amount paid for the spread minus transaction costs.

BE=Long Strike Price–Net Premium Paid–Transaction Costs

Risk

● Risk is limited to the amount paid for the spread plus transaction costs.

● The maximum loss is reached if at expiration the market is above the strike price of the long put option.

A bear put spread is known as a *debit spread* because the trader must pay to get into the trade. The trade is constructed by buying a closer to the money put and selling a put option with a distant strike price.

Because it is a debit spread, if the trade is held until expiration the long option has to be in-the-money enough to cover the premium paid for the spread just to break even. In the example noted in Figure 6.3, the trade has a total cost of 8 cents, or $400 (remember, the multiplier in soybeans is $50). The cost of the trade is calculated by subtracting the amount of premium collected for the short put from the amount paid for the long put. In this case, the trade involves buying a $7.30 put in soybeans for 12 6/8 and selling a $7.00 put for 4 6/8.

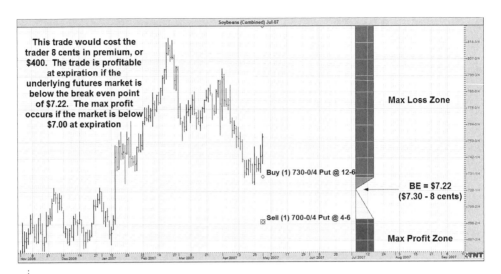

This trade would cost the trader 8 cents in premium, or $400. The trade is profitable at expiration if the underlying futures market is below the break even point of $7.22. The max profit occurs if the market is below $7.00 at expiration

Soybeans (Combined) Jul-07

Max Loss Zone

Buy (1) 730-0/4 Put @ 12-6

BE = $7.22 ($7.30 - 8 cents)

Sell (1) 700-0/4 Put @ 4-6

Max Profit Zone

Figure 6.3 This trade is a loser of 8 cents or $400 if the futures price is trading above $7.30 at expiration.

The break-even point of the trade is figured by subtracting the premium paid of 8 cents from the strike price of the long put, $7.30. Thus, this trade breaks even at expiration if the market is trading exactly at $7.22 before considering transaction costs (see Figure 6.4).

The maximum profit on the trade is 22 cents or $1,100 and occurs if the underlying futures contract is trading at or below the strike price of the short put, $7.00.

> A bear put spread is one way to buy a close-to-the-money put option at a discount, but it also limits profit potential. Thus, it is a good idea to sell the short put of the spread just beyond support levels.

One seemingly negative aspect of a bear put spread is the lack of unlimited profit potential. If the market "crashes" well below $7.00, this trade doesn't benefit. For every cent that the market is beyond the $7.00 mark at expiration, the long put option will be making as much as the short put option is losing. In essence, below $7.00 all the profits made on the long $7.30 put are given back in the form of losses on the short $7.00 put.

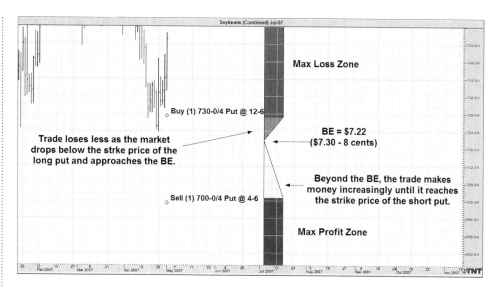

Soybeans (Combined) Jul-07

Max Loss Zone

Buy (1) 730-0/4 Put @ 12-6

Trade loses less as the market drops below the strke price of the long put and approaches the BE.

BE = $7.22
($7.30 - 8 cents)

Beyond the BE, the trade makes money increasingly until it reaches the strike price of the short put.

Sell (1) 700-0/4 Put @ 4-6

Max Profit Zone

Figure 6.4 **The benefit of limited risk comes at a price. With this strategy the market must move below the break-even point before the options expire. There are a lot of factors working against trade, leaving little room for error.**

The most that the trade could lose at expiration, assuming that the spread was kept intact, is the amount of premium paid for the spread, which is 8 cents or $400. Even if soybeans go to an all-time high and beyond, the trade will only lose $400.

As the market trades beyond the break-even point of $7.22, the trade becomes more and more profitable until the market reaches $7.00. For instance, if the underlying futures contract was trading at $7.20 at expiration, this trade would be making a profit of 2 cents ($7.22–$7.20), or $100. Likewise, if the underlying futures market was at $7.10 at expiration, the trade would be profitable 12 cents ($7.22–$7.10), or $600, before commissions and fees.

It is somewhat common practice for traders to leg out of a debit spread such as a bull call spread or a bear put spread. In the case of the bear put spread, this may involve buying back the short put and holding on to the long put or selling the long put and holding on to the short put. Of course, doing so increases the risk of the trade and alters the BE point.

chapter 7

Synthetic Swing Trading

Close proximity to the options and futures markets, trial and error, and experience have led us to a keen understanding of the trading game. We have acquired a basket of knowledge and skills that we believe to be imperative to financial success in this vicious arena. Although having this knowledge and understanding in no way, shape, or form guarantees profits; nothing does. However, the premise of this chapter is to alter your perception of option trading by sharing some of our ideas.

Because markets tend to trade in a defined range, we have concluded that outright long option positions are priced to lose in most cases. As a matter of fact, studies conducted by the Chicago Mercantile Exchange (CME) suggest that far more options than not expire worthless, and we trust that much of the peril in long option trading boils down to the market's tendency to trade relatively sideways a majority of the time. As a result, constant awareness of levels of support and resistance is crucial.

Within the aforementioned trading ranges, are short-lived trends in which many traders look to exploit through futures swing trading. However, it is also possible to profit from a range bound market using a combination of long and short options. We like to refer to this as *synthetic swing trading*.

In the realm of trading, a synthetic position is any financial instrument that is artificially created by using a combination of other assets whose features, as a whole, are comparable to the instrument that it is designed to replicate. Synthetic swing trading describes the use of option spreads or a combination of options and futures to trade the markets in a capacity that is normally done using futures contracts. In other words, we are synthetically creating a "quieter" version of a futures contract.

In this particular instance, we are using the term "synthetic" loosely. Most references to synthetic indicate the mimicking of an identical risk and reward profile, while we are simply creating positions that are *comparable* to trading outright futures. For example, a truly synthetic strategy may include the purchase of an at-the-money call option and the sale of a futures contract. This strategy provides the trader with similar, or even identical, risks and potential rewards as simply buying a put. Accordingly, such a trading approach is often referred to as a synthetic put. We will go over this concept in much more depth in Chapter 10, "Synthetic Long Option Plays."

Synthetically swing trading offers traders a more flexible position relative to outright futures trading with seemingly less exposure to market volatility. While the profit and loss diagram may differ from that of an outright futures trade, the market approach is the same.

Swing traders are not looking to predict the overall direction of the market or to hold a bullish or bearish bias. Instead, the goal is to simply profit from the natural ebb and flow of the market. In other words, swing traders attempt to capitalize on both the trending and retracement phases of the market. The theory of this strategy is based on the assumption that all upward action must result in a corrective period, or vice versa. If this can be done with futures, why not use a similar approach in option trading?

Why Swing Trading with Option Spreads?

While there are traders who opt to swing trade using futures contracts as opposed to options, we argue that option spreads can be effective in ironing out some of the market's volatility. This is important in that it allows more room for error, and in the case of incorrect speculation on market direction less immediate risk may be involved. As we cover some trading examples, this concept will become clearer.

As with most things in life, in terms of volatility, less is often more.

Once a futures position is executed, you are immediately exposed to theoretically unlimited risk, and the profit and loss begins to become a reality. In an option spread, any naked leg exposes the trader to theoretically unlimited risk, but unlimited risk doesn't occur until the market travels beyond the strike price of the short option. This can be a big advantage in that you don't have to be 100% perfect in timing or execution. It is possible for the market to move against you without causing as much financial burden as a futures contract might. Later in this chapter we will discuss the scenarios in which this is the case as well as the accompanying risks involved.

Of course, there is always a catch. The downside of swing trading with options versus futures contracts is the fact that the profit potential is often limited. With the exception of the synthetic options and futures, all other strategies involve theoretically unlimited risk beyond a certain point and limited profit potential. Another potential pitfall is the ease of entry and exit (market liquidity) and the possibility of the extrinsic handcuff becoming an obstacle. However, this shouldn't discourage you. We deem that such strategies offer much better odds of success, which, in our opinions, outweigh any potential downfalls.

When looking to synthetically swing trade a market, our tool belt is loaded with the following strategies:

- Bull call spread with a naked leg

- Bear put spread with a naked leg

- Ratio call spread

- Ratio put spread

- Synthetic options and futures

Here is a description of each of these trading methods along with examples of how they may help you achieve your trading goals.

Trading Naked (It's Not What You Think)

When we use the term "naked" to refer to an option, we are not referring to its wardrobe, or lack thereof. Naked is often used to describe a short, or sold, option that exposes the seller to unlimited risk. Any option that is not executed in direct conjunction with a long option of the same type but differing strike price, or a futures contract that benefits from a price move in the opposite direction of the short option in question is considered to be naked. For example, a short call may be "covered" by a long futures contract.

Being naked in public is punishable; being naked in a market is risky, but it may be rewarding.

A good broker will clearly be able to decipher the difference between a covered option and a naked option. Unfortunately, through our experiences we have come to realize that many brokers do not understand option theory and often make the false assumption that any short option involves unlimited risk, but this is obviously not the case. As you saw in Chapter 6, "Limited Risk Option Spreads," credit spreads entail short options but do not subject the seller to unlimited risk. A common error that beginning brokers, or those who simply aren't competent enough to be taking or advising client orders, make is to assume that an iron butterfly is a marginable trade. As you see in Chapter 9 "Limited Risk Range Trades," an iron butterfly consists of two long options and two short options. The risk of each of the short options is covered by the long options. Your brokerage firm should not charge margin on this trade because the risk is limited to what you pay for the spread. If it does, you should begin shopping for a new clearing firm.

By now, we all know that options are an eroding asset and that they are essentially priced to lose. As we have repeatedly stated throughout the book, this makes it difficult to make money as an option buyer. We believe that a trader can increase her odds of success by financing trades through premium collection.

Specifically, traders who are expecting prices to rise can increase their leverage, and probability of success, by executing an option spread in which the purchase of call options is financed by the proceeds of short options. Trading naked may take the form of various options spreads, but it will always involve the sale of more short legs than long or at least more short option premium than long option premium. Examples of such are ratio spreads, or bull call and bear put spreads with naked legs.

In their simplest form, each of these spreads is an expansion of either a bull call or a bear put spread. For example, a bull call spread with a naked leg is in essence a sale of an uncovered put to pay for a bull call spread. Similarly, a trader can finance a bear put spread by selling a naked call option. Likewise, a trader could collect the premium needed to purchase a bull call spread by selling an extra call. Naturally, the decision on which strategy to use depends on your risk tolerance and market conditions. We discuss some examples a little later.

Understanding the Risk and How to Cope

Sellers of naked options are subjected to theoretically unlimited losses. Therefore it is critical that traders assess the technical and fundamental circumstances of the market to choose an appropriate strike price for a short option.

For obvious reasons, you wouldn't want to sell a put option above critical support levels or sell a call option below critical resistance levels, as illustrated in Figure 7.1. As a trader, you are in the business of increasing your odds. Selling an option for no other reason than that it will bring in a lot of premium is padding the cash in your trading account, but it is also putting the odds in favor of your competition. Just as this would be financial suicide in any business, the repercussions that you may experience in futures trading can and will be extremely fierce.

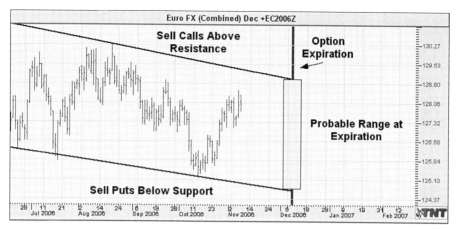

Figure 7.1 The secret to option selling is proper placement of strike prices. Call options should be placed above resistance and put options should be placed below support.

Bull Call Spread with a Naked Leg

Buy an at-the-money or out-of-the-money call option.
Sell a call option with a distant (higher) strike price.
Sell an out-of-the-money put option.

When to Use

● You think the market will go up but purchasing a near-the-money outright call option is very expensive.

● The goal is to produce a inexpensive, or even free, trade without regard to commissions.

Profit Profile

● Profit is limited to the difference between the strike prices plus premium collected for the spread and minus the transaction costs if done as a credit, or minus the premium paid and minus the transaction costs if done as a debit.

- At expiration the break-even is equal to the long call strike price plus the net amount paid for the spread plus commissions and fees if executed as a debit, or the reverse break-even is equal to the strike price of the short put minus the amount of premium collected plus the transaction costs if executed as a credit.

BE (if a debit)=Long Strike Price+Net Premium Paid+Transaction Costs

RBE (if a credit)=Short Put Strike Price–Net Premium Collected+Transaction Costs

Risk

- Risk on the downside (short put) is theoretically unlimited.
- The market trading below the short put is similar to being long the futures from the put strike price.
- At expiration if the market is between the short put and long call you lose the net debit paid for the spread. If it was executed as a credit, the trader keeps the premium collected.

Example

Let's take a look at a trade that may have been possible in mid June 2006, illustrated in Figure 7.2. Throughout May and much of June, the stock market managed to erase most of the gains that had been achieved over the first two quarters of the year. The catalyst to the selling was fear of inflation and an aggressive Federal Reserve campaign to control price pressures. On June 14, using the September options you could have executed the following trade at a debit of less than $100. Buying the September Dow 10,800 call, selling the 11,200 call and the 10,400 put. In other words, for just under $100, without regard to commissions or margin, a trader could have purchased an at-the-money call option. Buying the 10,800 call option outright (without selling the additional call or put) would have cost 425 points or $4,250 (425 x $10). The break-even point of buying the 10,800 call would have been 11,225 (10,800+425). However, by selling the 10,400 put and the 11,200 call the break-even is moved all the way down to about 10,808 to increase the probability of success tremendously. The risk on this trade is below 10,400 and is theoretically

We often use the term synthetic futures to describe a strategy that includes a combination of long and short legs with the short options outnumbering the long. This is because the option spreads can be created with a relatively high delta value. Remember, a futures contract has a delta of 1. These spreads are optimal in that they are flexible and offer a trader some room for error.

unlimited. Under this level, it is nearly equivalent to being long the futures contract. The maximum profit potential of this spread is the distance between the strike prices of the long and short calls, which is 400 points, or $4,000 (400 x $10), minus the cost of the trade and the commissions. The maximum profit occurs if the market is above 11,200 at expiration.

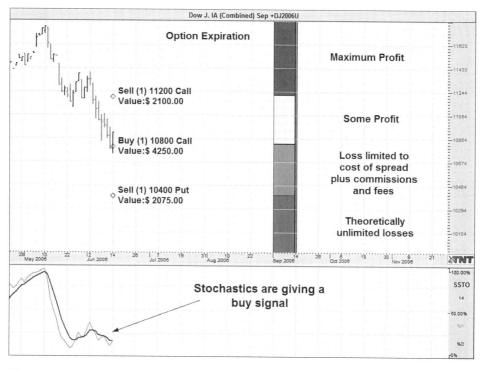

Figure 7.2 The market looks to be oversold, but picking a bottom can be like catching a falling knife. Here is way to enter the market with some room for error.

Now let's review a trade that didn't turn out exactly as planned, but eventually paid off. The September Dow Jones futures contract had satisfied its digestive needs by dropping to the 11,100 level following a bullish move. In anticipation of the market regaining strength to return to the highs experienced a few weeks earlier at 11,400 many were eager to execute an aggressive option trade. On July 12, according to these theoretical values it may have been possible to buy the August 11,200 call, sell the 11,400 call and the 10,900 put for even money or a small debit. The profit potential on this trade was $2,000 if the market was trading at or above 11,400 at expiration, as shown in Figure 7.3.

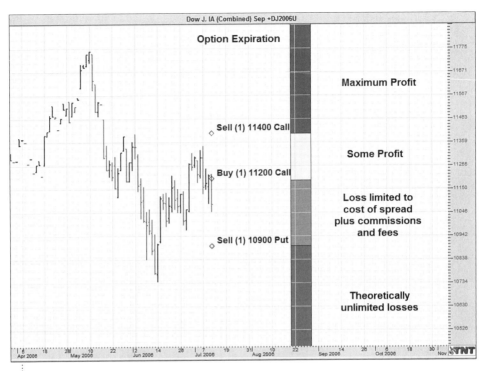

Figure 7.3   Unless the market is below 10,900 at expiration, this trade will either be a minimal loser or profitable.

Synthetic swing strategies such as a bull call or bear put spread with a naked leg may make it easier for traders to ride out the waves of the market when compared to trading futures contracts. A futures trader has to worry about being stopped out and has no hedge should the market go against the position. In the case of a bull call spread with a naked leg, as the market drops against the position, the trade is making money on the short call. This helps to take some of the sting out of the trade as the other two legs would be losing positions.

The day subsequent to entry, the market swiftly dropped to the recent low near 10,800. As illustrated in Figure 7.4, this was well below the strike price of the short put as well as a reasonable comfort zone. However, understanding that markets are in constant search for an equilibrium price, many were likely unwilling to give up on the trade. It is not uncommon to see dramatic but temporary moves as new information hits the marketplace triggering an "overreaction."

Unfortunately, many beginning traders fall victim to "false" market moves such as this. In their defense, you can never be certain that price changes are temporary until after the fact. As you can imagine, fear and greed play a big part in a premature exit of a trade. In this case, maintaining resolve and sticking with the trade would have paid. As you can see in Figure 7.5, the market was able to regain its composure and approach the option expiration date well within the profit zone.

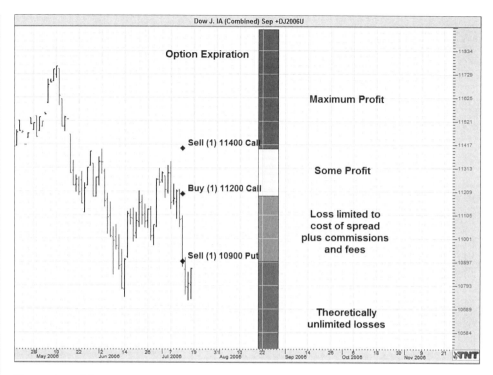

Dow J. IA (Combined) Sep +DJ2006U

Option Expiration

Maximum Profit

Sell (1) 11400 Call

Some Profit

Buy (1) 11200 Call

Loss limited to
cost of spread
plus commissions
and fees

Sell (1) 10900 Put

Theoretically
unlimited losses

Figure 7.4 With the market below the strike price of the short put, the trader is in a losing position intrinsically and potentially extrinsically. However, if the market recovers to a level above 10,900 at expiration the losses are limited to the cost of the spread.

"I never buy at the bottom and I always sell too soon."
Baron Nathan

In the heat of the moment, a trader might have mistakenly bought back the 109 put at a significant loss. In fact, though we don't remember details, we are almost positive that we remember a few clients who liquidated similar trades out of fear and we can't say that we blame them. After all, the market had just plunged more than 500 points in a very hasty fashion and didn't seem to be willing to stop for anything. However, an experienced trader may have had the frame of mind to stand back from the trade and objectively observe major technical and fundamental factors to make an educated decision. In this case, you can see that the market was simply forming a base of support from which it could forge a rally. A retest of the previous month's low resulted in an uncomfortable situation but didn't give traders any indication that the market was in store for continued selling pressure.

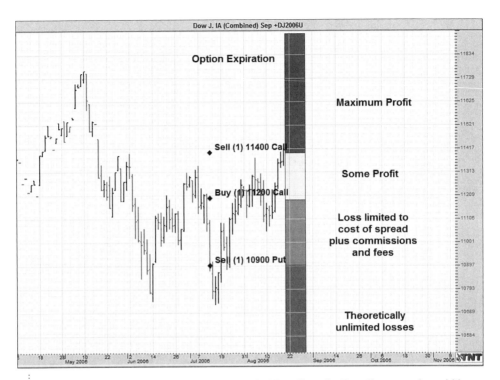

Figure 7.5 Assuming that the trade was held until expiration, the spread would have returned a handsome profit. Those who may have fallen victim to fear following the market downturn may have had a completely opposite result.

Naturally, it is much easier to grasp this concept as you are reading this text and looking at charts than it is if you are involved in the markets and have real money on the line. Keep in mind that all great traders suffered incredible losses in the beginning of their trading careers. The ability to manage your emotions is something that takes practice and experience to accomplish, and even then these capabilities will falter from time to time simply because even great traders are human.

The purpose of using this particular trade as an example isn't to lead you to believe that hanging on to a loser in hopes that it will turn around is always the right move. In fact, doing so could prove to be extremely detrimental.

We want you to walk away from this example with the understanding that your biggest obstacle to making money in futures trading is psychological. The premise that losses should always be cut short isn't always going to be possible or preferable. As brokers, we have seen too many traders suffer unnecessary losses at the hands of a panic liquidation. Whether we agree with our clients' decisions or not, an order is an order, and we are there to execute their requests.

Bear Put Spread with a Naked Leg

Buy an at-the-money put option or an out-of-the-money put.
Sell a put with a distant (lower) strike price.
Sell an out-of-the-money call option.

When to Use

- You think the market will go down, but an outright put option is very expensive and you want to be positioned close-to-the-money.

- The goal is to purchase a close-to-the money put for very little cost.

Profit Profile

- Profit is limited to the difference between the strike prices of the long and short puts plus premium collected minus transaction costs if executed as a credit. Or the distance between the long and short put strike prices minus the premium paid minus the commissions and fees if executed as a debit.

- At expiration the break-even is equal to the long put strike price minus the net amount paid for the spread minus transaction costs in the case of debit. If it is a credit spread, the reverse break-even will be the short call strike price plus the net premium collected minus transaction costs.

BE (if a debit)=Long Strike Price–Net Premium Paid–Transaction Costs

RBE (if a credit)=Short Call Strike Price+Net Premium Collected–Transaction Costs

Risk

- Risk on the upside (short call) is theoretically unlimited.

- The market trading above the short call is equivalent to being short the futures from the call strike price.

- At expiration if the market is between the long put and short call you lose the net premium paid for the spread if executed as a debit. If executed as a credit, the trader keeps the premium collected.

The premise of trading with "naked" legs is to create extremely cheap, or even free trades. The term free infers no cash outlay or collection but doesn't consider commission, margin, or risk. Many brokers refer to free as "even money" because nothing in life is free. Essentially the strategy is looking to use the market's money to finance a long option position in exchange for accepting unlimited risk beyond a stated point. The trade illustrated in Figure 7.6 involves a long Treasury bond 113 put, a short 111 put, and a short 115 call. If filled at the prices noted in Figure 7.6, the trade would be a credit of 3 ticks. This is figured by netting the premium paid for the long put against the premium collected for the short call and the short put. In the case of bond options, the simple process of netting can quickly become complicated. We hope that you paid attention in grade school when you were taught fractions.

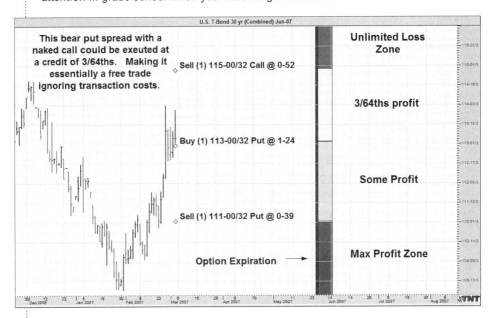

Figure 7.6   A three-legged spread such as a bear put spread with a naked leg provides a trader with some "room for error."

Bond options, unlike the futures contracts which are quoted in 32nds, are quoted in 64ths. This means that for every full handle of price movement, which is equal to $1,000, there are 64 minimum ticks. Likewise, in bond futures each full point is split into 32 ticks. Each tick of an option price is worth $15.625, or ($1,000 / 64). Thus, buying the 113 put for 1'24 would cost $1,375 ($1,000+(24 x $15.625)), selling the 115 call for 52 ticks would bring in $812.50 (52 x $15.625), and selling the 111 put for 39 would bring in $609.37 (39 x $15.625). If you took the net of the premium, you would get a credit of

3 ticks, or $46.87. Please note, that the premium of 1'24 regarding the 113 put is equivalent to 1 24/64ths, not 124/64ths.

If the bear put spread with a naked leg is executed at a credit, assuming that the market is not beyond the strike price of the short call, the trader would be profitable whether the spread ever becomes in-the-money or not.

The structure of this trade gives traders some room for error. Because the trade can be executed at a small credit without consideration of transaction costs, it is profitable by at least 3 ticks anywhere below 115. The maximum profit occurs if the market is trading below 111 at expiration. At the time of this trade, the market is trading near 113, approximately two full points below the strike price of the short call and thus the risk on the trade. In essence, this trade allows the trader to be wrong in the direction of the market by two price handles before incurring losses at expiration. With that said, at anytime prior to expiration extrinsic losses are possible even if the market never travels above the strike price of the short call option.

Naturally, it is much easier to be right in the direction of Treasury bonds with a two-point "cushion" than it would be with a futures position that immediately puts a trader at the mercy of the market.

A free trade simply implies that the trade collects more premium on the short options than is paid for the long options of the spread. It does not suggest that there are no commissions charged, margin necessary to execute the trade, or risk.

Because the trade was essentially free to get into, the trader's risk of loss at expiration is only existent if the market is above 115'01, (remember the 01 represents 1/32 not 64ths) once again ignoring commissions and fees. In other words, this is the reverse break-even point on the trade (see Figure 7.7). It is important to note that the reverse break-even point is well above the price where the market was trading at the time of execution. This makes it possible for the trader to be wrong in the direction of the market and still walk away a winner of 3/64ths before commission and fees.

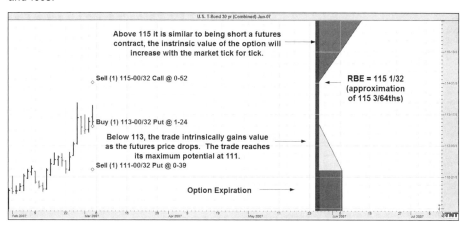

Figure 7.7 The reverse break-even point on the trade is nearly two full points above the market at execution. We believe that this provides increased odds of success.

The opportunity cost of having room for error and seemingly better odds of success on a trade such as a bear put spread or bull call spread with a naked leg is the burden of limited profit potential and unlimited risk. To mitigate the impact, it is important that when structuring the trade the short call of the bull call spread is placed at, or slightly beyond, resistance, and the short put of the bear put spread is placed at, or slightly beneath, support. Doing so decreases the potential impact of limited profit potential with the strategy.

Try mimicking this type of payout with a futures position without using a combination of options. It cannot be done. In futures trading there is no room for error; incorrect market assumptions result in immediate losses.

Above the reverse break-even price of 115'01 the risk is theoretically unlimited. At expiration, the trade will be losing tick for tick with the futures market above the RBE. To illustrate, if bonds are at 115'27 at expiration the loss on the trade would be 51 ticks or $796.87. Remember, bond options are quoted in 64ths, while futures are traded in 32nds. So the calculation to derive this loss would be (27/32 x 2)=54 /64, (54 -3) x $15.625=$796.87.

Of course, with all the benefits of trading a bear put spread with a naked leg over trading futures there are bound to be glaring disadvantages. For one, the trade provides only limited profit potential. Regardless of how far below the strike price of the short put option the market is at expiration, the profit potential is capped at $2,046.87 (see Figure 7.8). We reached that figure by calculating the spread between the strike price of the long put and the short put and adding the credit collected to initiate the trade, ((113–111) x $1,000+$46.87). If you recall, each full point in bonds is equal to $1,000, and the trade was executed at a credit of 3/64ths at which each of the three ticks was worth $15.625.

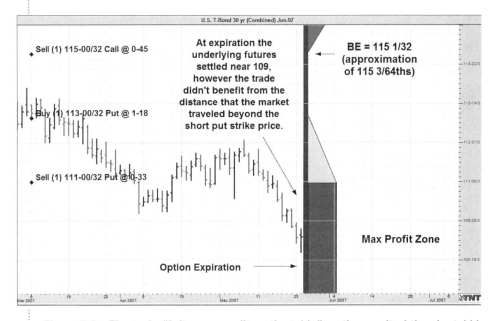

Figure 7.8 The trade "left some profit on the table" as the result of the short 111 put, but in our opinion the benefits of such a strategy outweigh the opportunity costs.

Call Ratio Spread

Buy an at-the-money call option.
Sell two or more out-of-the money call options.

When to Use

- When you expect the market to make a slight or moderate up move, but there is potential for the market to make a significant down move.
- The objective is to put this trade on as a credit, even-money (free), or small debit.

Profit Profile

- If the trade is done as a credit the profit on the downside (below the long call strike price) is limited to premium collected minus transaction costs.
- Profit on the upside (above the long call strike price) is limited to the difference between the long and short calls minus the transaction costs plus the amount collected if done as a credit, but minus the amount paid if executed as a debit.

Risk

- If the market expires below the long call and the trade wasn't executed at a credit, your risk is limited to any premium paid for the spread plus transaction costs.
- Holding more short calls than long, the upside risk is unlimited above the strike price of the short calls.
- Having unlimited risk, this trade needs to be watched closely.

BE (if debit)=Strike Price of the Long Call+Premium Paid+Transaction Costs

RBE (if debit)=Short Call Strike Price+Distance between the Long and Short Options–Premium Paid–Transaction Costs

RBE (if credit)=Short Call Strike Price+Distance between the Long and Short Options+Premium Collected–Transaction Costs

BE (if credit)=At expiration this trade profits in the amount of the credit from the strike price of the long call all the way to zero. This trade is profitable at any point below the RBE, thus a true break-even cannot be determined

Similar to the trades previously mentioned in this chapter, ratio spreads allow a trader to enter the market with little out-of-pocket expense in exchange for accepting theoretically unlimited risk beyond a specific point. In the case of a one-by-two call ratio call spread, the trade consists of buying a close to-the-money call option and selling two call options with distant strike prices. Depending on the premium paid for the long option and collected for the short options, this trade may be either a debit or credit spread, or simply you may be paying out more than you are collecting, or you may be collecting more than you are paying out.

Whether the spread is executed as a credit or a debit is dependent on the strike prices you choose and the extrinsic value of the options such as time, volatility, and demand. Of course, in most cases it is preferential to collect money on the trade rather than pay a premium for it. However, if executing the trade as a credit means that you have to narrow the distance between the strike prices to a point in which the delta values are too similar, or you have to get closer-to-the-money than you are comfortable with, then it is not worth it. The most important thing is that the construction of the trade is sound and is in line with your patience and risk tolerance.

Imagine the possibilities of such a trade. If you were able to get a one-by-two ratio spread filled at a credit, it is possible to be absolutely wrong in the direction of the market and still be profitable. Sure, the trade would have made more had the market gone in the anticipated direction, but to be wrong and still make money can be a great asset in the world of trading. Keep in mind, that there are traders who are very good at what they do (they actually make money in the markets) and are right less than half of the time.

The disadvantage to a ratio spread is that the risk in the trade lies beyond the strike prices of the short options. So it is possible to be *too right*. If the market travels in the anticipated direction but overshoots your targets, you may find yourself in a losing trade. Considering that your analysis was correct, at least in terms of the direction, this can be very frustrating.

An additional warning should be made here; if the market makes an extraordinarily violent move in the direction that you had anticipated, the combined value of the short options may appreciate faster than the value of the long option. Because you are long one and short two, the extrinsic value of the options may create a scenario in which, despite the fact that the underlying futures market is in the area that would be considered the "profit zone," the trade may be losing *prior* to expiration.

This is because when a market begins to move quickly, the demand for options in the given direction increases dramatically. As you can imagine, if everyone is buying options in the same direction, call or put, the prices will skyrocket. We argue that if the market has already begun moving to the point where the corresponding options are "overpriced" you may have already missed the move and should be a seller of these options rather than a buyer.

However, if you are not already in the market when the price explosion occurs, a ratio spread may be appropriate. This is because you are buying one "overpriced" option, but selling two "overpriced" options.

On the surface, this strategy seems to be extremely complicated and confusing; we feel that the only way to gain an understanding of the mechanics of the trade is to consider an example.

Example

Until 2008 soybean futures had only been above $10 a handful of times and in limited amounts of time but when this market begins to rally speculators quickly jump on the bandwagon in anticipation of the infamous "beans in the teens" scenario. High bean prices usually translate into seemingly overinflated call premiums, making ratio call spreads a viable strategy.

Buying an $8.40 soybean call option for 55 1/4 cents, and selling two $9.20 calls for 31 3/4 a piece would bring in a credit of 8 1/4 cents to the trader (55 2/8–(2 x 31 6/8)=8 2/8, reduced to 8 1/4 cents). This is significant in that it means that even if the market doesn't go up as anticipated, the trader still gets to keep the 8 1/4 cents, or $412.50 assuming that trade is held intact until expiration. Being wrong and still making more than $400 before commissions and fees puts the odds strongly in favor of the trade. In fact, the only way that this trade could be a loser at expiration is if the market was trading above the reverse break-even point of $10.08 1/4. As mentioned earlier, the market has only been above $10 on rare occasions. Because this trade was executed as a credit, we would use a reverse break-even calculation. The RBE is figured by measuring the distance between the strike price of the long call and the strike price of the two short calls and adding this to the strike price of the short call; we then add the net credit. Keep in mind that this example ignores commission and fees. Thus, the RBE=($9.20–$8.40)+$9.20+8 1/4 cents=$10.08 1/4 at option expiration (see Figure 7.9).

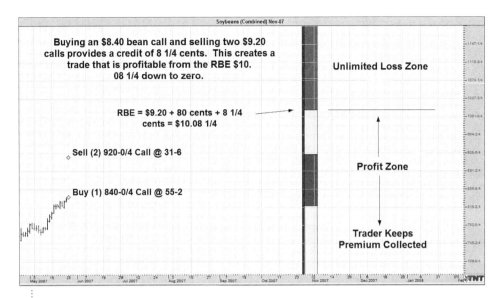

Buying an $8.40 bean call and selling two $9.20 calls provides a credit of 8 1/4 cents. This creates a trade that is profitable from the RBE $10. 08 1/4 down to zero.

Unlimited Loss Zone

RBE = $9.20 + 80 cents + 8 1/4 cents = $10.08 1/4

Sell (2) 920-0/4 Call @ 31-6

Profit Zone

Buy (1) 840-0/4 Call @ 55-2

Trader Keeps Premium Collected

Figure 7.9 One-by-two ratio spreads are capable of providing traders with large profit zones.

However, if there is one thing that we have learned through experience it is that putting the odds in your favor isn't always enough. You can never underestimate a market and should always be aware of the fact that almost anything can, and eventually will, happen in trading. Thus, although the profit zone on this trade is extremely large and seemingly likely, the trade is not without risk. If the market did rally above the RBE of $10.08 1/4, then the trade would be facing *theoretically* unlimited losses. In other words, as the market surpasses the RBE the trade loses increasingly with every tick higher.

As mentioned, if the option spread itself expires worthless the trader gets to keep the original premium collected of 8 1/4 cents. This occurs if the market is trading beneath $8.40 at expiration, assuming that the spread was left intact. Above $8.40 the spread is said to be in-the-money. Profits are increased with every tick that the market moves above the long call strike price until it reaches the maximum potential at the strike price of the short options. Beyond this point, the trade "gives back profits" until it runs out of money at the reverse break-even, $10.08 1/4. Once again, beyond this point the trader faces unlimited loss potential. Keep in mind that these calculations are based on values at expiration, or option premium without extrinsic value.

The maximum profit potential on this trade occurs if the underlying futures contract is trading at exactly $9.20, the strike price of the short call options. At this point, the trade would be profitable intrinsically by $4,000 (80 cents x $50); remember the multiplier for soybeans is $50. However, the trade was filled at a credit so the premium collected must be added to the profit potential of the spread making the total maximum profit on the trade $4,412.50 ($4,000+(8 1/4 x $50)) before taking into account the commissions and fees to execute the transaction.

Perhaps the best aspect of this trade is its ability to profit even if the market goes down. Beneath $8.40 all the way down to zero, the trade is profitable in the amount of the net credit minus commissions and fees (see Figure 7.10).

Many traders use ratio spreads as a counter trend strategy; in the case of a one-by-two call spread you may look to put this trade on at a credit in a swiftly rallying market. The result is a trade that profits on a rally or a decline, assuming that the market doesn't rally beyond the RBE of the trade, which may be substantially higher.

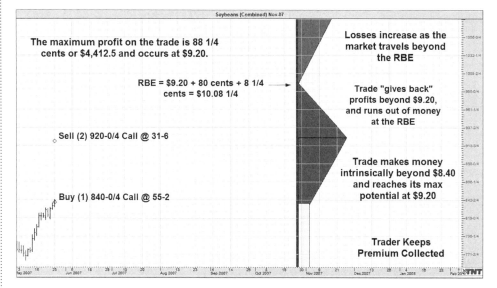

The maximum profit on the trade is 88 1/4 cents or $4,412.5 and occurs at $9.20.

RBE = $9.20 + 80 cents + 8 1/4 cents = $10.08 1/4

Sell (2) 920-0/4 Call @ 31-6

Buy (1) 840-0/4 Call @ 55-2

Losses increase as the market travels beyond the RBE

Trade "gives back" profits beyond $9.20, and runs out of money at the RBE

Trade makes money intrinsically beyond $8.40 and reaches its max potential at $9.20

Trader Keeps Premium Collected

Figure 7.10 One-by-two ratio call spreads can offer seemingly spectacular odds of success, but can be frustrating if you are "too right" and the market rallies above your RBE, at which point the trade faces unlimited loss potential.

Put Ratio Spread

Buy an at-the-money put.
Sell two or more out-of-the-money puts.

When to Use

● When you expect the market to make a slight or moderate down move, but there is potential for a significant up move.

● The objective is to put this trade on as a credit, even-money, or small debit.

Profit Profile

● If the trade is done as a credit the profit is limited on the upside (above the strike price of the long put) to premium collected minus transaction costs.

● Profit on the downside (below the strike price of the long put) is limited to the difference between the long and short puts plus the net credit minus transaction costs of the trade. If the trade is executed as a debit, the profit potential is limited to the difference between the long and short put strike prices minus the premium paid minus transaction costs.

Risk

● If the market expires above the long put, your risk is limited to any premium paid for the spread plus transaction costs if the trade was executed as a debit.

● Holding more short puts than long, the downside risk is unlimited below the strike price of the short puts.

● Having unlimited risk this trade needs to be watched closely.

BE (if debit)=Strike Price of the Long Put–Premium Paid–Transaction Costs

RBE (if debit)=Short Put Strike Price–Distance between the Long and Short Options+Premium Paid+Transaction Costs

RBE (if credit)=Short Put Strike Price–Distance between the Long and Short Options–Premium Collected+Transaction Costs

BE (if credit)=This spread is profitable in the amount of the premium collected beginning at the strike price of the long put infinitely higher. This trade is profitable from any price above the RBE, thus a true break-even point cannot be determined.

A one-by-two ratio put spread is normally implemented by those who are bearish but do not completely trust their assessment and believe that the downside price potential is limited. Or, it may simply be a ploy to take advantage of inflated premiums due to swiftly moving markets.

Similar to a one-by-two ratio call spread, a one-by-two ratio put spread allows entry into a market for very little money in exchange for theoretically unlimited risk, and margin of course. The trade can be executed as either a debit or credit, depending on market conditions and structure of the trade.

Keep in mind that if the trade is filled at a debit, meaning that it cost more to buy the long option than was taken in for the short legs, the trade will have both a break-even and a reverse break-even. This is because for the trade to be profitable at expiration, the market will have to be beyond the strike price of the long option enough to cover the amount of premium paid for the spread. A ratio spread executed as a credit will also have a reverse break-even point but cannot lose at any price higher than the RBE so a true break-even point can't be determined. If the market moves beyond the strike price of the short options, the reverse break-even will be the distance between the strike price of the long and short options plus or minus the amount of premium paid or collected. In the case of a put ratio spread, the RBE is calculated by adding the premium paid or subtracting the premium collected.

Naturally, if you pay to get into a trade it will make it that much harder to make money because it shifts your RBE further away. Again, if the difference between collecting and paying for a spread means structuring the trade in a way that makes the associated risks above what you would normally be willing to accept, it isn't worth it. Even a "free" trade, or a small debit, is a great way to increase your odds of success.

Example

As illustrated in Figure 7.11 the simultaneous purchase of a Dow 12,400 put for 290 points, or $2,900 (290 x $10), and the sale of two 12,000 puts for 167 a piece results in a net credit. Each tick in the Dow is equal to $10, so the credit collected would be $440 (((167 x 2)−290) x $10). If the market rallies against the preferential direction of the trade (down), the trader will keep the $440 at expiration. In fact, this trade pays off something anywhere between the RBE at 11,556 and infinitely higher. The only instance in which this trade would lose

In the case of a ratio spread, it pays to be right but not to be *really* right.

The one-by-two ratio write, especially when executed as a credit, provides traders with an impressive profit playground. However, this type of strategy can be somewhat frustrating if the market explodes in the direction of your spread. In such a case, the losses on the short options may temporarily outweigh any gains on the long option even if the market isn't beyond the calculated RBE at the time of expiration.

if held to expiration would be if the underlying futures market was trading under the RBE. This particular example happens to be similar to a trade that was executed for clients as a hedge against short puts in the S&P 500.

The RBE is calculated by subtracting the difference between the strike prices of the spread from the short put strike price as well as the premium credit originally collected (12,000–(12,400–12,000)–44)=11,556.

Below the RBE, the trade faces theoretically unlimited loss. This is where frustration from this strategy may set in. By implementing this trade, the trader is most likely looking for the market to head moderately lower. Below 11,556 the trader may have been right in the direction of price movement, but wind up losing money anyway. Beneath the RBE, the trade loses increasingly as the market trades lower.

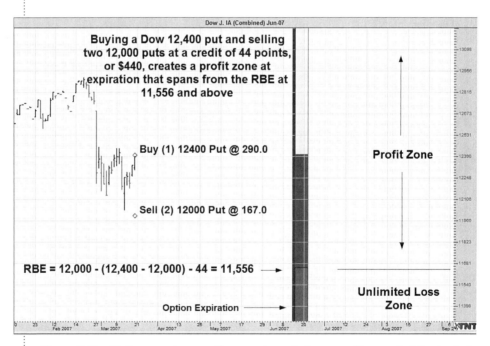

Dow J. IA (Combined) Jun-07

Buying a Dow 12,400 put and selling two 12,000 puts at a credit of 44 points, or $440, creates a profit zone at expiration that spans from the RBE at 11,556 and above

Buy (1) 12400 Put @ 290.0

Sell (2) 12000 Put @ 167.0

Profit Zone

RBE = 12,000 - (12,400 - 12,000) - 44 = 11,556 →

Unlimited Loss Zone

Option Expiration →

Figure 7.11   Ratio spreads can offer an extremely large profit zone, but the trade is not without risk.

This trade contains a maximum profit potential of the difference between the strike prices of the long put and the short puts plus the premium collected upon entry of the trade (see Figure 7.12). Thus, this trade can return as much as $4,440 (((12,400–12,000)+44) x $10). Such a payout would occur if the futures price settles at 12,000 at expiration.

It is important to realize that the chances of the underlying futures being exactly at 12,000 at expiration are slim to none. Nonetheless, knowing the mechanics of the trade, including profit and loss zones, is imperative to making educated decisions in terms of exiting or adjusting the trade.

Ratio spreads can be difficult to trade in certain markets, such as those that are highly volatile or thinly traded. If an option market has typically wide bid/ask spreads, it is probably not the venue to be doing ratio spreads. This is because if the trade goes violently against you and you opt to liquidate prior to expiration, it may be costly to pay the extrinsic value on top of the bid/ask spread. Of course a trade in a more liquid market can go against you at any given time, but you may be able to liquidate at a more manageable loss.

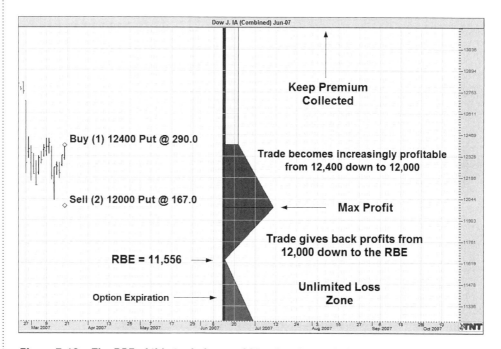

Figure 7.12   The RBE of this trade is over 800 points beneath the market price when this trade was implemented, accordingly it would take a very large adverse move for this trade to be in trouble at expiration.

If a one-by-two ratio spread is executed as a credit, but the spread expires worthless the trade is still profitable in the amount of premium collected minus the commissions and fees paid to initiate the trade. As you can imagine, it can be a valuable tool to profit on a trade in which your speculative direction is wrong. Once again, the downside of the strategy lies in unlimited risk beyond the reverse breakeven point of the trade.

The simplest way to understand the payoff of a ratio spread at expiration is to look at it logically. From the strike price of the long put to the strike price of the short puts the trade is making money intrinsically. That is, the long put is in-the-money, but the two short options are still *intrinsically worthless*. Intrinsically worthless refers to the fact that at expiration the options won't have any value if the market is trading at or above the strike price, not beyond. Once the price drops below the strike price of the short puts, they gain intrinsic value. Because the trade involves one long put, one of the short puts will simply offset gains on the long put as the market drops. However, the second short put is "naked." Once the market drops enough to erase the profits made on the long put between the long strike and the short strike, the trade becomes a loser. Plainly stated, the trade makes money at expiration from 12,400 to 12,000. Below 12,000 the trade is giving back intrinsic profits until it runs out of money at 11,600. Below 11,600, the trade is giving back the premium collected to get in until it runs out at the RBE, at which point the trade faces unlimited losses (see Figure 7.13).

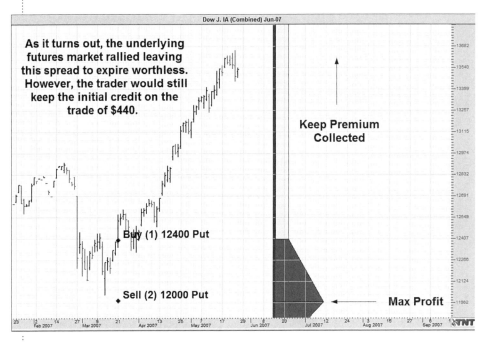

Figure 7.13   One of the most appealing characteristics of this strategy is the ability to make money despite flawed predictions in price movement.

chapter 8

The Other Ratio Spreads

As mentioned, ratio spreads come in various forms. A version that we less commonly use is the *back spread*. This trade involves the sale of a close-to-the-money option and the purchase of two options of the same type with distant strike prices. This trade is a mirror image of the previously covered ratio spreads.

A back spread comprises of either calls or puts, but not both, in the same expiration month. Because there isn't a naked, or uncovered leg in the spread, the trader is not liable for theoretically unlimited losses. Instead, a back spread trader faces limited risk and unlimited profit potential.

The trade can be executed as a credit (you collect more premium on the short option than you pay for the long options), debit (you pay more for the long options than you collect for the short option), or even money. In most cases, you would only look to do this trade if it will bring in a credit, or at least at even money. This is because it takes a substantial move for this trade to make money. Without a credit, it is a losing proposition in all instances other than a big move in the desired direction.

Traders typically utilize a back spread strategy if they think that the market is going to make an extreme move. In our opinion there are better ways to capture such a price move, but because this is a commonly covered strategy we thought that it would be appropriate to include it. Doing so may also help in your understanding of options and option spreads.

In our opinion, ratio back spreads are a difficult way to make money in the commodity markets. The strategy typically requires a substantial move to be successful.

Call Ratio Back Spread

Sell an at-the-money or out-of-the-money call.
Buy two or more out-of-the-money calls with a higher strike price.

When to Use

● When you expect the market to make a substantial move higher after a period of stagnation.

● The objective is to put this trade on at a credit, even money (free), or a small debit.

Profit Profile

● If the trade is done as a credit the profit is limited on the downside (below the strike price of the short call) to premium collected minus the transaction costs.

● Profit on the upside is unlimited beyond the reverse break-even

RBE 1 (if a credit)=Strike Price of Short Call+Net Credit–Transaction Costs

RBE 2 (if a credit)=Strike Price of Long Calls+Distance Between Long and Short Call Options–Net Credit

BE (if a debit)=Strike Price of Long Calls+Distance Between Long and Short Call Options+Net Debit

Risk

● Risk is limited to the difference between the strike prices of the short and long call options minus the net premium collected plus the transaction costs if done at a credit. If the spread is filled at a debit, the risk is limited to the difference between the short and long call strike prices plus the premium paid plus commissions and fees.

Call back spread traders are looking for the market to go lower, or much, much higher.

- If the market expires below the short call and the trade was executed as a debit, your risk is limited to any premium paid for the spread plus commissions.

- At expiration maximum loss is realized if the market is trading at the long call's strike price.

Example

Perhaps it will be easier to fully understand the mechanics of the trade by looking at a charting example shown in Figure 8.1. A trader anticipating that the stock market break trading range resistance in late August 2006, but unsure enough to actually pay out of pocket for a call option could have executed a call back spread. According to theoretical values, it would have been possible to sell a September 1280 call and buy 2 September 1290 calls for a small credit, about 50 cents in premium. Each dollar (full handle) move in the S&P is equal to $250 per contract, so the amount of the credit in terms of actual dollars would be $125.

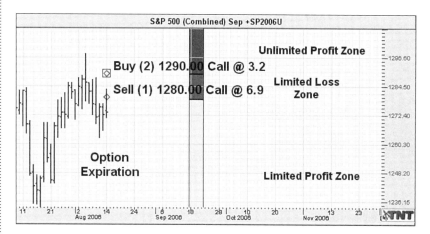

Figure 8.1 This call back spread brings a small credit to the trader before considering transaction costs, but to be successful beyond the original amount collected the market would have to be beyond 1299.50 at expiration.

Without regard to commissions or other transaction costs, this trade has a limited profit of $125 below the short strike price of 1280. This trade has a reverse break-even at 1280.50, the short call strike price plus the premium collected and another one at 1299.50 because the spread was executed at a credit. This is figured by adding the distance between the strike prices to the strike price of the long calls minus the net credit for executing the trade.

The maximum loss on the trade can be calculated by determining the dollar value of risk between the two strike prices minus the premium collected and occurs if the market is trading at 1290 at expiration. In this case it is $2,375, figured as follows.

Difference in Strike Prices=1290.00–1280.00=10.00

Premium Collected=.50

Multiplier=$250

(10.00–.50) (250)=$2,375 Maximum Risk

Please note that if the market is between the strike prices at expiration the loss will be the intrinsic value minus the premium collected. For example, if the market is trading at 1285 at expiration, the loss on the trade will be 4.50 or $1,125 (4.50 x $250).

The profit potential on this trade is theoretically unlimited. To calculate what the profit would be at expiration you would take the difference between the futures price at expiration and the strike price of the long call options and subtract the difference between the strike price of the long and short call plus or minus the premium paid or collected. This is because one of the long call options limits the risk, or covers, the short call option. The other long call option returns a profit. If the market is trading at 1308 at expiration, the profit on the trade would have been $8.50, or $2,125. This can be calculated as follows.

Difference in Futures and Strike Price=18.00

Premium Collected=.50

Distance Between Strike Prices of Long and Short Call=10.00

Multiplier=$250

(18.00+.50–10.00) (250)=$2,125 Profit at Expiration

Put Ratio Back Spread

Sell one at-the-money or out-of-the-money put.
Buy two or more out-of-the-money puts.

When to Use

● When you expect the market to make a substantial down move after a period of stagnation or expect a trend reversal.

● The objective is to put this trade on as a credit, at even money (free), or a slight debit.

Profit Profile

● If the trade is done as a credit the profit is limited on the upside (above the short put strike price) to premium collected.

● Profit on the downside (below the long put strike price) is unlimited.

RBE 1 (if a credit)=Strike Price of Short Put–Net Credit+Transaction Costs

RBE 2 (if a credit)=Long Put Strike Price–Distance between Long and Short Strike Price+Net Credit–Transaction Costs

BE (if a debit)=Long Put Strike Price–Distance between Long and Short Strike Price–Net Debit–Transaction Costs

Risk

● Risk is limited to the difference between the strike prices of the short and long put options plus the net premium paid plus transaction costs if executed at a debit. If done as a credit, the risk is limited to the difference between the strike prices of the long and short puts minus the premium collected plus commissions and fees.

● If the market expires above the short put your risk is limited to any premium paid for the spread plus transaction costs if the spread was executed at a debit.

● At expiration maximum loss is realized if the market is trading at the long put strike price.

● Being partially right is the worst-case scenario. In this strategy you want to be either very right or wrong.

Example

If ever there were a market capable of moving sharply, it is crude oil. We are not advocates of any type of back spread, but crude oil seems like a candidate for the strategy in that the volatility is high and the options are expensive.

As illustrated in Figure 8.2 selling a crude $62 put for $3.30, or $3,300, and buying two of the $57 puts for $1.37 each yields a credit of .56, or $560 (($3.30 –($1.37 x 2)) x $10). If the trader is wrong about the direction and the price of crude oil rises, he still gets to keep the initial credit for putting on the trade assuming that the trade is held intact until expiration. After all, $560 for being wrong doesn't seem to be a bad deal. However, it is being right that you have to worry about in this type of trade.

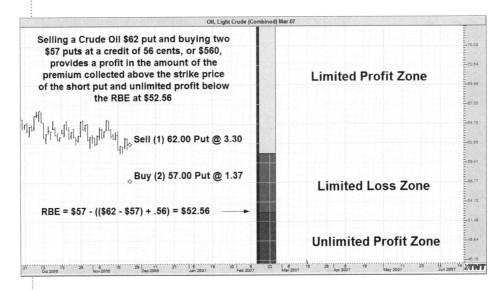

Figure 8.2 In the case of a back spread, being right in the direction isn't enough; you have to be extraordinarily right. This is the primary reason that we don't recommend this type of trade structure.

If the market drops, but doesn't move far enough to reach the RBE, the trade can lose as much as $4,440 ((($62–$57)–.56) x $10). The maximum loss occurs if the market is trading at the strike price of the long put at expiration, in this case $57. Keep in mind, this market will have to drop nearly $10 from the time of entry to reach the unlimited profit zone, which is beyond the reverse break-even. Even in crude oil, this seems unlikely. For reasons such as this, we don't find this to be a preferential strategy.

The RBE can be calculated by adding the net credit from the difference in the strike price of the short put and the long puts, and then subtracting that number from the strike price of the long option. In this example, the RBE=($57- (($62+$57) -.56)) $57=$52.56, before taking transaction costs into consideration. Once the market reaches the strike price of the short option, it will have to drop enough to make up the loss sustained on the short put from $62 to $57. Below $57, one of the long puts will simply cap the losses on the short put; the other will be recouping losses as the market declines.

"The inherent vice of capitalism is the unequal sharing of blessings; the inherent virtue of socialism is the equal sharing of miseries."
Winston Churchill

This trade will also have another reverse-break-even calculation. If the market trades sideways, or goes higher, the profit potential is the premium collected. However, once the market trades below the strike price of the short option the trade will intrinsically be giving back the money taken in until it runs out at $61.44 ($62–.56), the break-even point (see Figure 8.3).

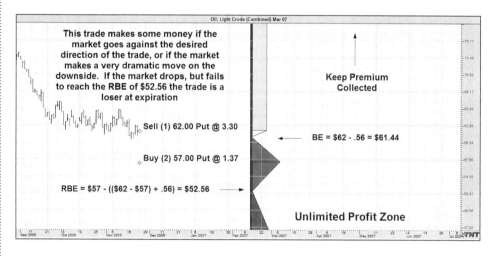

Figure 8.3 Not only do the odds of failure seem somewhat likely on a back spread, but it can be costly too. This trade has a total risk of more than $4,000.

A put back spread has the potential of unlimited profit with the benefit of limited loss; however, the odds of success appear to be less than attractive in most circumstances. Not only does the trader have to be right in the direction, but she must be extremely right and the market must move within the stated timeframe. If the market moves in the expected direction but doesn't move to the magnitude needed to reach the reverse break-even, or doesn't do it before option expiration the trade could be a substantial loser.

In our opinion, option back spreads are one of the hardest ways to make money when trading commodities. With so many other choices in terms of strategy, we fail to see how the benefits of this approach outweigh the downside. Although the risk on the trade is limited, depending on the structure of the spread and the market, the limited risk may be quite large (see Figure 8.4). Additionally, if limited risk is also *likely*, you may be much better off utilizing a strategy that contains theoretically unlimited risk but less probability of loss.

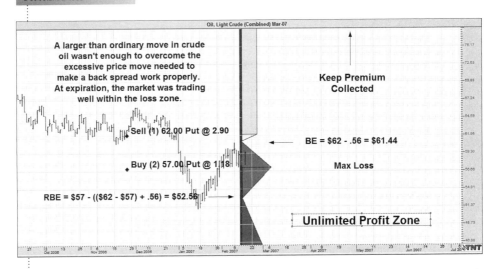

Figure 8.4 Even one of the biggest plunges in the history of crude oil wasn't enough to make this a profitable venture.

Recall the discussion in regard to long option strategies; similar to the back spread, the risk of loss is limited and the profit potential is unlimited. Yet neither the back spread nor a simple long option seems to provide the trader with reasonable odds of success. This is in line with just about everything that you have ever learned about finance in that risk and reward are highly correlated (see Figure 8.5).

Unlike a typical ratio spread, a back spread executed before an explosion in volatility in the direction of the spread may benefit from the dramatic increase in extrinsic value. This is because the trade is short one option, but long two. Even if the market has failed to travel beyond the reverse break-even and into the profit zone, at any point prior to expiration it is possible for the trade to be profitable due to the implied volatility of the options.

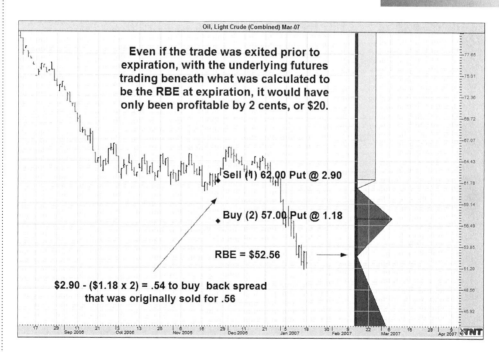

Figure 8.5 It seems as though the trader may have been able to exit the trade at a nice profit at sometime prior to expiration. However, even with the market near its lowest point, this trade would have returned only a marginal profit.

chapter 9

Limited Risk Range Trades

By definition a *butterfly* is an option spread consisting of more than two different options, usually consisting of a combination of both long and short options. It actually resembles a butterfly, having a central "body" as well as "wings."

An *iron butterfly*, sometimes referred to as a *diamond butterfly*, is an alternative to outright long option trading. It allows traders to enter the market with limited risk and provides a large range in which the trade returns a profit. We like to call this the *profit playground*.

Unlike outright long options or futures contracts, a diamond butterfly is capable of returning a profit in a market that is trading sideways. An iron butterfly consists of two long options and two short options with three equidistant strike prices, as shown in Figure 9.1.

> *An iron butterfly is similar to an iron condor; however, they differ in that the middle strike prices are identical in an iron butterfly. Additionally, an iron butterfly tends to be a bit more directional than an iron condor, which is typically neutral.*

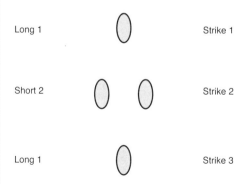

Long 1	Strike 1
Short 2	Strike 2
Long 1	Strike 3

Figure 9.1   An iron butterfly actually resembles a butterfly in that it has a "body" and "wings."

In the case of a call butterfly, a trader would simultaneously buy one call at both the highest and lowest strike prices and sell two calls at the center strike price. Likewise, a put diamond butterfly consists of the purchase of a put at both the highest and lowest strike prices and sale of two puts at the center strike price.

The result is the ability to purchase a close-to-the-money option with minimal out-of-pocket expense. The maximum profit occurs at expiration if the underlying futures market is trading at the center strike price and is calculated by taking the difference between the long and short option strike prices. However, the trade pays off something anywhere between the upper and lower strike price while the break-even point occurs at the upper or lower strike plus or minus the premium paid. Don't be alarmed if you are confused by this statement we will soon provide a much clearer explanation.

The maximum loss occurs if at expiration the underlying futures market is trading above or below the outer strike prices. The potential loss on the trade is limited to the amount of premium paid for the spread.

By the way, in the world of trading time is of the essence. Floor brokers often use slang terms and abbreviations to speed up the communication process. Iron call butterflies are simply referred to as a "call fly," while an iron put butterfly is known as a "put fly."

Why Use Diamond Butterflies?

- Affordability
- Increased manageability of market volatility
- Ability to adjust the trade
- Lack of margin

The primary reason for a butterfly spread is affordability. Purchasing options with strike prices close-to-the-money can be expensive. More options than not expire worthless; thus it is unwise to pay excessive amounts for options that are priced to lose.

In addition, diamond butterflies are useful in "taking the volatility" out of the futures market. In other words, the value of the spread fluctuates slowly relative to the futures price (see Figure 9.2). This is because the values of both the long and the short options are correlated. At any given time you may be profiting on the long options but losing on the short or vice versa.

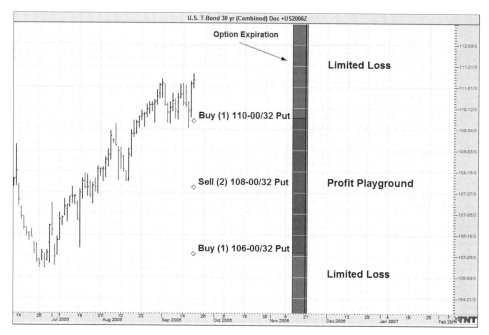

Figure 9.2 Iron butterflies are often directional in nature, but can be frustrating should the market move too far in your anticipated direction. It is possible that the move could push prices through and beyond your profit zone.

Furthermore, iron butterfly spreads can be easily adjusted. If the market makes a move above the boundaries of your put spread, you can take a profit on the short puts and hold on to the long puts in hopes of a bear move. This should be done if most, roughly 80% or more, of the short option premium has eroded and the market appears to be technically overbought. Doing so will leave the trader with two long options, no margin requirement of course, and theoretically unlimited profit potential, as illustrated in Figure 9.3.

It is also possible to "roll" the spread higher by purchasing the short puts back and using the existing long put for protection of a one-by-two ratio spread above the original trade (see Figure 9.4). In this case it might involve buying a 114 put and selling two 112 puts, should the market rally to that level.

Adjustments are often necessary, and the possibilities are unlimited. However, while your broker will let you into an iron butterfly with very little funding in your account, adjustments often involve margin and should only be done by those who have adequate funding. Your broker will be able to determine whether your account qualifies to adjust any particular trade. For those trading accounts without enough money to margin an adjustment you will typically have to hold an iron butterfly until expiration to see much in the way of a profit.

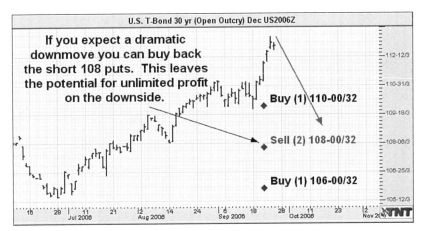

Figure 9.3 Assuming that you have enough margin in your account to do so, butter-flies can be easily adjusted in an attempt to take advantage of the ebb and flow of a market; this particular adjustment does not require additional margin.

Adjustments such as this can normally be done at even money, or for free, without regard to transaction costs. Such an adjustment would provide the trader with a payout anywhere below 113 and zero. This is because the protective put is placed one handle beneath the short option strike prices. Thus, the trade doesn't give back all of the gain made on the long put, but it does give back half of it. Even below 110, the trader keeps the $1,000 payout minus any debits incurred along the way. Note that this is simply a put ratio spread as covered in Chapter 7, "Synthetic Swing Trading."

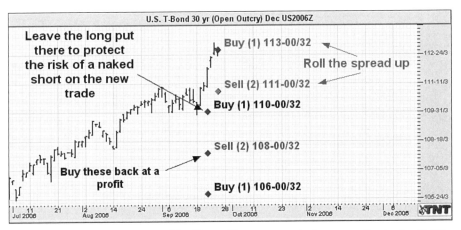

Figure 9.4 Rolling the spread is like getting a second chance on the trade. If the conditions are right, it may be possible to make the roll for very little additional cost or risk.

In the case of Treasury bonds as shown previously in Figure 9.4, the maximum payout on this trade would be $2,000 (2 handles x $1,000) minus the total debit paid for the original spread and any adjustments and would occur if the market is trading at 111 at expiration. The remaining long 110 put protects the risk of one of the short 111 puts. Naturally, risk on the other short 111 put is limited by the long 113 put. Unlike the previous adjustment, this move does not provide traders with unlimited profit potential, but it does offer limited loss and no margin requirement. This adjustment may be most appropriate if expectations are for modestly lower prices. However, it is an inexpensive adjustment and can potentially salvage an unsuccessful trade. Simply put, there isn't a good reason *not* to make this adjustment should the premium cooperate and the opportunity arise.

> "When you get to the end of your rope, tie a knot and hang on." Franklin D. Roosevelt

As you can imagine, the ability to roll the strike prices of your original trade to follow market prices is a great advantage. It is like having the ability to "mulligan" a trade. You may have been wrong on your original assessment of the market, but for a low-cost adjustment you get a "do over." Equally, the closer-to-the-money an option is, the greater the probability that it will be profitable. The ability to adjust the position to get closer-to-the-money is equivalent to having the ability to constantly skew the odds in your favor. Who wouldn't want that?

Long Call Iron Butterfly

Buy one at-the-money or out-of-the-money call option.
Sell two call options with distant (higher) strike prices.
Buy one call option with an equally distant (higher) strike price.

When to Use

● When you expect the market to make an up move but not go beyond a specific point.

Profit Profile

● The profit potential is limited to the difference between the long call and short call less the cost of the spread minus transaction costs.

● Maximum profit is achieved at expiration if the market is trading at the short call strike price.

Risk

● Being long the outside options and short the inside, the risk is limited to the premium paid for the spread plus transaction costs.

● To keep the risk limited to what you paid for the spread your long calls need to be equidistant to the short calls.

BE 1 = Primary Long Strike Price + Net Premium Paid + Transaction Costs

BE 2 = Secondary Long Strike Price – Net Premium Paid – Transaction Costs

An iron butterfly makes it possible for a trader to enter a market such as crude oil, which can be extremely expensive to trade, with a small amount of capital and limited risk. In the example that we are about to visit, it would cost a trader just under $3,000 to purchase an at-the-money call option, but by using the iron butterfly strategy the trader can buy the same option through the combination of a spread for a cost of under $500. The opportunity cost of executing the spread is giving up the potential for theoretically unlimited profit potential. However, we believe that the lower level of risk and more likely attainable break-even point makes the iron butterfly the optimal choice in most scenarios.

Example

As illustrated in Figure 9.5 buying a $54 crude call for $2.72, selling two $57 calls for $1.61 a piece, and purchasing the $60 call option for $0.92 to protect the trade from exposure to limitless risk creates an iron butterfly call spread for a total cost and risk of $0.42, or $420. Because this trade includes two long call options equidistant to the two short call options, the risk of loss on the trade is capped at the price paid for the trade, $420. If the underlying futures contract is trading below $54 at the time of expiration, the entire spread expires worthless to net the maximum possible loss on the trade.

If the market rallies, but exceeds the strike price of the distant long call option ($60) at expiration, all options in the spread expire in-the-money essentially canceling each other out as the exchange automatically assigns and exercises each of the options into futures contracts. Once this is done the trader will be flat the market and would have incurred the maximum loss in the amount of the original outlay, or $420.

The goal of a trade such as this is for the market to rally moderately higher to expire at or near the center strike price of the spread, $57. At this price, the payout to the trader is $2.58, or $2,580, before commissions and fees. This is calculated by subtracting the cost of the trade from the distance between the long and short options, ($57–$54)–$0.42=$2.58.

It is important to realize that if held intact, an iron butterfly spread typically won't show much of a profit until the options are close to expiring. This is because the time value of the short options will mitigate any profits, whether intrinsic or extrinsic, on the long option. Thus, this type of trade is what we like to call a "slow handed" approach to the markets.

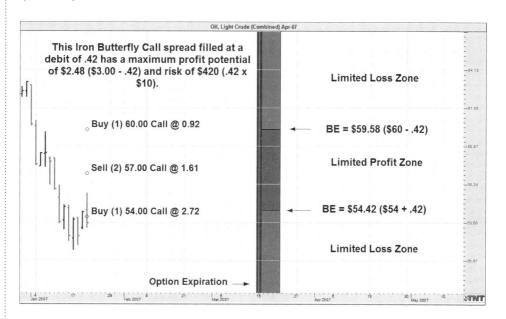

Figure 9.5 Iron butterflies are designed for affordable entry, limited loss, and wide profit zones.

An iron butterfly has two break-even points, one on each side of the spread. In this case the first break-even point is $54.42 calculated by adding the net cost of the trade to the strike price of the near-the-money call option. The second break-even occurs once the market has surpassed the maximum profit point and is approaching the protective long call option. The second BE for this iron butterfly is $59.58, calculated by subtracting the cost of the spread from the strike price of the distant call.

Consistent with a one-by-two ratio call spread, an iron butterfly gains intrinsic value as the futures price trades beyond the strike price of the primary long option. However, once the market surpasses the strike price of the two short options, the trade is essentially giving up intrinsic gains until it runs out of money at the strike price of the protective long call. Once you consider the cost to execute the spread, the actual profit on the trade at expiration occurs beyond the first BE and before the second BE, as shown in Figure 9.6. Likewise, as the market travels beyond the strike price of the primary call option and approaches the BE point, the trade is intrinsically recovering the cost of the trade. As the market surpasses the second BE and approaches the strike price of the protective long call the trade is giving back the money recouped to cover the cost of the trade. Thus, once the market reaches the strike price of the second long call, in this case $60, the trade is a loser of exactly the amount of premium paid for the trade.

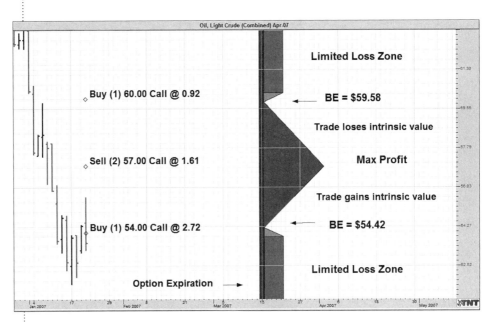

Figure 9.6   Iron butterflies don't require massive market moves to be profitable. The break-even point is normally relatively realistic.

Long Iron Butterfly Put

Buy one at-the-money or out-of-the-money put option.
Sell two put options with distant (lower) strike prices.
Buy one put option with an equidistant lower strike price.

When to Use

● When you expect the market to make a down move but not go beyond a specific point.

Profit Profile

● The profit potential is limited to the difference between the long put and short put strike prices less the cost of the spread and the transaction costs.

● Maximum profit is achieved at expiration if the market is trading at the short strike price.

Risk

● Being long the outside options and short the inside, the risk is limited to the premium paid for the spread plus transaction costs.

● To keep the risk limited to what you paid for the spread the strike price of the long puts need to be the same distance from the short puts.

BE 1 = Primary Long Strike Price–Net Premium Paid–Transaction Costs

BE 2 = Secondary Long Strike Price + Net Premium Paid + Transaction Costs

In essence, a put iron butterfly, sometimes referred to as a "put fly" by floor brokers, is a one-by-two ratio spread with an equidistant put purchased to limit the risk on the downside. Unlike a simple ratio spread, once the market drops below the profit zone of a put iron butterfly the trader will sustain a loss in the amount paid to get into the spread plus the commissions but is not exposed to the possibility of additional losses.

Example

As illustrated in Figure 9.7 purchasing an S&P 1430 put for $20.00 in premium, selling two of the 1400 puts for $12.10 a piece and then purchasing a 1370 put to protect the downside risk for $7.30 creates a debit spread of 3.10, or $775 (3.10 x $250). Essentially, the trade pays off something at expiration if the underlying futures market is within the break-even points at both ends of the butterfly. In this case the first break-even occurs at 1426.90, which is simply the strike price of the primary long put minus the amount of premium paid for the spread (1430-3.10). The distant break-even point is 1373.10, calculated by adding the premium paid for the spread to the strike price of the protective put option (1370 + 3.10). As you can see, the profit zone on this trade is relatively large. The profit playground covers 53.80 points in the S&P. It is important to note that just because the trade is intrinsically in-the-money doesn't mean that it is profitable; this trade (and all debit trades) is only profitable at expiration once the premium paid for the spread is recouped.

Had a trader opted to simply buy the 1430 put outright, leaving himself open for unlimited profit potential, it would have cost $5,000. Instead, this trade cost only $775 and also involves limited risk. The opportunity cost is the forgone profit potential. However, in this case especially, the odds seem to be grossly in favor of an iron butterfly as opposed to paying and risking $5,000 on a trade that will only be profitable at expiration if the S&P is trading more than 20 points lower than the strike price. To illustrate, the break-even on the iron butterfly is 1426.90 while the break-even on buying the 1430 put outright would be 1410. The butterfly requires much less of a move for the trade to be profitable.

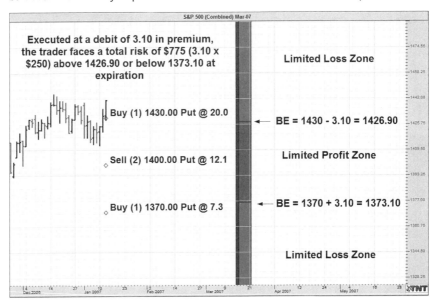

Figure 9.7   Iron butterflies provide limited risk and allow entry into a market at a highly discounted price.

Between the two break-even points, the profit potential of the trade at expiration peaks at the strike price of the short puts. If the underlying futures market was trading at exactly 1400 at expiration, this trade would provide the maximum profit of $6,725. To get this figure, subtract the strike price of the short puts from the strike price of the primary long put. Then subtract the original cash outlay to enter the trade and multiply that number by $250 (((1430-1400)–3.10) x $250=$6,725). Don't forget to subtract commissions and fees from the final figure; because four separate options are involved four transaction fees are charged.

Because this strategy involves the purchase of an equidistant put beneath the one-by-two ratio, the risk is limited to what is paid for the spread plus commissions and fees. Regardless of what happens to the S&P, crash or irrational exuberance, if the market is beyond the break-even points on either end of the butterfly the trader will not lose more than $775 (3.10 x $250) plus commissions and fees paid to get in (see Figure 9.8).

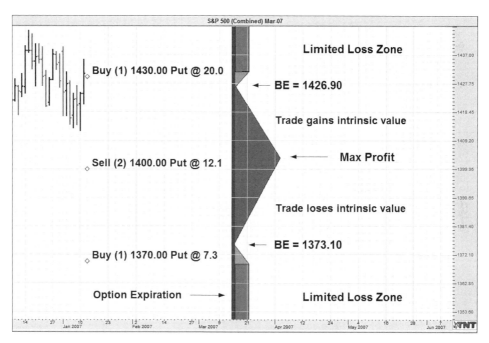

Figure 9.8 In exchange for unlimited profit potential, iron butterfly traders receive limited risk and a close-to-the-money market position.

Floor brokers may refer to the put iron butterfly as a "put fly"; they often get creative in speeding up the communication process.

Comparable to the one by two ratio put spread, this trade makes money intrinsically as the market travels beyond the strike price of the primary long put. Once it reaches the strike prices of the two short puts the profit potential has peaked. Beyond this point, the trade intrinsically "gives back" gains until finally running out of money at the break-even of 1373.10.

The disadvantage to a range trade such as the iron butterfly lies in the fact that if the market moves too far in the anticipated direction, the trade will be a loser. Naturally, this can be frustrating. However it is important to realize that in the world of trading, there is a big difference between being right and making money.

chapter 10

Synthetic Long Option Plays

A synthetic position is any financial instrument that is artificially created by using a combination of other assets whose features, as a whole, are comparable to the instrument that it is designed to replicate. For example, a trader can mimic the payout of a call option by simultaneously going long a futures contract and buying a put option. Likewise, the payout of a put option can be duplicated by selling a futures contract and buying a call option.

Why Use Synthetic Positions?

Synthetic options allow traders to easily adjust their trade should the market go against their original assessment. This makes perfect sense. If you are long a put option and long a futures contract in a falling market and you still strongly believe that the market is underpriced, you could take a profit on the long put and continue to hold the long futures contract. If things work out from there, you have just taken the best of both worlds. An obvious disadvantage can be found in the fact that if you liquidate your protective put, you are exposed to theoretically unlimited risk on the downside.

"What man's mind can create, man's character can control."
Thomas Edison

Synthetic positions can also be adjusted in the case of a market that does go in your favor. If the same trader buys a put and buys a futures contract and the market subsequently rallies, she has the option of taking profits on the futures contract and holding on to the long put. In this case, the trader would not be exposed to unlimited risk but would have unlimited profit potential on the downside. At this juncture, the worst possible outcome would be for the option to expire worthless. Hopefully, profits on the futures contract would be well above and beyond the value of the eroding option. As with anything in commodity trading, decisions must be made on a case-by-case basis. There are no clear-cut answers, only educated guesses.

The same applies to a trader who is long a call option and short a futures contract. The risk and payout are similar to the purchase of an at-the-money put, but this position provides the ability to leg out of the trade.

Another advantage of a synthetic long option is that it generally carries a lighter margin requirement and inherent risk, while providing the benefits of a futures contract. In theory, synthetic options contain no risk beyond the cost of getting into the trade; however, a "cash call" is a possibility. This can occur if you lose more money on the futures position than you have cash to cover the losses in the account. While the protective option will be gaining in value, options are treated as assets; they are not liquid cash and cannot be used to fund compromising futures positions. Should this occur you would treat it like any other margin call by either liquidating the trade or sending money to re-fund the account.

Be "Cheap"

Synthetic long options can be a viable trading strategy, but the same rules apply to synthetics that do to outright option buying: be cheap. As we have previously mentioned, more options than not expire worthless. Thus, in the long run being an option buyer is simply a no-win venture, even if you are buying the option as an insurance policy against a futures position.

This creates a dilemma in that the strategy requires the purchase of an at-the-money option for protection. For this reason, we recommend synthetic long options only in markets that involve relatively inexpensive premiums or at least, during times of low volatility and depressed option values. Some of the appropriate candidates are corn, soy meal, bean oil, orange juice, and sugar. This is by no account an all-inclusive list, but it gives you a general idea of the types of markets that you should be focusing on.

Under most circumstances, we would not advocate doing such a strategy in a market such as natural gas or crude oil. For instance, an at-the-money option in natural gas with two weeks to go commonly goes for $4,000 or more. Yet, once again, trading is a game of rules of thumb. Perhaps if natural gas or heating oil is trading at an all-time low and put premium is at a discount to the norm, executing such a trade might be a wise endeavor.

Synthetic Long Call Option

Go long a futures contract.
Buy an at-the-money or out-of-the-money put option.

When to Use

● When you are very bullish, but want limited risk.

● The more bullish you are the further from the money (lower strike price put) you can buy, although a true synthetic call would involve an at-the-money put option.

● This position is sometimes used instead of a straight long call option due to increased flexibility.

● Like the long call it gives you substantial leverage with unlimited profit potential and limited downside risk.

Profit Profile

● Profit potential is theoretically unlimited.

● The break-even at expiration is equal to the futures entry price plus the premium paid and transaction costs.

BE=Futures Entry Price+Premium Paid+Transaction Costs

● For each point the market goes above the break-even, the profit at expiration increases by one point.

Risk

● This trade involves limited risk.

● Your losses are limited to the difference between the entry price of the long future and the strike price of the long put plus the amount paid for the option along with transaction costs.

● Maximum loss is realized if the market is below strike price at expiration.

Late in the summer of 2006, December corn futures were trading near contract lows after suffering a decline of nearly 50 cents in a very short period of time. While it appeared to be an opportune time to get long, there was significant doubt in the market's ability to recover due to its seasonal tendency to trade lower throughout the fall. It wouldn't be rational to go long a futures contract during what is normally a bearish time of year, but doing so along with a protective put purchase is a sound trading strategy.

In this case, a trader could have gone long a futures contract near $2.40 on August 29. An at-the-money put option could have simultaneously been purchased for 13 1/2 cents, or $675 (each cent in corn is worth $50).

This seems like a logical time to review the difference between how grain options and grain futures are quoted. In Figure 10.1 you can see that the 240 put could have been bought for 13-5, which is meant to denote 13 5/8 cents. While options trade in eighths of a cent, futures trade in quarters. Futures prices will either have a 0 at the end of the quote meaning that it is trading in a full number such as 400'0 or simply $4.00. 400'2 can be read as $4 and a quarter of a cent, 400'4 can be read as $4 and a half cent, and 400'6 can be read as $4 and three-quarters of a cent. For the sake of simplicity in calculating this example, we are going to round the price of the 240 put to 13'4 or thirteen and a half cents.

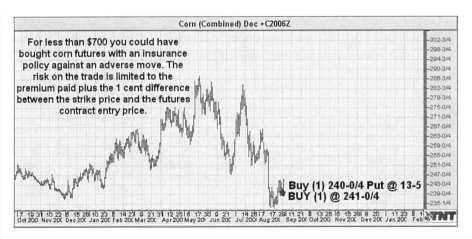

Figure 10.1   Synthetic option trades allow a trader to be involved in the market with limited risk and with a considerable amount of "lasting power."

The risk on this trade is equivalent to the amount paid for the insurance (long put) plus the difference between the entry price of the futures contract and the strike price of the long put. This may look complicated, but if you approach it logically it makes perfect sense. By buying a $2.40 put, the intrinsic value of the option will offset losses in your futures contract penny for penny below $2.40. If you are long from $2.41, you are unprotected from $2.41 to $2.40.

It is important to note the use of the term *intrinsic*. If you recall, intrinsic value can most easily be described as the value of the option if it expired right now. In other words, it is how deep in-the-money the option is and does not account for extrinsic value such as time, volatility, and so on.

Before expiration, it is certainly possible for a trader to be suffering from a difference in intrinsic value and losses on the futures position. This is because of the option's delta value. To review, if an option has a delta of .50, common for an at-the-money strike price, its premium will fluctuate by about half a cent for every cent that the futures market moves. An at-the-money option will not always appreciate or depreciate tick for tick with the futures market. However, at expiration the values will come together, and the gains and losses of such will be offset.

As shown in Figure 10.2, the break-even point at expiration is equal to $2.54 1/2; this is calculated by adding the cost of the long option to the entry price of the futures contract ($2.41+13 1/2 cents). Above this level, the trader enjoys unlimited profit potential. Below the break-even point, the trader is exposed to limited risk, regardless of how low the commodity price goes.

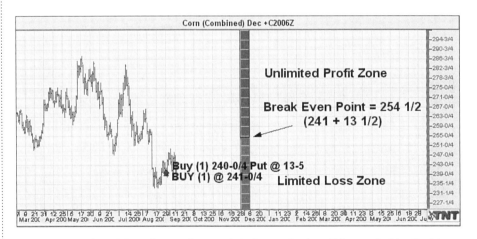

Figure 10.2   The risk and reward potential of a synthetic call is nearly identical to a long call option. The advantage to such a trade is the ability to adjust according to market moves. This may mean taking profits on the put and holding the long futures contract or vice versa.

Hopefully, you were a bullish participant in the late summer/early fall grain rally of 2006. Had you had a trade similar to this, the rewards would have been handsome.

On Wednesday November 8, the December 2006 corn contract reached $367 1/2 (see Figure 10.3). It is highly unlikely that a long trader would have offset the trade at the exact high, in fact almost impossible. However, this is an example—and it is always fun to daydream. Had the trade been liquidated at that day's highest price, the futures position would have yielded a profit of well more than $6,000. At this point, the long put option would have been nearly worthless had you not liquidated it early. Any premium lost on the long put option would be subtracted from the net profit of the trade. Nevertheless, it would be petty to complain about the decay of a $675 insurance policy on a trade that eventually paid out nearly ten times the amount.

Please note that this is a very favorable example. Although this trade went extremely well, there is a chance that trades can go just as wrong as this one went right.

Figure 10.3   **If the trade was held intact until expiration, the put would have expired worthless. However, gains on the futures contract would have overcome any loss on the put plus much more. Too bad they aren't all this easy.**

Bear in mind that this strategy is a synthetic call option. In other words, the trader could have reaped similar rewards by simply buying an at-the-money call option with a strike price of $2.40 and still been exposed to limited risk. In theory, the cost of the $2.40 call option would be comparable to the cost of the protective $2.40 put option in this example. Thus, the risk on the trade would have been nearly identical. Yet, what the synthetic call option offers traders is the ability to adjust the risk and reward profile after the trade has been executed. We will soon look at an example of a synthetic long put in which adjustments to the position can be made by simply liquidating one portion of the trade and leaving the other.

Synthetic Long Put Option

Go short a futures contract.
Buy an at-the-money or out-of-the-money call option.

When to Use

- When you are very bearish, but want limited risk.

- The more bearish you are the higher the strike price of the call can be, although a true synthetic put involves an at-the-money call option.

- This position is sometimes used instead of an outright long put due to its flexibility.

- Like the long put, this position gives you substantial leverage with unlimited profit potential and limited risk.

Synthetic options involve limited risk and no margin requirement. But it is possible to receive a cash call. A cash call is similar to a margin call, but instead of being margin deficient the trader is cash deficient. This might occur if the market goes strongly against a synthetic option position because although the long option is gaining as the market goes against the position, the loss on the futures contract may exceed the available cash in the account. Remember, a long option is not the same as cash. In fact, cash is taken out of the account to buy an option.

Profit Profile

- Profit potential is theoretically unlimited.

- At expiration the break-even is equal to the short futures entry price minus the premium paid minus the transactions costs.

BE=Futures Entry Price–Premium Paid–Transaction Costs

- Each point the market goes below the break-even the profit at expiration increases by a point.

Risk

- Your loss is limited to the difference between the futures entry price and call strike price plus the premium paid for the option.

- Your maximum loss occurs if the market is above the option strike price at expiration.

A long synthetic put is the exact inverse of the long synthetic call option. A trader who executes this strategy is anticipating that the price of the commodity will move lower. Essentially, the trade involves selling a futures contract and buying an at-the-money call option to limit the risk of the trade. The resulting position has a payout that is identical to a long put option at expiration. Prior to expiration, the profit and loss of the synthetic may be slightly different from that of an identical put option due to factors such as market volatility, demand, and so on. In other words, differences in extrinsic value, or delta value, might make the synthetic position slightly more or less profitable at any given time prior to expiration.

It is also important to note that the math necessary to calculate the break-even point and determine risk for a synthetic option, whether call or put, is slightly more complicated than that of a long option. Many beginning traders are intimidated by this, but because the concepts are so similar to long options, the mechanics of synthetic options are much easier to learn than it may seem on the surface.

> "It's not that I am so smart; it's just that I stay with problems longer."
> Albert Einstein

Just as a synthetic call is easily adjustable, so is the synthetic put. Once in the trade, if the market rises against the position it may be possible to sell the long call at a profit and use the money made on the long call to move the break-even on the short futures to a higher price. This is a risky adjustment in that it eliminates the insurance that made the position a limited risk trade. Without the benefit of the long call, the trader is subject to theoretically unlimited losses as any other outright futures position would be.

Conversely, if the market drops to oversold levels you may want to take a profit on the short futures contract, by buying it back, and hold onto the long call in hopes of a market recovery. If circumstances allow, your timing is right, and luck is on your side, it is possible to make money on both legs of the trade. Unlike offsetting the long call, this adjustment doesn't increase the risk of the trade at all. In fact it has the opposite effect. Locking in a profit on the short futures position that covers the entire cost of the protective call option ensures that the trade is profitable regardless of whether the call expires worthless.

Example

In a swiftly rallying market it may be tempting to sell a futures contract in an attempt to capitalize on a potential market correction. However, doing so can feel like jumping in front of the proverbial freight train. To protect the trade from unlimited risk it is possible to buy a call option for protection. At expiration, the call option will offset losses in the futures contract tick for tick above the strike price of the long call. Prior to expiration this may not necessarily be the case because the delta value of the call option probably won't be equal to that of the futures, but you will be glad that you have the protection.

Imagine a trader selling wheat near what were then multiyear highs and buying a $6.25 call as an insurance policy against being wrong, as illustrated in Figure 10.4. As the trade stands, the risk is limited to the amount of premium paid for the long call option and any difference between the entry of the futures market and the strike price of the protective call option.

Figure 10.4 A synthetic put is identical to being long a put at the same strike price of the synthetic. Like buying an outright option, the market must make a relatively substantial move to return a profit to the trader, but unlike an outright put option a synthetic can be adjusted by legging out of the trade.

While commodities are known for trading within a range, those ranges can sometimes be expanded. Thus, selling a market near the highs of its historical range is a relatively high probability trade, but there are certainly no guarantees that it will work out. If you were following this market in 2007 you know exactly what we mean. For this reason, it is often wise to use a combination of long and short options or futures to mitigate the exposure when trying to pick a market top or bottom.

In this example, the trader was actually filled at $6.24 1/4 (see Figure 10.5) on the short futures contract and paid 27 6/8 (referred to as 27 and three quarters) cents for the $6.25 call option. Wheat, like most of the other grains, has a point value of $50, making the total cost of the option $1,387.50 ($50 x 27 6/8). The risk on the trade is actually the cost of the option plus 3/4 of a cent. This is determined by the distance between the fill price of the short futures, $6.24 1/4 and the strike price of $6.25. This makes sense, because the option only protects the position above $6.25. From the entry of the futures position and the strike price the position is "naked."

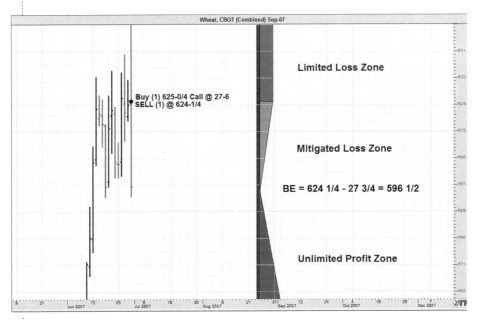

Figure 10.5   **This trade requires that the market be below $5.96 1/2 at expiration before consideration of commissions and fees to be profitable.**

Picking the top or bottom of a market can incur devastating losses if the proper strategy is not utilized. If premiums are relatively cheap, a synthetic long option may be the answer. Limited risk, unlimited reward, flexibility, and the ability to withstand adverse moves are all distinct benefits of the strategy.

Now that we have talked about the risk, let's discuss the reward. This trade contains unlimited profit potential, but will only return a profit to the trader at expiration if the underlying market has fallen enough to recapture the original outlay for the protective call option. Ignoring commissions and fees, the market would have to be below the break-even point of $5.96 1/2 to be intrinsically profitable. As the underlying futures price travels below the strike price of the long call and toward the break-even point, intrinsic losses are mitigated until reaching the break-even on the trade.

As previously mentioned, one of the distinctive qualities of a synthetic long option play is the ability to adjust the position. Adjustments are possible whether the market travels in favor of the trade or against it. In the case of a synthetic long put; if the underlying commodity price drops to a point in which either the premium paid for the protective call option is recovered or the trader simply believes that the market has bottomed out, it may be possible to liquidate the futures contract at a profit. This would entail buying it back at a lower price than the original entry and holding on to the long call option hoping for a market reversal (see Figure 10.6).

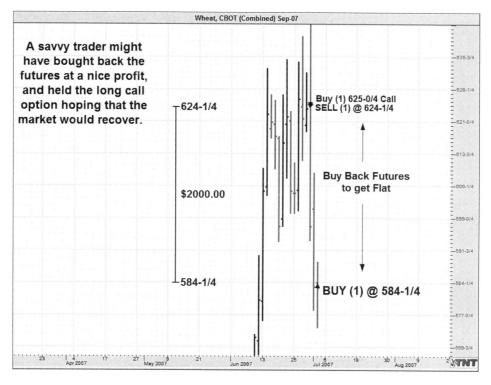

Figure 10.6   A trader may choose to adjust the trade by lifting one of the legs. In this case it would have been possible to take a profit on the futures position and hold the long call in hopes of a recovery.

If the timing is accurate and the market moves in a big enough magnitude it may be entirely possible to liquidate, or sell, the call option for more than what was originally paid. In this case the trader would have "had his cake and eaten it too" by profiting on both the futures and the option portion of the trade. With that said, it is important to realize that this is not nearly as easy in practice as one might think, but it is achievable.

Synthetic long options are not always the best way to approach a market. In fact, because a synthetic long call or long put has nearly identical characteristics of buying a call or put, the strategy faces the same drawbacks. The biggest disadvantage is the potential premium erosion of the protective call or put and the amount that the futures market must move to overcome the premium paid for the insurance. Thus, just as in long call or put trading, this is a viable strategy only when either premium is "cheap" and/or the market is trading at such an extreme that a substantial move in the desired direction is believed to be probable.

In this example, wheat prices dropped well below the break-even point calculated earlier of $6.24 1/4; offsetting the futures position by buying back the short contract would guarantee a profitable trade by at least the difference between the futures profit and the original cash outlay for the $6.25 call option. As you can see in Figure 10.6, it may have been possible to buy the futures contract back at a price of $5.84 1/4 resulting in a profit on the futures position alone of 40 cents. Even if the call option expired worthless, the trade would net a profit of 12 1/4 cents (40 cents – 27 3/4 cents), or $612.50 before considering transaction costs (see Figure 10.7). This is calculated by taking the profit on the futures contract and subtracting the cost of the $6.25 call option.

This adjustment alters the risk and reward involved in the position considerably in that the trader no longer has risk of loss. Simply put, the new trade offers unlimited profit potential on the upside in exchange for the trader potentially giving back a portion of profits in the form of an eroding call option. The amount of profit forfeited can never leave the trader with less than $612.50. This worst-case scenario would occur if the $6.25 call expired worthless.

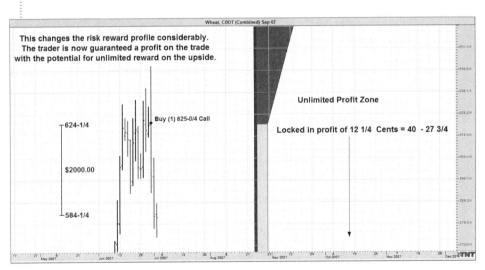

Figure 10.7   Offsetting the futures contract at a profit above and beyond the original cost of the long call ensures that the trade will be profitable by at least 12 1/4 cents regardless of the direction of the market.

In a better case scenario, wheat prices would rally to a point in which the trader could sell the option to recover some, all, or in excess of the premium originally paid. Assuming that the option was held to expiration, the profit on the trade would increase by every tick that the underlying futures market was trading above the long call strike price. For example, by adding 27 3/4 cents to the strike price of $6.25 we know that $6.52 3/4 completely recovers the cost of the option; with the futures price at $6.52 3/4 the trade would be profitable by $2,000. This is because at that price, the long call option would be worth the amount originally paid (27 3/4 cents), and the futures contract was liquidated at a profit of 40 cents or $2,000.

While adjustment examples such as this may make it seem easy to time the market and maximize profits, we assure you that it is not. Even experienced and trained traders have a hard time predicting price movement with certainty.

chapter 11

An Option Trade from Top to Bottom

Good traders do their homework. This includes watching the markets on a daily basis, doing chart work, and studying the daily price action. Good traders are constantly on the lookout for patterns and recurrences that could hint at future price moves. It is imperative to properly understand and utilize the various tools available, such as those that measure volatility and momentum, identify emerging trends, and attempt to gauge the all-important fundamental value of the underlying market.

Identifying an Opportunity

Let's take a look at the coffee market in December 2005 using the May 2006 contract. This simply means that we will be using a coffee contract scheduled to expire in May 2006 in the December time frame.

Of course, the most valuable means of doing this is a price chart (see Figure 11.1). Looking at the recent price action we see many possibilities. However, at a glance we are unsure of whether we are in a downtrending market, a bottoming market, or even a market that is becoming range bound. Beginning to analyze a market can seem overwhelming, thus, an orderly approach is necessary.

Coffee futures and options are not for the faint of heart. This is the type of market that can allure traders with relatively tame price movement, but eventually explode in a way that can be financially devastating—or like hitting the lottery if you happen to be on the right side of the move.

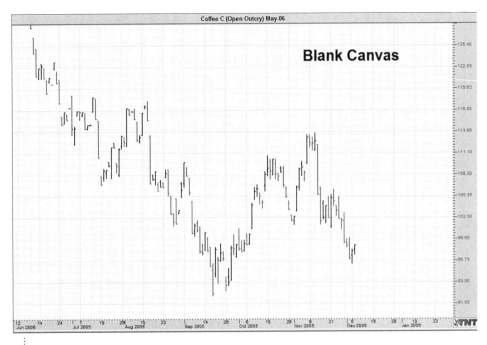

Figure 11.1   Think of a price chart as a blank canvas.

We start with a clean chart, and proceed to "dress it up" by overlaying various indicators to determine what the market is trying to tell us. The first step is to get a better idea of where this market has been—in other words, where this market is really trading at in comparison to its past.

The question we are trying to answer is: "Is the current price we see a high price or low price for this commodity?" *To get a better idea of where a market is going, you need to know where it's been*! While this seems to be a relatively obvious concept, it is often overlooked by overzealous or inexperienced traders.

A daily chart alone does not contain enough information, but the information that we need is readily available on weekly, as well as monthly, charts. These are typically contained in almost every software or charting application. You may be wondering, "Why do we need daily charts if they do not contain all the information needed to trade; why don't we just trade off long-term charts?" It's a logical question; long-term charts do give you an overview of the price history of a given commodity, but they tend to gloss over the important day-to-day things essential to trading. Also, long-term charts do not reveal the small signs that some traders miss such as price gaps and the day-to-day stats that reveal minor areas of support and resistance. By the way, it is often said that roughly 80% of all gaps are filled, but it is important to realize that the time frame is questionable. It can sometimes take several months for a gap to be filled. However, gap trading is becoming less and less viable as technology advances. Most markets are now traded electronically nearly 24 hours per day; this eliminates many of the price gaps that used to occur between trading sessions.

Looking at a 20-year chart, shown in Figure 11.2, may give us a better idea of where the market is currently trading in relationship to what we refer to as the trading "envelope."

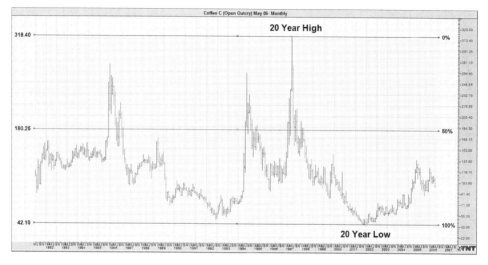

Figure 11.2 With the exception of a few upward spikes, coffee prices have fluctuated between about $1.80 and $0.42.

They say a picture is worth a thousand words, and this picture is no different. As you can see the price of coffee has been as low as 40 cents and as high as $3.20 over the last 20 years. With a contract size of 37,500 pounds and a multiplier of $375, the profit or loss sustained in a coffee futures position can be substantial. Knowing the multiplier, we can calculate the value of the total range to be about $105,000 (($3.20–.40) x $375). That's nice if you happened to buy at the lowest price and sell at the highest; however, things like that only happen in fairy tales, so stop dreaming. This book deals with reality.

Although this market is currently trading at the lower quarter of its "envelope," it is in an area that it has traded before and has spent much time in. This is key! *This tells us that the current pricing level is where the market is most comfortable.*

Too many traders make the mistake of only seeing the highs or lows, and plan their trades on the basis of the market's reaching these prices again. This is a major mistake! You need to understand that for the market to return to these "extremes" something extreme needs to happen, and the ability to predict such an unforeseen event is IMPOSSIBLE!

"No profession requires more hard work, intelligence, patience, and mental discipline than successful speculation." Robert Rhea

A great example was in 1994, when the coffee market was trading near $1.00 at the close of trade on a Friday. Over the weekend an unexpected freeze hit South America, causing severe damage to the coffee crop. A floor trader from the Coffee, Cocoa, and Sugar Exchange was later quoted as saying; "I must have missed the memo on Friday that there was going to be a freeze" in answer to a reporter's question to why the market was caught off guard. Unfortunately, many traders were caught in the move. Short options that looked to be destined to expire worthless on the Friday before the freeze were worth several thousand dollars on the following Monday. This is the perfect example of why it is always a good idea to buy short options back once most of the premium has evaporated; failing to do so could be catastrophic.

Hopefully, as you look at a long-term chart you will also notice that one price extreme is usually followed by another, but in the opposite direction. This is not an unusual occurrence and is logical once you think about it. When prices are low, production shrinks due to the lack of profit margin, which then shifts the scales of supply and demand causing prices to rise (lower supply supports prices because there are less goods to go around). To illustrate: Eventually low prices will increase the demand for the commodity; likewise as the price drops producers look to more profitable crops. As you can imagine, together these factors (increased demand and lower supply) are capable of triggering a sharp rally.

On the other extreme, higher commodity prices equal higher profits for growers and producers. Once again the balance of supply and demand is thrown out of whack. The production of the commodity is then pushed to its limits. Subsequently, with an ample supply on the market, prices slide lower and eventually start the cycle all over again.

This cycle is a common occurrence in all grown commodities where the normal production outcome is, or can be, affected by unforeseen events such as droughts, floods, disease, and pestilence.

Now that we have determined that the market is currently trading in its comfort zone, we dig deeper, looking for opportunity. To do this we need to dress up our chart with the tools or indicators we need to identify the possibility of what *could or should* happen next. Please note the use of the terms "could" or "should" instead of "will"; this is important. As a trader you must be willing to admit to yourself that the only thing that you truly know is that you don't know; nobody does. Only a fool actually believes that he has the ability to see the future. Remember, Wall Street is strewn with the bleached white bones of foolish and egotistical traders; so never be a fool, in the words of Dirty Harry, "a man has got to know his limitations."

Back to the coffee chart; as shown in Figure 11.3 we begin by adding a trend indication tool. We like to keep it simple; a three-line simple moving average composed of the 4, 9, and 18 day moving average. A crossover of these is a combination introduced by another professional trader in 1989. Over the years we have experimented with different combinations, changing the number of lines, trying different values, but always coming back to the original.

Next we add a couple of momentum-based computer generated oscillators; in this case we employ both a slow stochastic as well as the MACD (Moving Average Convergence Divergence). Why those? Well in truth almost all oscillators, even though they look different, are nearly the same. They are all based on a combination of equations used to determine momentum of some sort along with overbought or oversold conditions. The primary difference between most oscillators is the speed of the signal. For example, the MACD tends to be a slow-moving oscillator with relatively sluggish signals. Despite the name, slow stochastics tend to be quicker in calling for a trend change.

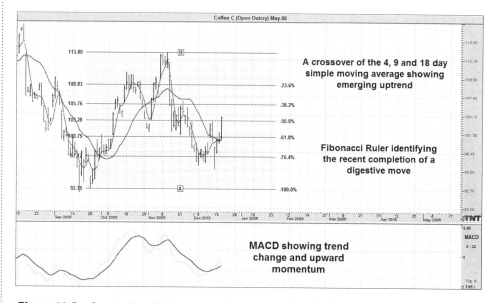

Figure 11.3 As a trader, it is important to use a basket of indicators to confirm justification of executing a trade.

There are only so many new ideas available in the world, so the guys that dream these things up (an attempt at immortality) usually take what is available, change it a little by adding a mathematical formula or some other special flavoring, and then put their name on it. In the 1990s, salesmen were pitching "The Ultimate Oscillator!"; however, since we don't know anybody who uses it nor do we ever see any reference to it, it apparently didn't live up to its name.

Anyway, we prefer to use the standard SST (slow stochastic) settings, but the MACD we have altered by changing the settings to a more aggressive stance. We set the MACD as an 8/20 single line combo with a 9 trigger. The goal is to identify the market's current momentum, but also where it is in its shorter-term range. The evidence of a buy signal using either of these indicators is a crossover in the two lines followed by momentum up or down.

We are looking at the combination of the moving averages to be in accord with the underlying oscillators, or simply pointing in the same direction. For additional confirmation we employ a Fibonacci ruler to verify whether the recent turning point is a valid area of support; this is how we begin to get an idea of what could or should happen in the coming days or weeks (see Figure 11.4). Again, *could* OR *should* is the key phrase. There are no guarantees or magic indicators. That's what makes trading commodities so exciting and adventurous. Remember, the infamous line from the movie *Trading Places*: "This is the last bastion of pure true capitalism!"

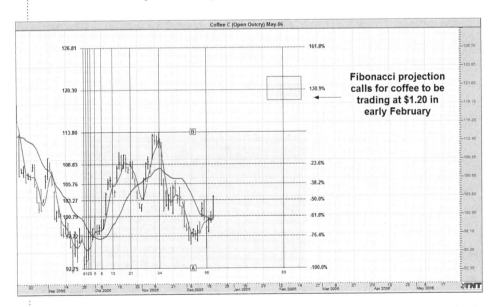

Figure 11.4   A Fibonacci projection ruler is yet another tool that we often refer to when analyzing a market.

Organization is key, so for the sake of being thorough we perform a mental checklist to be sure we can justify entering the market. Just as a pilot and co-pilot do a preflight check before going into the air, traders should make sure that their analysis is capable of supporting their actions. Keep in mind that different markets or trading conditions will alter the components of the checklist. Also, you may prefer a different set of oscillators; nonetheless structure is important.

- **Moving average**—Crossover occurring and pointing higher—Check.

- **Computer-generated oscillator**—Buy signals confirmed—Check.

- **Market positioning favorable**—Check. Recent support level confirmed by Fibonacci.

- **Long-term positioning**—Check. Favorable to the upside due to the fact the market is in the lower portion of its long-term price envelope.

As Gil Grisham of the television show *CSI* would say: "The evidence doesn't lie." And the evidence at hand points to a buying opportunity. However, it is important to note that the evidence we are basing our decision on is not always constant and is subject to change without notice. Different types of indicators may work favorably in one scenario but not in another; this is where experience comes in. Hence, a good trader constantly monitors the markets and reviews charts and positions on a daily basis, looking for possible changes.

Once we have determined our expected market direction and magnitude, we begin to explore what type of strategy would be appropriate. As you have learned, there are various levels of risk and reward, as well as directional bias, depending on the chosen strategy. This is harder than you might think; the decision can't be based on a mathematical formula, and it certainly isn't rocket science. Nonetheless, it is difficult because it is based on personality and where-withal. The best strategy is the strategy that depends on the trader not the vehicle.

This is where traders have to review themselves and their abilities from both a financial and a mental standpoint. A trader's self-checklist should primarily focus on the following two items:

- **Wherewithal**—This is the capitalization of the account as well as the available risk capital located elsewhere. One of the biggest mistakes a trader can make is overtrading or *churning* themselves. As brokers we would be breaking the moral code of conduct (not to mention face legal trouble) if we were to *churn* an account. Unfortunately, clients tend to do it to themselves relatively often. We are not only talking about the volume of trading, but also the ratio of margin to equity. This is how much of the dollar amount of the account you are committing to the trade. We usually suggest not exceeding 50% to 70%, but that is our opinion, and it is your money. Keep in mind that less is usually better and don't forget the lessons learned from the 1990s. Despite what Gordon Gecko from the movie *Wall Street* says, greed is not good. You have probably heard the old adage, bulls and bears go to market, but hogs get slaughtered.

● **Risk tolerance**—This is where the math gets fuzzy. An individual's ability to absorb and withstand risk goes beyond financial calculations due to the fact that it is blended with psychological factors and personalities. In other words, not everybody looks at a dollar the same way. This is why the casinos in Las Vegas have penny slots and dollar slots. They also have gaming tables where the betting starts as low as a dollar as well as the "High Stakes Rooms" that are cordoned off with a velvet rope. Just because two individual traders may have the same account size, doesn't mean that their individual risk tolerance is similar.

A person with a low risk tolerance, although perhaps able to afford to play using the same risk parameters as a person with high risk tolerance, will be uncomfortable and more susceptible to letting nerves get the best of him when the going gets rough. Overly nervous traders may make decisions based on fear, thus making irrational moves instead of rational decisions. They often fold their hands too early in the game. Accordingly, traders need to look at themselves with open honesty and assess where they are on the scale. We are not implying that a low tolerance to risk is a bad thing; it is the traders' misinterpretation of their tolerance to risk that causes harm.

The strategy you use should be dictated by the financial capabilities of the account, your tolerance to risk, and your speculation on price movement. Additionally, use your head not your ego. Don't convince yourself that you are superior to the market. Always look at the worst-case scenario and ask yourself if you are prepared to pay the consequences if you are wrong. Don't forget that markets are unpredictable, living and breathing things. By the term "breathe," we mean that they gyrate within the ranges of support and resistance, bouncing back and forth as they make their way higher and lower. By the way, markets have a mind of their own, regardless of what you or anybody else believes.

This day-to-day volatility beats most futures traders; they are often taken out of the market prematurely due to stop orders being placed too tight or by intimidation and second guessing. Paul Brittain calls these traders "the weak sisters" and "the shoe string salesmen." They are nervous and usually trading with scared money—that is, money they really shouldn't be trading with. Don't forget that only risk capital should be used to trade futures and options. There is a big difference between trading and investing.

A trader who lacks conviction is constantly switching his posture, going from bullish to bearish in the blink of an eye but constantly being one step behind the market. Regrettably, these traders feed the market and make up a huge portion of the estimated 80% of traders who lose in the 80/20 rule.

For those of you who are unaware of the 80/20 rule, it applies to many aspects of the commodity market. While these figures may not be exact, they likely aren't far off and drive home the point. In terms of trading, it is often said that roughly 20% of market participants make 80% of the money. If you haven't already guessed it, the remaining 80% of market participants typically don't fair as well.

Too many novice traders fall victim to the personality disorder of an addicted gambler in that their decisions are emotionally based and in total disregard of any perceivable logic. The lack of justifiable judgment most often stems from fear of loss. While under the "spell" of fear and greed, they often take profits too soon and hold losses too long. In their minds, it isn't really a loss unless they get out of it. They trade on the hope that they will be lucky—at this point they are prayers, not players, and this may lead to self-destruction.

Too many traders truly believe that there is some sort of Holy Grail and are always switching strategies, brokers, analysts, and firms in their search. These traders are the fodder of the trading system salesmen, as well as trading mentors and coaches. They are the perfect target for industry salesmen who know exactly what they want to hear. Don't fall victim to the "guaranteed profit" trap. The closest thing to a guarantee in the world of finance is a T-Bill because there is no perceived risk of the U.S. government defaulting. Trading options and futures is as far from a T-Bill as you can get.

Your understanding that there is no magic when it comes to predicting market moves is where you will really discover the true beauty of using options in your trading. Through options, a trader has the ability to take advantage of a market's potential move while having a certain degree of control over exposure to the risk that exists in any trade. Better yet, they are able to mitigate the volatility of the market through the use of option spreads.

An option trader has the ability to choose her level of risk exposure through the strategy implemented. Although there will always be a certain degree of risk in any trade, options can soften your risk exposure regardless of the method; you can even limit your risk completely when using a long option strategy. As we have demonstrated in this book, in some cases you can cushion your risk by blending long and short options in a way that will accomplish a common goal.

Based on the chart work that we have completed and the technical setup of the market, several different but similar option plays can be employed. Take into account that options are flexible. There are an infinite number of possibilities involving combinations of options months, types, and strike prices. We don't have enough room in this book to demonstrate each of them, but we would like to think that we have given you a stepping stone and provided you with the most common and arguably the most useful.

Our assessment of a bullish price move from current levels may justify a long call, a short put, a bull call spread, or something in between. If we were interested in trading *futures* rather than options we may decide that a long futures trade would need a sell stop placed below the recent low, which is 92.10. Based on the current futures price of 104.60, the stop order would be 12.5 cents below the market. A coffee futures contract represents 37,500 pounds of coffee; at $375 of profit or loss per penny of futures movement, the risk of the trade equates to about $4,687.50 before transaction costs. This can be calculated by subtracting the stop price of 92.10 from the current price of 104.60 and then multiplying that number by $375. Understandably, this amount of risk shakes the nerve of many traders regardless of the amount of risk capital and experience at play.

Rather than buying a futures contract, which exposes a trader to theoretically unlimited risk (this is even true with a stop order placed) immediately upon entering the trade, you could buy a call option, which provides limited risk. A close-to-the-money option, the 107.50 call, would cost you about 4.40 cents or $1,650. Thus, even though a long option strategy limits your risk to the premium paid, in this case the risk is high, and we believe the odds of success to be low. After all, the market would need to increase in value from its current close of 104.60 to nearly 112 to reach the option's intrinsic break-even point. If you recall, the break-even point of a long call option is calculated by adding the premium paid (plus transaction costs) to the strike price of the call option. In this case, if a trader paid 4.40 cents for the option, the break-even point would be at 111.90. This is calculated by adding 4.40 to the strike price of 107.50. Remember, 4.40 in premium is equivalent to $1,650.

If the market fails to reach the break-even point by option expiration, you could lose some, but probably all the cost of the option. In the situation where the market is at or below the strike price of 107.50, the option would expire worthless providing the buyer with the maximum loss but the seller with the maximum profit. Of course, when buying an option outright, the max loss is equal to the amount of premium paid to purchase the option. Based on studies that suggest that more options than not expire worthless, option buyers seem to have the odds stacked against them.

In this case, after taking into consideration the current market price and the cost of buying an option outright, we decide that the optimal trade is to create a synthetic futures contract using a blend of both long and short options. If constructed correctly, the trade will give us the delta that we desire and the ability to profit from the trade if we are right. It may also not pose immediate risk to the downside as a futures contract would. It is important to note that the goal is to form a spread in which the overall delta of the spread exceeds that of buying an outright call but is less than that of a futures position (the delta of a futures contract is one). The net result is a directionally biased trade with less volatility.

As we have attempted to drill into your trading mindset, selling options allows traders to collect premium that can be used to pay for the primary option, or long option. In other words selling premium lowers the cost of the long option. In turn, this favorably shifts the distance from the strike price to the break-even point, or brings it to a more realistically attainable level. In the case of a credit spread it becomes a reverse break-even, which completely removes the break-even point on the upside because the trade makes money even if the long option of the spread expires worthless. Of course, all this is true only as long as the market stays within the reverse break-even. If you recall, a credit spread simply means that more premium was collected for the short options than was spent for the long options.

Due to the shift in break-even points we believe that using a combination of long and short options also balances out the odds of a trade making money. In our eyes, option spreads are capable of leveling the playing field. Assuming that the CME study regarding expiring options is accurate and somewhere between 70% and 80% of options expire worthless, selling two options for every one that you buy increases the probability of making money relative to a long option strategy. With that said, doing so doesn't guarantee profits.

From another perspective, the probability of a market going in favor of a trader's expected direction is roughly 1 out of 3. After all, a market has the ability to go up, down, or sideways. A three-legged spread may profit in two of these scenarios, while a futures position can profit only in one of them. Accordingly, we have opted to go with a strategy known as the bull call spread with a naked leg.

Based on theoretical values, we could have bought the 107.50 call for about $1,683 (or 4.49 cents in premium); this is our primary option (see Figure 11.5). We then could have sold an out-of-the-money call to collect additional premium. According to the data provided, the 117.50 call would have brought in nearly $700, or 1.86 cents. By doing so we are lowering the cost of the 107.50 by the amount collected for the 117.50 call option to create a net debit (cost) of $986.25 or 2.63 cents in premium.

As it stands, this trade is a bull call spread. It is a long option strategy with limited risk; there is no margin requirement, and the intrinsic break-even is lowered from 111.99 (107.50+4.49) to a more desirable 110.13 (107.50+4.49−1.86). In plain English, this trade now makes money at expiration above 110.13. The negative side is that it also limits your profit potential to the distance between the strike prices of the long and short call options minus the net debit. In this case it is 7.37 cents ((117.50 − 107.50 − 2.63) or $2,763.75 (7.37 x $375); however, the odds of the market skyrocketing out of control look to be slim. Rather than trying to hit the ball out of the park, look for base hits to avoid striking out.

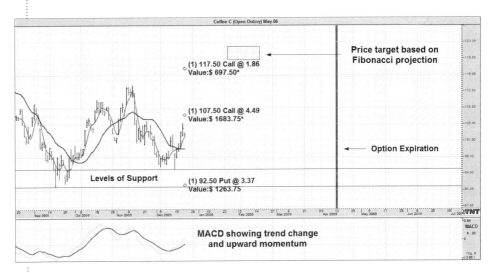

Figure 11.5 **Looking at technical support, and the expected market direction, it makes sense to sell a put at or under support and a call at or above the price target.**

Although limited risk and no margin are appealing, the bull call spread "as is" is still relatively expensive. As mentioned, it doesn't make sense to pay a lot of money out of pocket for an option, or option spread, which will probably expire worthless. Accordingly, we could sell a put below the market to collect additional premium. The addition of this naked leg changes the overall risk of the trade in several ways. In this case, selling the 92.50 put for about $1,263.75 creates a credit spread; instead of paying for the option spread the trader collects money, about $277.50 or .74 cents. This also erases the intrinsic break-even and creates what we refer to as a reverse break-even. Assuming that we could collect 3.37 cents, or $1263.75 for the 92.50 put, the reverse break-even on the trade would be 91.76. In other words as long as the market is above the reverse break-even of 91.76 (92.5–.74), this trade will be profitable. Yes you are reading this right, the market can actually fall 10 cents against the trade, and as long as it is above the reverse break-even at expiration, the trade can show a profit.

However, there is a catch. Below the short put strike price there is unlimited risk, similar to that of a futures contract. Nevertheless, keep in mind that level is 10 cents lower than the current price. Also, with the market anywhere above the long call strike price at expiration, this trade can show a profit above and beyond the original credit of $277.50. If the market is at or above the *short* call, this trade can return a profit of 10 cents or $3,750 (10 x $375) plus the premium collected when the trade was initiated for a net profit of $4,027.50 before commission and fees.

Don't forget, this trade involves a margin requirement based on the futures margin adjusted by a method referred to as *SPAN*, or *Standard Portfolio Analysis of Risk*.

Another disadvantage to point out is that at any time before expiration the trade may show a loss even if the market is above the strike price of the short put, 92.50 in this example. This can occur due to an increase in extrinsic value resulting from changes in any of the components of time value, namely volatility or demand.

Furthermore, a phenomenon that we refer to as the extrinsic handcuff can often lead to frustration for beginning traders. Extrinsic handcuff occurs when traders have either misconstructed their option spread or have been exposed to a market that has experienced a sharp increase in volatility.

The aggravation stems from similar delta values of the long call option and the short call option in a bull call spread. As the market rallies, the trade is making money on the long call but may be giving up much or all of the profits thanks to losses on the short call. The result is a trade that, although positioned in the correct market direction, fails to make respectable money unless held until expiration. At anytime before expiration, the trader is free to liquidate but may not be able to do so anywhere near the intrinsic value of the trade or even worse at a profit.

The wrath of the extrinsic handcuff can be diminished by properly placing strike prices at distances that will allow for differing delta values. If you recall, the delta value is the rate at which the value of an option reacts to price movement in the underlying futures contract. If a trader is willing to accept more risk, it is also possible to retaliate against the extrinsic handcuff by lifting one leg of the spread at a time. This is illustrated later in this example.

In trading, there are several ways to gain exposure in any given market. It is important to realize that there is no "Holy Grail," and that each approach to the market has advantages and disadvantages that may or may not be viable based on market conditions. It is up to the trader to be able to weigh the risks and rewards of each strategy and most important look to capitalize on probabilities. Much of this analysis is purely common sense, and that is one thing that can't be covered within the confines of a book.

Rolling the chart ten days ahead (see Figure 11.6), you see the shift in option premium as the market moves. In a rallying market, the calls increase in value while the put decreases in value. You can also see one of the drawbacks of this strategy discussed previously, the extrinsic handcuff. When the market moves in your direction too fast, the short call will explode in value to absorb some of the profit. Conversely, if you keep in mind that the cost of the trade was less than nothing (ignoring transaction costs and margins) because it was initiated as a credit, it is still a phenomenal return.

Once again, the figures provided in this trading example don't include the transactions costs. All premium paid must be increased by the commission that you pay per trade. Likewise, all the premium collected should be reduced by the commission paid.

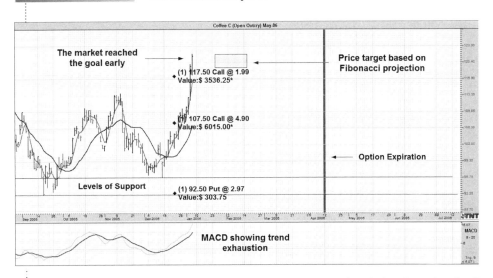

Figure 11.6   Coffee prices reached the original target early; obviously trades don't always work out this well, but it is nice when they do.

Trading these "balanced blends" of long and short options gives a trader the flexibility to adjust the trade to suit his needs and goals as the market fluctuates. The trader can lift legs, add legs, or liquidate the entire position, hopefully to lock in a profit. The choices are many and varied, and if we had an endless amount of time we would cover each one of them. At this point, you should have learned enough to get the idea, so let's finish this trade.

As the short put loses a majority of its value, it is imperative to take the risk off the table by buying it back. We had originally collected $1,293 in premium; now its value has eroded to under $100 (see Figure 11.7). Because there is still time before expiration, it still exposes us to unlimited risk, and common sense says we should close it out by buying it back; doing so locks in a profit of more than $1,000 on that particular leg of the trade. Besides, there are a lot easier ways to make less than $100. Don't get greedy; you may be sorry.

Figure 11.7 When trading short option strategies, it never pays to be greedy. When most of the short option premium has eroded, buy it back even if it seems highly unlikely that it will have any value at expiration.

By buying back the put, we have transformed the trade from a bull call spread with a naked leg into just a bull call spread. We have removed the margin requirement because we have removed the unlimited risk involved with the trade, and we did all this for under $100. Don't forget that we actually just locked in a profit on this leg of the trade. Consider this, we sold the option (by itself) for $1,263 and closed it out for $86.25, or a profit of $1,176.75 before commission. Nonetheless, keep in mind that the money that was originally collected was spent on the rest of the trade, so don't open the champagne bottle just yet.

A few more days pass by and the opportunity to adjust this trade more aggressively develops, open your mind to the possibilities. Unlike most "option gurus" we trade using charts and not an arbitrary risk graph, so we are conscious of the underlying market and the technical signals it sends out. Seeing that the market may have possibly run its course we begin to look at exit strategies. At this point we can liquidate the entire bull call spread, or go short the market (anticipate lower prices) by merely liquidating the long call portion of the trade and holding on to the short call. In essence, we have just converted our bullish trade into a bearish position with unlimited risk on the upside.

We are now fundamentally "short" the market via a short naked call. The new position entails unlimited risk to the upside, but don't forget about the cushion. We closed out the 107.50 call for 13.91 cents or $5,216.25 (13.91 x $375); taking the money off the table gives the remaining short position a cushion in that amount.

Look at it this way. We entered the trade at a credit, so by taking a profit on the long leg we have, in essence, added the proceeds of the long call to our credit. As a result, the break-even points on the "new" short position are significantly wide. To be specific, this trade (as a whole) will be profitable all the way up to 131.92. Let's take a detailed look at how we came to this conclusion.

Given these adjustments to the trade, it may be difficult to identify the new reverse break-even on the position. After all, we have taken profit on two legs of the trade. The monies made on these components are now "cushion" for the remaining leg. The simplest way to look at it is this: Our original credit of $277.50 was reduced by the amount paid to buy back the 92.50 put, $86.25. We then increased our net credit by the amount received in the sale of the 107.50 call, $5,216.25 (see Figure 11.8). To calculate the current RBE, we use a net credit of $5,407.50. First, it is necessary to convert the dollar value into premium based on the multiplier for this particular market. Once again, the multiplier in coffee is $375, thus the net credit is 14.42 cents ($5,407.5/$375). This is the amount that will be added to the strike price of the short 117.50 call that remains open. Hence, the RBE is now 131.92 (14.42+117.50). With the existing position, the only way that the trader will lose at expiration is if the market is trading above 131.92.

At this point we have taken a profit on the short 92.50 put, as well on the long 107.50 call, but we do have unlimited exposure with the remaining 117.50 short call. According to hypothetical valuation the remaining short call has a premium value of $2,703, that's the amount it would cost us to buy it back. Due to our belief that the market will continue to sell off, or likely to digest the recent run up, we sit back and watch.

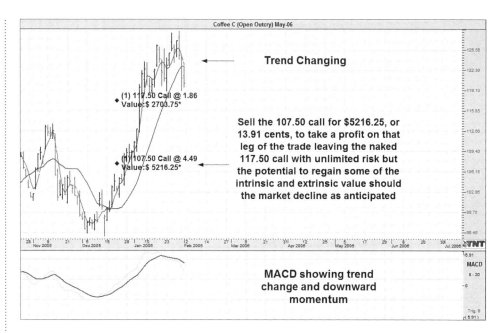

Figure 11.8 Aggressive adjustments are all a part of trading option spreads, but only traders willing to accept the associated risk should participate.

Forty days later (of course we watched it everyday) we see that the technical setup of the market didn't lie to us, and coffee prices did sell off. The short call depreciated in value not only due to the direction of the market but due to the passing of time as well.

With option expiration coming up we close out the trade; yes we close it out instead of risking everything we have gained on chance (see Figure 11.9). Moments like this remind us of the coffee spike in the mid 1990s where coffee prices opened one day of trading 40 cents higher than its previous close without warning. As a reminder, 40 cents in coffee is equivalent to a gain or loss of $15,000. Again, it is wise to buy back the option once about 80% of the original option value has eroded. Naturally, market conditions may be cause to alter this rule of thumb, but it is a good idea to exit the trade once a majority of the profit potential is attained. In this example, the 117.50 call was originally sold for 1.86 cents or $697.50. Sticking to the 80% rule, a trader would have exited this leg of the trade by buying the call option back for $139.50; according to hypothetical values the option could have been offset for a cost of $112.50 to lock in a profit on this leg of the trade of $585; we will be happy to take it.

Holding on to the short 117.50 call until closer to expiration may lead to buying the option back for next to nothing, but the risk is high. More often than not, holding out in hopes of collecting the last shred of time value is harmless; however, such greed may result in financial ruin should you be caught in a suddenly violent market. Experienced traders realize that it is better to simply exit the trade than trip over dollars trying to pick up pennies.

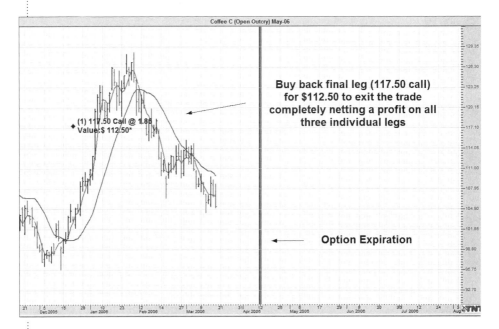

Figure 11.9   Never leave a short option position open if most of the premium has eroded; doing so leaves the trader exposed to theoretically unlimited risk compared to a small potential reward.

So, now you have seen a trading example from start to finish. We started with our standard analysis to determine what we expected the market to do. We then created a trading strategy that we not only understood but were comfortable with based on our interpretation of the market and risk tolerance. We employed this strategy and made the necessary adjustments to not only amend the risk but to also enhance the profit potential. The net result of our efforts returned a profit of $5,294.25 (1,176.75+3,532.50+585). Don't forget to subtract transaction costs.

Using a total commission and fee of $35 per round turn, the trade would have yielded $5,189.25 ($5294.25–($35 x 3)). We use this as an example; your costs depend on what you pay, and that varies from customer to customer and from firm to firm. In this case the profit was reduced by $105 because three commissions would have been charged on the trade at an assumed rate of $35. Likewise, if you pay $50 per round turn you would need to reduce the total profit by $150.

This style of trading allows greater flexibility by giving traders more control in their exposure to risk and reward. Unlike a futures position, in which the profit and loss is immediate, option spreads allow a trader more room for error. Depending on how the trade is constructed, and whether it was filled at a credit or debit, it is possible for a trade to be dead wrong in timing and direction and still come out with a profit. The ability to make money through a directional play and preserve capital should that directional speculation prove to be wrong is priceless.

chapter 12

The Wizard of Oddz: Applying Option Strategies in the "Real World"

Option trading is not unlike other industries that are in the business of "playing the odds." For example, casinos bring in gaming revenue confident that over time they will collect more that they pay out in winnings. Although comparing the financial markets directly to gambling may not be a popular perspective, they both have obvious similarities. In the same way, insurance companies collect premium in anticipation of the probability of future payouts. Option traders may be able to benefit from the same logic through option selling, thus capitalizing on probabilities as opposed to entering a position hoping to profit on a "long shot."

It is not a big secret that casinos have a distinct edge over the average gambler. That is what makes the Las Vegas strip possible; extravagant buildings and upkeep are all part of the billion dollar industry. In fact, the gaming industry has enjoyed so much success that Nevada legislation has put much of the state's tax burden on casinos. Similarly, states such as California and Illinois derive much of their cash flow from the sales of lottery tickets. Perhaps the secret to making money in commodities is thinking like the house, and we believe that understanding and incorporating option selling is a good start toward this goal.

Video poker is quickly becoming the casino game of choice based on the perceived odds. A popular version, Double Double Bonus Poker, has been known to offer a theoretical payout ratio of up to 100.067% if played with a perfect strategy. However, few players play perfectly, especially after a few free cocktails. If you have ever played video poker you know that your goal is a royal flush. The other payouts may keep you in the game longer, but most players don't consider cashing out anything less than the jackpot. This is, of course, what the casinos want. What most don't realize is that the odds of hitting a royal flush are slightly worse than 1 in 40,000 hands played. You can see how this can be a thriving industry. Our point is, instead of striving to be the lucky winner of a jackpot you may be better off turning the tables and looking for smaller, yet more consistent, gains. Doing this certainly doesn't guarantee profits, but it does put the odds in your favor, and that is the ultimate goal of a trader.

Therefore, option trading should be approached in the same manner that a casino owner looks at gambling. Would you rather be the buyer of a lottery ticket, or a seller? Would you rather be emptying the bill collector of a video poker machine, or aimlessly stuffing money into a machine in search of that 1 in 40,000 shot at a jackpot?

To be clear, the odds of success on a long option are far greater than the odds of winning the lottery or hitting a royal flush, but you can see the similarities in logic. Successful traders are looking to frequently make small profits as opposed to "investing" several years in search of extraordinary profits.

While a degree of luck is involved in futures trading, consistent profitable trades can only be consistently realized by those who tilt the probabilities in their favor. As mentioned previously, despite the widespread belief that trading is a zero sum game, it really isn't. While it is true that there will be one winner and one loser to every executed trade, there is a third party to the transaction. Don't forget that the brokerage firm always gets paid for executing your trade. Whether you are paying a full service or a deep discount commission rate there is a cost to executing a trade, and it must be considered in your overall prospective ability to profit in this game. Additionally, all transactions involve exchange fees that need to be accounted for. With that said, unless you are paying an outrageously high commission rate for the strategy that you are employing, successful trading stems from the trades themselves not necessarily the transaction costs. Too many beginning traders focus on saving a dollar in round turn commission rather than making profitable trades. This can be extremely detrimental to those who simply aren't ready to place self-directed trades online. Please note, if you are comfortable with your knowledge and ability to enter your own trades there is really no reason for you not to do so. After all it will save you money on transaction costs and in the long run enhance your ability to be a profitable trader. However, if you are just beginning you should strongly consider using a full service broker until you are ready to go out on your own. Trade entry mistakes can be surprisingly costly.

> **Commission is baggage, but focusing on the trades and execution will save you more money than knocking a few dollars off the transaction costs.**

It is our credence that the odds of a successful futures contract trade is approximately 1 in 3. This assumption is based on the fact that after execution of a futures contract the market will do one of three things: it will either go up, down, or sideways. Of course, if you are long a futures contract you will only make money if the market goes up. You will lose money on the trade if the market goes sideways (don't forget transaction costs) or lower and you exit the trade.

> You have likely been introduced to the premise that trading commodities is a zero sum game; but this isn't necessarily the case. For every individual trade (buy and sell), there is a winner and a loser. However, transaction costs paid interfere with the theory of each participant having a 50/50 chance of success.

Adjusting the Oddz

As mentioned previously, the only way to make money in these markets in the long run is to put the probabilities in your favor. We have come up with four primary actions to put you well on your way to favorable odds:

> There is a big difference between being a trader and being a craps shooter. It is up to you to make the distinction in your own trading.

- Trading extremes (markets near all time highs or lows).
- Take advantage of various degrees of volatility.
- Avoid playing economic or agricultural reports.
- Avoid buying options outright (unless they are cheap, $500 or less).

Trading Extremes

Unlike stocks, commodities tend to trade in defined ranges over the longer term. These "trading envelopes" provide opportunities for disciplined traders. Trading extremes such as prices near all-time highs and lows tend to significantly increase the odds of a successful trade (see Figure 12.1). This is especially the case with prices at the lower end of the trading range; searching for market lows is sometimes referred to as *bottom fishing*.

The premise of this strategy lies in the knowledge of supply and demand and a market's tendency to seek an equilibrium price level (see Figure 12.2). The fact that commodities trade in a defined range makes perfect sense. Remember, commodities are goods not "bads." Although they can become cheap, they will never be worthless. Once a commodity approaches the lower end of the price band, production of that commodity becomes less attractive to farmers, miners, and so on. As a result, supply of the product begins to dwindle over time, which in turn pushes prices higher. Thus, it is a continuous cycle.

An opposite but similar occurrence unfolds if prices become too expensive. Higher commodity prices lure producers to bring goods into the markets. Eventually the increase in supply forces prices back into a more normal price range.

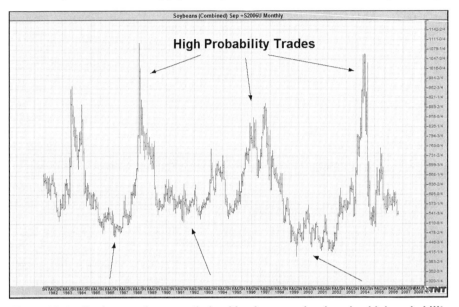

Figure 12.1   Traders can increase their odds of success by choosing high probability trades such as markets trading near long-term extremes.

Additional price pressure results from a decrease in commodity consumption. After all, if the price of orange juice doubles you will probably find an alternative beverage. As consumers shift their purchasing power from orange juice to a substitute product, the decrease in demand allows for price movement toward an equilibrium level.

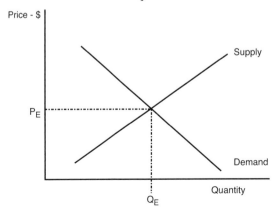

Figure 12.2   Fundamental traders are ultimately speculating on their interpretation of the supply and demand equation for a given commodity.

The concept of supply and demand applies to all markets, but is perhaps more obvious in the commodity markets. One of the most basic fundamental tools used in an attempt to predict a fair market price, or what future price movement may be, is the supply and demand curve. Economic theory is based on the relationship between these two factors. In fact, economists have developed equations to define the direct connection.

In its simplest form, the downward slope of the demand curve suggests that a greater quantity of goods will be demanded when the price is at lower levels. Likewise, the upward slope of the supply curve depicts that higher market prices will lead to an increase in supply. This is because producers are willing to produce more goods in search of exceptional profits.

The point at which these two points meet is known as the equilibrium. At equilibrium, producers are willing to supply Q number of goods for price P. Buyers will also demand quantity Q at market price P. Thus, the market is in equilibrium. It is important to note that a supply and demand curve is drawn as a function of price, and not as a function of each other.

Fundamental traders are assuming that they know more than all other market participants.

Before you get too carried away with this, remember that while it is relatively easy to draw a supply and demand chart, it is nearly impossible to make a realistic prediction of market price using a model such as this. An equation is only as good as the data that is input. While there are data sources for supply and demand available they are often less than accurate and tend to lag the market pace. Commodity prices almost always reflect current supply and demand factors long before governmental reports are released to the press.

Take Advantage of Variations on Volatility

Just as commodity prices tend to trade within a range, so does the volatility associated with a given contract (see Figure 12.3). Identifying these patterns and capitalizing on these changes in volatility are critical to being a profitable trader.

It is often said that volatility is synonymous with opportunity, but what you must understand is that it can also be associated with despair. Volatility is a double-edged sword, not unlike leverage. Successful traders realize that too much of a good thing is just that, too much. Sometimes it is best to be on the sidelines of a fast-paced market, rather than in the trenches without the proper ammo.

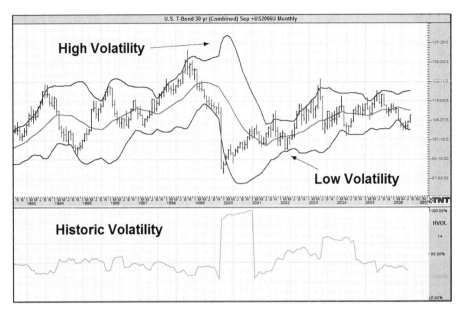

Figure 12.3 Trading volatility is as important as trading the price of a commodity. In essence, you would like to sell options in periods of high volatility and buy during times of low volatility.

It is possible to use various levels of volatility to your advantage by adjusting your approach to the market. For example, in a market that is experiencing high levels of volatility, it may be wise to avoid futures positions altogether. In fact, it may be a good time to be an option seller.

> Think of volatility as you would price, "buy low and sell high."

As a rule of thumb, option traders should avoid purchasing options during times of increased volatility. Instead they should look to sell naked options for premium collection, or potentially multileg credit spreads. This is because when market volatility is high so is the extrinsic value of the corresponding options. Likewise, during times of low volatility options values are low. Don't you feel better buying items from the sales rack rather than paying full price?

Additionally, market volatility tends to fluctuate greatly and has difficulty sustaining high levels over a long period of time. Thus, if you time it correctly by selling options in high volatility and buying them back in low volatility you may stand to profit regardless of the direction of the market. This is because the extrinsic value (time, volatility, demand, and so on) will be grossly overvalued during times of high volatility. Once the volatility subsides, the extrinsic value can implode surprisingly quickly.

The downside of selling option premium into volatility is that if there is an explosive move that you simply don't have the capital to "ride out," you may be left in a less than desirable position. For example, if you sell premium into high volatility but the volatility still manages to increase, it can become insanely expensive to buy back your options, which can create a substantial loss on paper. If you don't have the margin posted, or the psychological wherewithal, to allow you to hold the positions through the "storm," the situation can get ugly making that paper loss a brutal reality.

As illustrated previously in Figure 12.3 and in Figure 12.4, you can see that although a substantial amount of time has gone by, an at-the-money call option is much more expensive following the increase in volatility. In this case, a little more than a month in time has passed leaving the life of the May options that much shorter (about 1/3); however, it is about $1,300 more expensive to get into the market with an at-the-money call option. This discrepancy is created by the market's belief that bigger price swings could lead to higher potential profits should speculation on market direction prove to be accurate. As you can see, the opportunity to be part of a market that is seeing unusual price movement comes at a "premium."

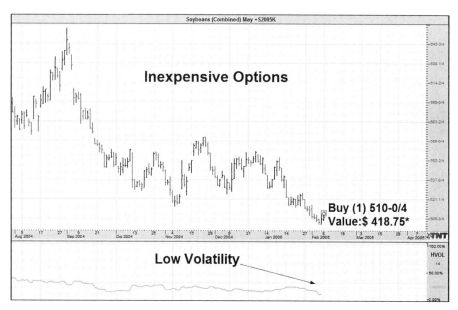

Figure 12.4 Times of low volatility typically create inexpensive option prices, thus creating a buying opportunity.

As stated in previous chapters, more options expire worthless than not, which put the odds in favor of premium sellers rather than buyers. Thus, we believe that purchasing expensively priced options provides traders with little probability of success (see Figure 12.5).

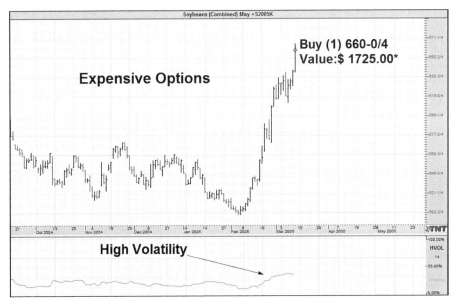

Figure 12.5   High volatility circumstances create inflated option premium making it advantageous to sell rather than buy.

Ideally option sellers look to sell premium in highly volatile market conditions and buy them back after market volatility has decreased. Just like it is impossible to predict market price with absolute certainty, it is impractical to assume that changes in volatility can be accurately predicted.

Conversely, selling options during periods of elevated volatility provides a golden opportunity for sellers. Based on our experience, we agree that in times of high volatility the probabilities of an option expiring in-the-money are increased, but the premiums collected are increased *dramatically*.

Volatility creates opportunity, but it can also cause misery.

Avoid Playing Economic or Agricultural Reports

The release of new information into the marketplace often creates a knee-jerk reaction that can be difficult for a futures position to absorb, as illustrated in Figure 12.6. While it would be impossible and irrational to avoid the release of all reports, it is prudent to avoid major occurrences such as the Employment Report or GDP readings.

Figure 12.6 Despite the "folklore," trading economic reports isn't always a lucrative venture. For it to be lucrative, you would have to be on the right side of the market (without being pushed out on a knee-jerk reaction).

Futures traders and long option strategy traders should avoid placing trades immediately before or after the release of data; however, option sellers may find it an opportune time to take advantage of the upswing in volatility. Nonetheless, market moves tend to be swift and often directionless, which may result in a risky proposition with little room for success. Entering orders in front of a potential "whipsaw" isn't wise—unless you have inside information on the report; in that case, it is just illegal.

Only Buy Options Outright If "The Time Is Right"

The primary message that we have attempted to convey is that long option strategies should be used sparingly. While there are times in which buying options outright may be the optimal strategy, we believe that more often than not there are better alternatives.

Rather than purchasing options, traders willing to post margin and accept unlimited risk, should look to construct strategies that involve selling premium along with any options that they are looking to buy. The short option premium is meant to finance the long options. Of course, conditions may be ripe for simply selling options outright.

More options than not expire worthless.

As mentioned previously in this book, a study conducted by the Chicago Mercantile Exchange (CME) estimated that an average of 70% to 80% of all options held to expiration at the CME expired out-of-the-money—that is, worthless. It is important to note, however, that most options are not held until expiration, and many that are may be components of an option spread or even a combination of futures and options. Thus, it isn't fair to assume that by purchasing an option you are automatically facing an 80% chance of loss. With that said, we interpret the findings to mean that when you sell options you are putting the odds in your favor because you are allowing time to work in your favor rather than against you.

Thus, whether you are selling options for the sole purpose of premium collection or doing so to make long option strategies more affordable, in our opinion the odds of success are increased.

When constructing a strategy with short options it is important to identify the prospects of incurring a loss, and know the extent of the potential damages. Obviously this is something that you should know before ever executing a trade. The less likely an option is to be profitable to the buyer, the more desirable it is for the seller. However, the option must also be capable of bringing in enough in premium to ensure that the reward is worth the risk. For example, it is irrational to sell an option for $50. After transaction costs are taken out of the equation there isn't a lot of profit potential for the trader, but the risk is still unlimited.

Many traders look to the delta value of an option to provide an estimate of the probability that a particular option will expire in-the-money. If you recall, the delta is equal to the change in the option value for each unit of change in the underlying futures contract. It can be considered a "rough" estimate of the chances that a particular option will expire in-the-money. For example, an at-the-money option typically has a delta of .50. In other words there is a 50% chance that the underlying contract will be trading favorable to the option's strike price at expiration.

When selling options, it is preferential to choose strike prices that have a delta value of 30 or less. Conservative traders may want to keep it under 10 or 15. Once again, the delta value is simply the amount of sensitivity that an option has to changes in the price of the underlying. We interpret this to imply that at the time of the trade the probability of that particular option expiring in-the-money is *roughly* 30%. We cannot emphasize enough that this is a ball park figure. Changes in market conditions such as price or volatility could significantly alter original estimates in the blink of an eye.

Similarly, the prospects for the sale of a credit spread yielding the maximum loss can be figured by analyzing the deltas. Remember, a credit spread involves the sale of an option along with the purchase of an option with a distant strike price for insurance purposes.

Example

As illustrated in Figure 12.7, if you sold a Dow 12,600 call option with a delta of .30 and bought the 12,800 call with a delta of .15 for protection, the probability of the market trading over 12,800 is estimated to be about 15% at the time of the trade execution. This is the worst-case scenario for the seller of the spread resulting in a loss of $2,000 minus the premium collected. In the hypothetical case shown in Figure 12.7, the maximum loss is equal to $1,200 ($2,000 - $800).

Likewise, given the theoretical delta values, a seller of this spread would theoretically avoid the maximum loss approximately 85% of the time and would collect the entire premium roughly 70% (1.00-.30) of the time based on the probabilities at the time of trade execution. In this case, the maximum profit potential is $800 before transaction costs.

To reiterate, using delta values as measures of probability should be viewed as an estimation rather than an exact science. There are more precise measures of chance, however, the difference in results is likely not worth the additional effort.

Keep in mind that this approximation is based on the probability of an option expiring in-the-money, not necessarily the odds of this trade being successful. After all, it is possible for a short option to expire in-the-money and still be profitable intrinsically. Also, delta values are not constant; along with the likelihood of the option expiring worthless, deltas can change quickly.

It is also important to note that these calculations assume that the trade will be held until expiration. However, due to the extrinsic value of the options, between the date of execution and option expiration it is entirely possible that the trade could show a substantial paper loss only to become profitable at expiration, or vice versa. The point that we are trying to make is that there will likely be significant swings in option prices as well as emotion before the trade expires. Trading isn't as easy as calculating the odds and then holding on for the ride. Fear and greed will almost always come into play and may have an extremely adverse effect on trading results if you aren't properly prepared.

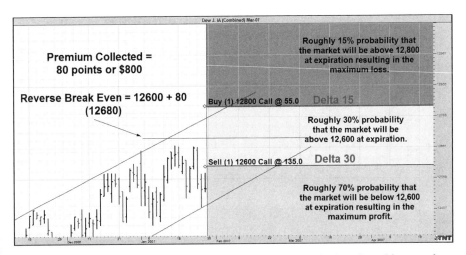

Figure 12.7   Using the delta value to get a rough idea of what the odds are of an option expiring in-the-money, you can determine whether the risk is worth the reward.

chapter 13

Margins and Option Trading

There is a lot more to commodity option trading than knowing the difference between a call and a put or even understanding the basics of the futures markets. Unlike stocks, which for the most part require that traders have the cash available to pay the face value for each security or option trade they execute, futures traders are able to borrow buying power from the exchange to execute trades.

While some stock traders are granted the ability to borrow from their brokerage firms, they are required to pay hefty interest charges and often have to jump through hoops for permission to do so. Futures traders, on the other hand, are simply required to put down a "good faith deposit" of a fraction of the value of the underlying commodity, which is nearly equivalent to an interest free loan. Options on futures traders, if implementing unlimited risk strategies, are required to post similar highly leveraged margin deposits. However, the amount of short option margin required by the exchange is much more difficult to determine. Nonetheless, being aware of the approximate required margin of each type of trading strategy is important to ensuring that you will be getting the most "bang for your buck" as well as trading within your means.

As we have attempted to make very clear, leverage is a two sided luxury. Being exposed to large fluctuations in position value with relatively low amounts of capital can result in excessive volatility in your account balance not to mention your mental well being. For this reason, many are of the belief that the leverage available to speculators may actually be a *disadvantage*. Despite your opinions on leverage, it is important that you fully understand the concept and how it works.

Many beginning traders are under the false pretense that option traders do not need to post margin or are not at risk of a margin call. While this is true if you are following a strict, long option only trading strategy, option sellers are subject to margin requirements just as futures traders would be. This is because, similar to futures traders, option sellers are exposed to unlimited risk.

> For every short option that outnumbers long options, there is margin.

How Margin Requirements Are Determined

Futures exchanges levy futures margin based on the daily fluctuations of each futures contract, while short option margin is calculated by a complicated equation developed by the Chicago Mercantile Exchange. The software program capable of this calculation is known as *SPAN, Standard Portfolio Analysis of Risk*. SPAN is designed to take into account the aggregate risk of each individual trading account by assessing the correlation of a given contract relative to other positions in the account. For example, a futures position in combination with a long or short option may have less inherent risk than having only a futures position and will be margined by SPAN accordingly.

Futures buyers and sellers, as well as option sellers, are required to meet margin requirements. Option buyers and those with limited risk option spreads such as a bull call spread, bear put spread, or an iron butterfly are not exposed to margin. This is because their risk is limited to the amount of premium paid for the spread or outright option. Naturally, the exchange wouldn't require you to have a good faith deposit on a trade in which the risk is limited, and that risk is already locked into the premium paid to execute the position. This is because even in the worst-case scenario there cannot be any additional negative cash outflows, unless of course the option expires in-the-money and is exercised into a futures contract. At that point, the trade would be margined according to that of the underlying futures contract.

What Happens If I Get a Margin Call?

Many beginning investors cringe at the thought of getting a margin call. This is understandable, but isn't nearly as traumatic as many have assumed it to be. In fact, in futures trading the practice is commonplace and is simply part of the "game."

> Think of a margin call as a friendly warning.

Should you receive a margin call, you will typically have a three-day grace period in which you can submit the funds necessary to bring the account within margin or liquidate positions. A good broker will have ideas to mitigate margin through position adjustments, or even eliminate it altogether, to avoid premature liquidation of a position.

For example, a trader who is short a call option and has been issued a margin call may not be comfortable with refunding the account. Nevertheless, she may still believe in the prospects of her position and would prefer to continue to have a speculative play in the market. In an instance such as this, not only would it be expensive to buy the short call option back, but it would take the trader out of the market completely. A cheaper alternative, one that would allow the trader to hold a varied version of the original trade, would be to purchase a call option above (at a higher strike price) the short option for protection. This would reduce the margin on the trade because it limits the trader's potential risk, yet still allows the trader to remain in the market with the chance of recovering some of the losses. The resulting trade is referred to as a bear call spread and was covered in Chapter 5, "Credit Spreads."

Adjusting Margin Once a Margin Call Occurs

Just as there is a theoretically unlimited number of option spread combinations, the possibilities of reducing margin and potentially satisfying a margin call are endless. In fact, covering all of them would require a second book. However, a few rules of thumb may be enough to get you out of a compromising situation.

Sometimes selling premium can be an effective tool to fending off a margin deficiency.

Depending on the situation, it may make sense to sell more option premium in an attempt to lower the margin requirement and satisfy a margin call. The same trader discussed in the previous section may have been able to sell a put to spread the risk of the trade as well as bring cash into the account. In this case, if the circumstances are right, SPAN margin on the new spread trade would be favorable to that of a single short option. This isn't to say that the actual margin charged would be dramatically less, but the cash collected from the short put is partially used toward the required margin.

Table 13.1 demonstrates the overall effect of selling an option spread in terms of margin. As you can see, the margin required for a two-sided spread can be similar (in this hypothetical case it is identical) to that of selling an option on one side of the market. To clarify, in most circumstances the exchanges see the risk of being short a call *and* a put similar to that of being short either a call *or* a put. This is due to the fact that you can lose only on one side of the trade. In fact, looking at Table 13.1, by adding a short 1350 put to the existing short 1450 call the excess margin is actually increased. In other words, despite the fact that the initial margin requirement remained constant, selling the put brought cash into the account and increased the tradable equity. Prior to selling the put, the account only had $3,500 of excess margin. This is the amount of equity above and beyond the initial margin requirement. Subsequent to adding a short put to the account, the excess margin increased to $5,000. Had the trader had a margin call of $1,500 or less, selling the put would have done the trick.

In essence, the seller of an option strangle can lose on the short call option if the market rallies but will be profitable on the short put. Obviously, this goes both ways. If the market drops, the trader may be underwater on the short put, but the call will become profitable as the market drops. The exchange, or more specifically SPAN, recognizes this. As a result, the margin on a short option spread is only charged on one side of the trade.

Table 13.1   Selling option strangles, as opposed to directional one-sided short option plays, can be margin beneficial.

Trade	Net Liquidation Value	Account Equity	Margin Required (Initial)	Excess Margin
Short S&P Futures				
1450 call	20,000	21,500	18,000	3,500
Short S&P Futures				
1450 call	20,000	23,000	18,000	5,000
1350 put				

In addition to selling more premium, converting a naked option into a limited risk credit spread is often a great alternative to adding money to an account or simply liquidating the trade. To demonstrate, if a trader is short a naked call option and receives a margin call, the purchase of an option with a distant strike price and the same expiration month, or a similar strike priced option in a closer month, may do the trick. Let's use the previous example to illustrate this point.

A trader short a naked 1450 call option in the S&P faces unlimited risk and a hefty margin requirement. On the other hand, through the purchase of a 1500 (further out-of-the-money) call option the margin required to hold the trade would be greatly reduced, and the risk of loss would become limited. If this looks familiar you are correct; adding the long call option with a distant strike price converts the naked short call to a limited risk credit spread known as the bear call spread.

As you can see in Table 13.2, assuming that the trader collected $1,500 for the 1450 call and later paid $500 for the 1500 call, the largest loss that the trader could sustain is $11,500 ($250 x (1500-1450) - $1000). If you recall from Chapter 5, this is calculated by multiplying the distance between the long strike and the short strike by the point value of the contract and subtracting the net credit. With that said, the most margin that the exchange will charge on the spread should be $11,500 and, in this instance, would clearly be enough to eliminate a margin call. Nonetheless, in most cases the margin required to hold a bear call or bull put spread is far less than the maximum potential loss.

Table 13.2 The purchase of an out-of-the-money option greatly reduces the risk and margin of a short option position.

Trade	Net Liquidation Value	Account Equity	Margin Required (Initial)	Excess Margin
Short S&P Futures				
1450 call	20,000	21,500	18,000	3,500
Short S&P Futures				
1450 call				
Long				
1500 call	20,000	21,000	11,500 (or less)	9,500 (or more)

You can see that credit spreads arguably provide more risk than naked options to those traders who abuse the corresponding increased amount of leverage. In this example, a trader could not only eliminate a margin call but likely squeeze another credit spread into the $20,000 trading account. Essentially the trader would be "doubling his bet" and facing a risk of $23,000, more than the amount on deposit. When trading credit spreads, remember, just because you can doesn't mean that you should.

Despite the trepidation of getting a margin call, it isn't the end of the world. Unless you are the type of client who has chronic and excessive margin deficiencies, brokerage firms should be willing to work with you by giving you a three-day grace period.

chapter 14

Commodity Trading Myths

There are as many misconceptions of the commodity markets as there are contracts traded on the Chicago Board of Trade each day. We have picked out a few of our favorites to share with the intention of "squashing" some of the assumptions that new traders make. We aren't trying to come across as cynical but feel that in order to become a successful trader you must open your mind to the realities as well as the rewards. Good luck.

It Is Easy to Make Money Trading

When first introduced to the world of futures trading and the leverage that comes with it, it is easy to get drawn into the hype. Software vendors, trading course writers, brokerage firms, and authors profit from the public's misconception of commodity trading. It is in their best interest to use a "smoke and mirror" approach when communicating to beginning traders. After all, their income depends on it.

> "There are no secrets to success. Don't waste your time looking for them. Success is the result of perfection, hard work, learning from failure, loyalty to those for whom you work, and persistence."
> Colin Powell

The truth is, trading is tough. Few people have found a way to consistently make money trading futures, and those who have didn't always have it so easy. Some of the most famous traders in the industry wiped out their accounts countless times before getting it right.

Remember Michael Marcus, the trader who turned a $30,000 proprietary account into $80 million? Prior to acquiring the patience and skill necessary to accomplish such a feat, he blew out several trading accounts, including one that contained $20,000 borrowed from his mother. Losses of that magnitude can be gut wrenching. It takes a persistent personality to subject himself to such torture to gain a grasp on the most critical aspect of trading—emotion.

The one thing that all successful traders will tell you is that you cannot learn to make money by reading a book or spending $5,000 on a trading course. These things are only the beginning; from there it takes practice and discipline.

I Made Money Paper Trading, So I Will Make Money in the Markets

If we had dollar for every time that we heard beginning traders tell us that they made money paper trading, therefore they will make money in the markets, we wouldn't be writing this book. Instead we would be on a tropical island (that we own) sipping on a Mai Tai.

Paper trading, in case you are unfamiliar with the term, is simply tracking fictitious trades to sharpen your trading skills. However, it is human nature to cheat. As much as we would like to tell ourselves that we are honest, when it comes to picking trades and making an honest estimate of where we would have been filled on entry and exit there are definite discrepancies.

This is especially true in the case of option trading. Paper traders think that it is realistic to assume that a closing option price, or even an intraday quote, is a realistic fill price. Doing this is far from accurate.

Just like futures prices, option prices are subject to a bid/ask spread. In other words, if you simultaneously bought and sold an option, you would lose the spread between the two prices. You will always pay more for an option than you can sell it for in that particular moment. The difference between the two prices is the spread that compensates the executing broker for filling the trade.

Imagine if you were a market maker, would you be comfortable taking the other side of each and every trade if there wasn't some sort of incentive? The bid/ask spread widens and narrows based on the risk of executing the trade. The most prominent determinant of this is market liquidity. Brokers require less compensation for trades in a market that has a lot of participants because they know that they will be able to offset the trades with little hassle. In some markets, the bid/ask spread can be significant and can skew paper trading results enormously.

The biggest discrepancy between paper trading results and actual trading results is emotion. As we have mentioned in previous chapters fear and greed guide the market, and this is definitely the case. A paper trader can easily take a step back from the market and look at it objectively. A trader who is making or losing money on every tick that the market moves will have to overcome emotion to make a rational decision. This is easier said than done.

Once into a trade with money on the line, it can be difficult to admit you are wrong when the market goes against you. Many traders make the mistake of holding onto a loser to the point of depleting their trading account out of fear of taking a loss. In fact, many inexperienced traders hold onto massive losers while cutting profits short simply because they are scared of losing a trade.

On the same token, greed often leads to traders failing to take profits in a timely manner. We have seen a beginning trader triple his account with long sugar calls only to allow them to expire worthless. Markets don't go up forever; if you are fortunate enough to catch a move of great magnitude be sure to come out of the trade ahead. Putting too much into the adage "The trend is your friend" can be damaging. Remember, the trend is only your friend until it ends.

If It Is on TV or in the Newspaper It Must Be True

Too many beginning traders get their trading ideas from newscasters on CNBC or another form of business news. Believe it or not, news providers are typically the last to hear the news. Markets are efficient, and their participants are sophisticated. Once a news story is released, the markets have likely already reacted to it.

Don't confuse brains with a bull market, and don't forget that the trend is only your friend until it ends.

For instance, in the summer of 2005, a client of ours heard a newscast about a drought in Illinois. The news source showed images of dried out and useless corn crops, insinuating that this was the norm rather than the exception. Along with the visuals, the newscast prompted investors to take a look at a possible corn rally.

Naturally, the phone calls began to pour in. Everyone was excited about going long corn in hopes of the drought causing enough damage to force prices to levels seen in the late 1990s. One of the respondents was an accomplished professional with a sizeable trading account. He was willing to bet his entire account, nearly $180,000 on the trade. After some persuasion, we were able to talk him into a much smaller position. Neither he nor the many others who went long corn on the advice of the newscast came out of the trade profitably.

Naïve crude oil traders also suffered in mid-2006 following a string of newscasts and analyst recommendations regarding higher crude prices. The general public ignored crude oil as it climbed from the teens toward $40 per barrel. With the market trading slightly above $40, the market started to garner some attention. However, TV commentators weren't oil bulls until much later. With crude toppling $80 per barrel in the mid 2000s there began to be widespread prediction of $100 crude oil and eventually much higher. Not only were we getting phone calls from people who had never traded commodities and wanted to open trading accounts to take advantage of the energy rally, we were getting a lot of walk-in business. In the brokerage industry, it is somewhat uncommon for random passers by to notice the office and come in to open a futures trading account. Of course, this was the top of the market at the time. It wasn't until late 2007 that crude oil prices finally made their way toward $100 per barrel, and much higher. By this time those responding to the original hype were likely scorned. Markets have a tendency to pull everyone in just before it has run its course. For those who are unfortunate enough to be late to the party, it can be a painful experience.

If I Listen to the Experts, How Can I Go Wrong?

Be careful whom you call an expert and whom you listen to for trading advice. This industry has a lot of self-proclaimed expert traders. Many of those selling software, courses, trading signals, and so on aren't all that they claim to be.

You will find that most of these "salespeople" are not registered with any governmental body. In this business, that means that they are for the most part unregulated. Unlike a registered broker, CTA (Commodity Trading Advisor), FCM (Futures Commission Merchant), or IB (Introducing Brokers) who must account for their claims, unregistered parties in the industry have the right to freedom of speech. They can manipulate data, mislead the trading public, and even make unrealistic claims with a decent chance of avoiding repercussion. Simply put, don't believe everything that you read or hear.

For example, a former client claimed to have written and published a futures trading course that was selling on what seemed to be a nicely developed and reputable Web site. We have never actually seen or read the material that he is selling, and don't care to either. The client is often calling us to ask about the difference between a limit order and a stop order. He is unfamiliar with the differences between open outcry and electronically traded markets, and he has no comprehension of how order execution takes place on the exchange floor.

Perhaps the biggest misconception in the industry is the knowledge of the typical commodities broker. This is not to say that they are all incompetent, but a large percentage of them are surprisingly inexperienced.

Being a broker has few perks, unless you are good at what you do. The job is commission based and can be lucrative for those who put forth the effort to educate themselves, provide a higher level of service, and network with those on the trading floor to ensure proper fills for their clients. The hours are long, but it is easy to fall in love with the excitement of it all.

For those who fail to put forth the effort necessary to make a decent living as a commodity broker, the pay is hardly worth the time. In fact, a fast-food restaurant or even unemployment would expectedly pay more. Based on our estimates, approximately 80% of brokers fall into this category; the other 20% make a respectable living and provide their clients with the service that they deserve.

A big problem facing the industry is the fact that the brokers are compensated in commission. Brokers who are short-sighted and fail to realize simple business practice are tempted to churn accounts. In other words, they will push clients to trade as a means of increasing their commission check with little regard to whether the client has a chance to make money on the transaction. Ironically, we believe that most of the brokers who approach their clients this aggressively for commission fall into the 80% of brokers who struggle to survive. There are a few steps that you should take to make sure that your broker is there for you and can properly meet your needs:

- **NFA Web site (www.nfa.futures.org)**—This Web site offers access to a database called *BASIC* (*Background Affiliation Status Information Center*). BASIC contains Commodity Futures Trading Commission (CFTC) registration and NFA membership information as well as futures-related regulatory and nonregulatory actions contributed by the NF/A, the CFTC, and the U.S. futures exchanges. In other words, by simply typing in the name of your broker, or prospective broker, you can access information such as how long this particular person has been registered and active in the industry. You will also see a list of any regulatory actions, NFA arbitration awards, and CFTC reparations cases that the broker has been involved with. Please note, that CFTC reparations claims are not enforcement actions. They are customer attempts to resolve futures-related disputes. The number of reparations claims filed does not mean that the individual violated any rules. Some or all of the claims may have been dismissed, settled, or withdrawn. NFA arbitration is a dispute resolution forum; it is not a regulatory action. Unlike CFTC reparations, the NFA only discloses information concerning arbitration cases for disputes involving customers and NFA members if an award exists. Regulatory actions are just that and include the case history of such offenses and may also disclose the outcome of the case. As you can imagine, knowing whether your broker has been involved in questionable activity in the past can be important.

- **Talk to them**—Getting to know your broker before you begin trading with him is significant. Key points to discuss are educational background, experience in the industry, and most important general market knowledge. A good broker doesn't necessarily have to be a college graduate, and certainly doesn't have to be in the business for 20 years, but she should have a well-rounded grasp of market characteristics. A 20- to 30-minute conversation will give you a good idea of how "with it" the individual is. Don't be afraid to ask questions and pry into personal experiences as a broker.

- **Education**—As mentioned previously, a college education doesn't make someone a great broker or even a successful trader. Even finance and economic majors don't necessarily have an advantage in the world of trading. However, knowing the basis of your broker's knowledge may give you some insight into a broker's strong points, work ethic, and so on.

- **Prior jobs**—This may seem a bit awkward, but you probably don't want to take trading advice from, or even leave trade execution up to, someone who was working at a car wash last month. Remember, the only requirement to being a commodity broker is passing the series 3 exam. You could be living in a "van down by the river" with no brokerage or trading experience and still manage to pass the test and get hired as a broker. This isn't meant to scare you, just to open your eyes so that you are aware of whom it is that you are dealing with.

- **Trading experience**—Ask a prospective broker how long she has been involved in trading. This is not the same thing as asking how long she has been a broker. Before becoming a registered broker, she may have traded for friends, family, or herself; studied the markets, and so on. The answer to this question shouldn't be the primary determinant of whether you choose this person as your account executive. After all, a broker is primarily an order taker. You tell the broker what you want, and the broker executes it for you. However, many people like to get their broker's opinion. With this said, you probably don't want an opinion from somebody who has never traded, or more important, had real money on the line.

- **Does the broker trade in his personal account?**—Don't be afraid to ask a prospective broker if he trades personally. You may be surprised to find that many of them do not. Several brokerage firms highly discourage their brokers from trading in personal accounts because they believe it to be a conflict of interest. After all, would you rather your broker be monitoring and servicing your account, or would you want the broker to be focusing on his own account? Obviously, a broker who is preoccupied with personal trading activities may not be giving clients the attention that they need. Thus, don't be entirely turned off if the answer to this question is no.

- **Execution**—When shopping for a broker, we have found that the single most important factor to consider is the broker's ability to give you proper and precise execution. In terms of electronically traded options and futures such as the e-mini S&P or the ECBOT Z-Bonds execution among brokers and brokerage firms will be almost identical. However, when it comes to open outcry option contracts the difference between an efficient and effective broker may mean the difference between trading successfully or unsuccessfully. A good retail broker will have connections to clerks on the floor who in turn have relationships with filling brokers standing in the pit. There is a good chance that a broker with a "floor presence" will have the ability to get quicker and more efficient fills reported than one without floor access. Keep in mind, that the more contracts you are trading the easier it will be for your broker to get cooperation from the floor.

The futures industry tends to attract individuals with a "get rich quick" mentality. This is true in the case of market participants as well as brokerage employees. Being a commodity broker requires nothing more than to pass a standardized test. With so many under the assumption that being a broker can be lucrative with minimal effort, it seems as though many are brought to the industry for the wrong reasons. Accordingly, the business is known to be transient. Make sure that your broker is going to be in it for the long haul before you invest too much time into the relationship.

Futures Contract Specifications

Contract	IM	Minimum Tick	Contract Size	Expiration Months
10-year Note	$1,148	.005 = $15.625	$100,000	H,M,U,Z
100 oz. Gold	$2,025	.1 = $10.00	100 oz	1st 3 Consecutive
2-year Note	$878	.005 = $15.625	$200,000	H,M,U,Z
30-day Fed Fund	$540	.005 = $20.835	$5,000,000	All Months
30-year Bond	$1,620	.01 = $31.25	$100,000	H,M,U,Z
5-year Note	$878	.005 = $15.625	$100,000	H,M,U,Z
5000 oz. Silver	$3,375	.001 = $5.00	5000 oz	1st 3 Consecutive
Aluminum	$2,025	.0005 = $22	44,000 lbs	All Months
Aussie Dollar	$2,430	.0001 = $10.00	A$100,000	H,M,U,Z
Big Dow Future	$14,063	1pt. = $25.00	$25 x Index	H,M,U,Z
British Pound	$1,485	.0001 = $6.25	£62,500	H,M,U,Z
Bund/10-year note	1400	.01 = €10.00	100000	H,M,U,Z
Buxl/30-Year bond	2850	.02 = €20.00	100000	H,M,U,Z
Canadian Dollar	$1,485	.0001 = $10.00	C$100,000	H,M,U,Z
Class III Milk	$2,025	.01 = $20	200,000 lbs	All Months
CME $ Index	$1,958	.01 = $10.00	1000 x Index	H,M,U,Z
Cocoa	$1,260	1.00 = $10.00	10 metric tons	H,K,N,U,Z
Coffee 'C'	$2,520	.05 = $18.75	37,500 lbs	H,K,N,U,Z

Contract	IM	Minimum Tick	Contract Size	Expiration Months
Copper	$6,413	.0005 = $12.50	25,000 lbs	All Months
Corn	$1,350	.0025 = $12.50	5000 bu	Z,H,K,N,U
Cotton #2	$1,680	.01 = $5	50,000 lbs	H,K,N,V,Z
Dax	13950	.5 = €12.50	€25 x Index	H,M,U,Z
DJ Euro Stoxx	3150	1 = €10.00	€10 x Index	H,M,U,Z
Dow Future (Regular)	$5,625	1pt. = $10.00	$10 x Index	H,M,U,Z
Ethanol	$3,375	.001 = $29	29,000 gal	All Months
Euro FX	$2,025	.0001 = $12.50	125000	H,M,U,Z
Euro Index	1197	.01 = €10.00	€1000 x Index	H,M,U,Z
Eurodollar	$743	.01 = $25.00	$1,000,000	H,M,U,Z 10 yrs out
EuroYen	¥12,150	.005 = ¥1250	¥100M	H,M,U,Z 5yrs out
FCOJ 'A'	$1,890	.05 = $7.50	15,000 lbs	F,H,K,N,U,X
Feeder Cattle	$1,350	.00025 = $12.50	50,000 lbs	F,H,J,K,Q,U
Frozen Porkbellies	$1,620	.00025 = $10	40,000 lbs	G,H,K,M,Q
Gold	$2,700	.1 = $10.00	100 oz	All Month
Hard Red Spring Wheat	$1,690	.0025 = $12.50	5000 bu	H,K,N,U,Z
Hard Red Winter Wheat- KC	$1,500	.0025 = $12.50	5000 bu	N,U,Z,H,K
Heating Oil	$6,075	.0001 = $4.20	42,000 gal	All Months
Jap Yen	$2,700	.000001 = $12.50	¥12,500,000	H,M,U,Z
Lean Hogs	$810	.00025 = $10	40,000 lbs	G,J,K,M,N,Q,V,Z
LIBOR	$473	.0025 = $6.25	$3,000,000	All Months
Lite-Sweet Crude Oil	$4,050	.01 = $10.00	1000 bbl	All Months
Live Cattle	$945	.00025 = $10	40,000 lbs	G,J,M,Q,V,Z
Mexican Peso	$1,875	.000025 = $12.50	MP 500,000	H,M,U,Z
Mini - Corn	$270	.00125 = $1.25	1000 bu	Z,H,K,N,U
Mini - Dow Future	$2,813	1pt. = $5.00	$5 x Index	H,M,U,Z
Mini - Euro FX	$1,013	.0001 = $6.25	62,500	H,M,U,Z
Mini - Eurodollar	$338	.50 = $6.25		H,M,U,Z
Mini - Gold	$675	.1 = $3.32	33.2 oz	All Months

Contract	IM	Minimum Tick	Contract Size	Expiration Months
Mini - Heating Oil	$2,869	.001 = $21	21,000 gal	All Months
Mini - Lite Sweet Crude	$2,025	.025 = $12.50	500 bbl	All Months
Mini - Nasdaq 100	$3,250	.25 = $5.00	$20 x Index	H,M,U,Z
Mini - Natural Gas	$2,869	.005 = $12.50	2500 mmBtu	All Months
Mini - RBOB Gasoline	$3,038	.001 = $21	21,000 gal	All Months
Mini - Russell 2000	$4,000	.10 = $10.00	$100 x Index	H,M,U,Z
Mini - Russell 1000	$2,900	.10 = $10.00	$100 x Index	H,M,U,Z
Mini - S&P 500	$3,500	.25 =$12.50	$50 x Index	H,M,U,Z
Mini - S&P Midcap 400	$3,750	.10 = $10.00	$100 x Index	H,M,U,Z
Mini - Silver	$675	.001 = $1.00	1000 oz	1st 3 Consecutive
Mini - Soybean	$486	.00125 = $1.25	1000 bu	U,X,F,H,K,N,Q
Mini - Wheat	$378	.00125 = $1.25	1000 bu	N,U,Z,H,K
Mini - Yen	$1,350	.000001 = $6.25	¥6,250,000	H,M,U,Z
Nasdaq - 100	$16,250	.25 = $25.00	$100 x Index	H,M,U,Z
Natural Gas	$10,800	.001 = $10.00	10,000 mmBtu	All Months
Nikkei 225	$5,000	1pt. = $5.00	$5 x Index	H,M,U,Z
NYH RBOB Gasoline	$6,750	.0001 = $4.20	42,000 gal	All Months
Oats	$1,013	.0025 = $12.50	5000 bu	N,U,Z,H,K
Palladium	$1,688	.0005 = $12.50	100 oz	All Months
Platinum	$2,700	.1 = $5	50 oz	All Months
Propane	$2,363	.0001 = $4.20	42,000 gal	All Months
Random Length Lumber	$1,650	.10 = $10	110,000bdft	F,H,K,M,U,X
Rough Rice	$810	.5 = $10.00	2000 cwt	U,X,F,H,K,N
Russell 2000	$20,000	.05 = $25.00	$500 x Index	H,M,U,Z
Russian Ruble	$3,000	.00001 = $25.00	RR 2,500,000	H,M,U,Z
S&P 500	$17,500	.10 = $25	$250 x Index	H,M,U,Z
S. Amer. Soybeans	$1,215	.0025 = $12.50	5000 bu	F,H,K,N,Q,U,X

Contract	IM	Minimum Tick	Contract Size	Expiration Months
SGX Eurodollar	$743	.0025 = $6.25	$1,000,000	4 nearest +1/4s
Silver	$4,050	.005 = $25	5000 oz	F,H,K,N,U,Z
Soybean Meal	$1,823	.1 = $10.00	100 tons	V,Z,F,H,K,N,Q,U
Soybean Oil	$810	.0001 = $6.00	60,000 lbs	V,Z,F,H,K,N,Q,U
Soybeans	$2,430	.0025 = $12.50	5000 bu	U,X,F,H,K,N,Q
Sugar #11	$910	.01 = $11.20	112,000 lbs	H,K,N,V
Swiss Franc	$1,350	.0001 = $12.50	SF 125,000	H,M,U,Z
Wheat	$1,890	.0025 = $12.50	5000 bu	N,U,Z,H,K

**The information contained herein is provided as a courtesy and the publisher assumes no liability for its accuracy. The margins listed are for general reference only; margin requirements can be adjusted by the exchanges or your brokerage firm without notice.

Glossary

A

abandon To elect not to exercise or offset a long option position.

actuals The physical or cash commodity, as distinguished from a futures contract. See cash commodity and spot commodity.

American option An option that can be exercised at any time prior to or on the expiration date. See European option.

arbitrage A strategy involving the simultaneous purchase and sale of identical or equivalent commodity futures contracts or other instruments across two or more markets to benefit from a discrepancy in their price relationship. In a theoretical efficient market, there is a lack of opportunity for profitable arbitrage. See spread.

arbitration A process for settling disputes between parties that is less structured than court proceedings. The National Futures Association arbitration program provides a forum for resolving futures-related disputes between NFA members or between NFA members and customers. Other forums for customer complaints include the American Arbitration Association.

ask The price level of an offer, as in bid/ask spread.

assignment Designation by a clearing organization of an option writer who will be required to buy (in the case of a put) or sell (in the case of a call) the underlying futures contract or security when an option has been exercised, especially if it has been exercised early.

associated person (AP) An individual who solicits or accepts (other than in a clerical capacity) orders, discretionary accounts, or participation in a commodity pool, or supervises any individual so engaged, on behalf of a futures commission merchant, an introducing broker, a commodity trading advisor, a commodity pool operator, or an agricultural trade option merchant.

at-the-market An order to buy or sell a futures contract at whatever price is obtainable when the order reaches the trading facility. See market order.

at-the-money When an option's strike price is the same as the current trading price of the underlying commodity, the option is at-the-money.

audit trail The record of trading information identifying, for example, the brokers participating in each transaction, the firms clearing the trade, the terms and time or sequence of the trade, the order receipt and execution time, and, ultimately and when applicable, the customers involved.

automatic exercise A provision in an option contract specifying that it will be exercised automatically on the expiration date if it is in-the-money by a specified amount, absent instructions to the contrary.

B

back months Futures delivery months other than the spot or front month (also called deferred months).

back office The department in a financial institution that processes deals and handles delivery, settlement, and regulatory procedures.

back spread A delta-neutral ratio spread in which more options are bought than sold. A back spread will be profitable if volatility increases. See delta.

backwardation Market situation in which futures prices are progressively lower in the distant delivery months. For instance, if the gold quotation for January is $360 per ounce and that for June is $355 per ounce, the backwardation for five months against January is $5 per ounce. (Backwardation is the opposite of contango.) See inverted market.

basis The difference between the spot or cash price of a commodity and the price of the nearest futures contract for the same or a related commodity. Basis is usually computed in relation to the futures contract next to expire and may reflect different time periods, product forms, grades, or locations.

basis grade The grade of a commodity used as the standard or par grade of a futures contract.

basis quote   Offer or sale of a cash commodity in terms of the difference above or below a futures price (for example, 10 cents over December corn).

basis risk   The risk associated with an unexpected widening or narrowing of basis between the time a hedge position is established and the time that it is lifted.

bear   One who expects a decline in prices. The opposite of a bull. A news item is considered bearish if it is expected to result in lower prices.

bear call spread   The simultaneous sale of an at-the-money or out-of-the-money call option with the purchase of a call option of the same expiration month but distant strike price.

bear market   A market in which prices generally are declining over a period of months or years. Opposite of bull market.

bear market rally   A temporary rise in prices during a bear market. See correction.

bear put spread   A strategy involving the simultaneous purchase and sale of options of the same class and expiration date but different strike prices. In a bear put spread, the option that is purchased has a higher delta than the option that is sold. Accordingly, the long put is closer-to-the-money than the short put.

bear vertical spread   See bear spread.

beta (beta coefficient)   A measure of the variability of rate of return or value of a stock or portfolio compared to that of the overall market; typically used as a measure of risk.

bid   An offer to buy a specific quantity of a commodity at a stated price.

bid/ask spread   The difference between the bid price and the ask or offer price.

Black and Scholes Model   An option pricing model initially developed by Fischer Black and Myron Scholes for securities options and later refined by Black for options on futures.

block trade   A large transaction that is negotiated off a trading floor or facility and then executed on an exchange's trading facility, as permitted under exchange rules. For more information, see CFTC Advisory: "Alternative Execution, or Block Trading, Procedures for the Futures Industry."

Board of Trade   Any organized exchange or other trading facility for the trading of futures and/or option contracts.

boiler room An enterprise that often is operated out of inexpensive, low-rent quarters (hence the term "boiler room"), that uses high pressure sales tactics (generally over the telephone), and possibly false or misleading information to solicit generally unsophisticated investors.

break A rapid and sharp price decline.

break-even (BE) The point at which a particular long option or long option spread executed as a debit will monetarily break even at expiration. Beyond this point, the trade becomes profitable at expiration.

broker A person paid a fee or commission for executing buy or sell orders for a customer. In commodity futures trading, the term may refer to: (1) floor broker, a person who actually executes orders on the trading floor of an exchange; (2) account executive or associated person, the person who deals with customers in the offices of futures commission merchants; or (3) the futures commission merchant.

bull One who expects a rise in prices. The opposite of bear. A news item is considered bullish if it is expected to result in higher prices.

bull market A market in which prices generally are rising over a period of months or years. Opposite of bear market.

bull put spread The simultaneous sale of an at-the-money or out-of-the-money put option and the purchase of a put with the same expiration month but distant strike price.

bull call spread (1) A strategy involving the simultaneous purchase and sale of options of the same class and expiration date but different strike prices. In a bull call spread, the purchased option has a higher delta than the option that is sold. Accordingly, the strike price of the long call option is closer-to-the-money than the strike price of the short call option.

bull vertical spread See bull spread.

bunched order A discretionary order entered on behalf of multiple customers.

butterfly spread A three-legged option spread in which each leg has the same expiration date but different strike prices. For example, a butterfly spread in soybean call options might consist of one long call at a $5.50 strike price, two short calls at a $6.00 strike price, and one long call at a $6.50 strike price.

buyer A market participant who takes a long futures position or buys an option. An option buyer is also called a taker, holder, or owner.

buyer's call A purchase of a specified quantity of a specific grade of a commodity at a fixed number of points above or below a specified delivery month futures price with the buyer allowed a period of time to fix the price either by purchasing a futures contract for the account of the seller or telling the seller when he wants to fix the price. See seller's call.

buyer's market   A condition of the market in which there is an abundance of goods available and hence buyers can afford to be selective and may be able to buy at less than the price that previously prevailed. See seller's market.

buying hedge (or long hedge)   Hedging transaction in which futures contracts are bought to protect against possible increases in the cost of commodities. See hedging.

buy (or sell) on close   To buy (or sell) at the end of the trading session within the closing price range.

buy (or sell) on opening   To buy (or sell) at the beginning of a trading session within the open price range.

C

C & F   "Cost and Freight" paid to a point of destination and included in the price quoted; same as C.A.F.

calendar spread   (1) The purchase of one delivery month of a given futures contract and simultaneous sale of a different delivery month of the same futures contract; (2) the purchase of a put or call option and the simultaneous sale of the same type of option with typically the same strike price but a different expiration date. Also called a horizontal spread or time spread.

call   (1) An option contract giving the buyer the right but not the obligation to purchase a commodity or other asset or to enter into a long futures position; (2) a period at the opening and the close of some futures markets in which the price for each futures contract is established by auction; or (3) the requirement that a financial instrument be returned to the issuer prior to maturity, with principal and accrued interest paid off on return. See buyer's call, seller's call.

called   Another term for exercised when an option is a call. In the case of an option on a physical, the writer of a call must deliver the indicated underlying commodity when the option is exercised or called. In the case of an option on a futures contract, a futures position will be created that will require margin, unless the writer of the call has an offsetting position.

call rule   An exchange regulation under which an official bid price for a cash commodity is competitively established at the close of each day's trading. It holds until the next opening of the exchange.

carrying charges   Cost of storing a physical commodity or holding a financial instrument over a period of time. These charges include insurance, storage, and interest on the deposited funds, as well as other incidental costs. It is a carrying charge market when there are higher futures prices for each successive contract maturity. If the carrying charge is adequate to reimburse the holder, it is called a "full charge." See negative carry, positive carry, and contango.

cash commodity   The physical or actual commodity as distinguished from the futures contract, sometimes called spot commodity or actuals.

cash market   The market for the cash commodity (as contrasted to a futures contract) taking the form of: (1) an organized, self-regulated central market (for example, a commodity exchange); (2) a decentralized over-the-counter market; or (3) a local organization, such as a grain elevator or meat processor, which provides a market for a small region.

cash price   The price in the marketplace for actual cash or spot commodities to be delivered via customary market channels.

cash settlement   A method of settling certain futures or option contracts whereby the seller (or short) pays the buyer (or long) the cash value of the commodity traded according to a procedure specified in the contract.

Also called financial settlement, especially in energy derivatives.

CCC   See Commodity Credit Corporation.

CEA   Commodity Exchange Act or Commodity Exchange Authority.

certificated or certified stocks   Stocks of a commodity that have been inspected and found to be of a quality deliverable against futures contracts, stored at the delivery points designated as regular or acceptable for delivery by an exchange. In grain, called "stocks in deliverable position." See deliverable stocks.

CFTC   See Commodity Futures Trading Commission.

charting   The use of graphs and charts in the technical analysis of futures markets to plot trends of price movements, average movements of price, volume of trading, and open interest.

chartist   Technical trader who reacts to signals derived from graphs of price movements.

churning   Excessive trading of a discretionary account by a person with control over the account for the purpose of generating commissions while disregarding the interests of the customer.

C.I.F.   Cost, insurance, and freight paid to a point of destination and included in the price quoted.

circuit breakers A system of coordinated trading halts and/or price limits on equity markets and equity derivative markets designed to provide a cooling-off period during large, intraday market declines. The first known use of the term circuit breaker in this context was in the Report of the Presidential Task Force on Market Mechanisms (Jan-uary 1988), which recommended that circuit breakers be adopted following the market break of October 1987.

clearing The procedure through which the clearing organization becomes the buyer to each seller of a futures contract or other derivative, and the seller to each buyer for clearing members.

clearing association See clearing organization.

clearing house See clearing organization.

clearing member A member of a clearing organization. All trades of a nonclearing member must be processed and eventually settled through a clearing member.

clearing organization An entity through which futures and other derivative transactions are cleared and settled. It is also charged with assuring the proper conduct of each contract's delivery procedures and the adequate financing of trading. A clearing organization may be a division of a particular exchange, an adjunct or affiliate thereof, or a freestanding entity. Also called a clearing house, multilateral clearing organization, or clearing association. See derivatives clearing organization.

clearing price See settlement price.

close The exchange-designated period at the end of the trading session during which all transactions are considered made "at the close." See call.

closing-out Liquidating an existing long or short futures or option position with an equal and opposite transaction. Also known as offset.

closing price (or range) The price (or price range) recorded during trading that takes place in the final period of a trading session's activity that is officially designated as the "close."

combination Puts and calls held either long or short with different strike prices and/or expirations. Types of combinations include straddles and strangles.

commercial An entity involved in the production, processing, or merchandising of a commodity.

commission (1) The charge made by a futures commission merchant for buying and selling futures contracts; or (2) the fee charged by a futures broker for the execution of an order. Note: When capitalized, the word "Commission" usually refers to the CFTC.

Commitments of Traders report (COT) A weekly report from the CFTC providing a breakdown of each Tuesday's open interest for markets in which 20 or more traders hold positions equal to or above the reporting levels established by the CFTC. Open interest is broken down by aggregate commercial, noncommercial, and nonreportable holdings.

commitments See open interest.

commodity A commodity, as defined in the Commodity Exchange Act, includes the agricultural commodities enumerated in Section 1a(4) of the Commodity Exchange Act, 7 USC 1a(4), and all other goods and articles, except onions as provided in Public Law 85-839 (7 USC 13-1), a 1958 law that banned futures trading in onions, and all services, rights, and interests in which contracts for future delivery are presently or in the future dealt in.

Commodity Credit Corporation A government-owned corporation established in 1933 to assist American agriculture. Major operations include price support pro-grams, foreign sales, and export credit programs for agricultural commodities.

Commodity Exchange Act The Commodity Exchange Act, 7 USC 1, et seq., provides for the federal regulation of commodity futures and options trading. See Commodity Futures Modernization Act.

Commodity Exchange Authority A regulatory agency of the U.S. Department of Agriculture established to administer the Commodity Exchange Act prior to 1975. The Commodity Exchange Authority was the predecessor of the Commodity Futures Trading Commission.

Commodity Exchange Commission A commission consisting of the Secretary of Agriculture, Secretary of Commerce, and the Attorney General, responsible for administering the Commodity Exchange Act prior to 1975.

Commodity Futures Modernization Act The Commodity Futures Modernization Act of 2000 (CFMA), Pub. L. No. 106-554, 114 Stat. 2763, reauthorized the Commodity Futures Trading Commission for five years and overhauled the Commodity Exchange Act to create a flexible structure for the regulation of futures and options trading. Significantly, the CFMA codified an agreement between the CFTC and the Securities and Exchange Commission to repeal the 18-year-old ban on the trading of single stock futures.

Commodity Futures Trading Commission (CFTC) The federal regulatory agency established by the Commodity Futures Trading Act of 1974 to administer the Commodity Exchange Act.

commodity option An option on a commodity or a futures contract.

commodity pool An investment trust, syndicate, or similar form of enterprise operated for the purpose of trading commodity futures or option contracts. Typically thought of as an enterprise engaged in the business of investing the collective or "pooled" funds of multiple participants in trading commodity futures or options, where participants share in profits and losses on a pro rata basis.

commodity pool operator (CPO) A person engaged in a business similar to an investment trust or a syndicate and who solicits or accepts funds, securities, or property for the purpose of trading commodity futures contracts or commodity options. The commodity pool operator either itself makes trading decisions on behalf of the pool or engages a commodity trading advisor to do so.

commodity price index Index or average, which may be weighted, of selected commodity prices, intended to be representative of the markets in general or a specific subset of commodities, for example, grains or livestock.

Commodity Trading Advisor (CTA) A person who, for pay, regularly engages in the business of advising others as to the value of commodity futures or options or the advisability of trading in commodity futures or options, or issues analyses or reports concerning commodity futures or options.

confirmation statement A statement sent by a futures commission merchant to a customer when a futures or options position has been initiated, which typically shows the price and the number of contracts bought and sold. See P&S (purchase and sale statement).

congestion (1) A market situation in which shorts attempting to cover their positions are unable to find an adequate supply of contracts provided by longs willing to liquidate or by new sellers willing to enter the market, except at sharply higher prices (see squeeze, corner); (2) in technical analysis, a period of time characterized by repetitious and limited price fluctuations.

contango Market situation in which prices in succeeding delivery months are progressively higher than in the nearest delivery month; the opposite of backwardation.

contract (1) A term of reference describing a unit of trading for a commodity future or option; (2) an agreement to buy or sell a specified commodity, detailing the amount and grade of the product and the date on which the contract will mature and become deliverable.

contract grades Those grades of a commodity that have been officially approved by an exchange as deliverable in settlement of a futures contract.

contract market   A board of trade or exchange designated by the Commodity Futures Trading Commission to trade futures or options under the Commodity Exchange Act. A contract market can allow both institutional and retail participants and can list for trading futures contracts on any commodity, provided that each contract is not readily susceptible to manipulation. Also called designated contract market.

contract month   See delivery month.

contract size   The actual amount of a commodity represented in a contract.

contract unit   See contract size.

convergence   The tendency for prices of physicals and futures to approach one another, usually during the delivery month. Also called a "narrowing of the basis."

corner   (1) Securing such relative control of a commodity that its price can be manipulated, that is, can be controlled by the creator of the corner; or (2) in the extreme situation, obtaining contracts requiring the delivery of more commodities than are available for delivery. See squeeze, congestion.

correction   A temporary decline in prices during a bull market that partially reverses the previous rally. See bear market rally.

cost of tender   Total of various charges incurred when a commodity is certified and delivered on a futures contract.

COT   See Commitments of Traders report.

counter-trend trading   In technical analysis, the method by which a trader takes a position contrary to the current market direction in anticipation of a change in that direction.

cover   (1) Purchasing futures to offset a short position (same as short covering); see offset, liquidation; (2) to have in hand the physical commodity when a short futures sale is made, or to acquire the commodity that might be deliverable on a short sale.

covered option   A short call or put option position that is covered by the sale or purchase of the underlying futures contract or other underlying instrument. For example, in the case of options on futures contracts, a covered call is a short call position combined with a long futures position. A covered put is a short put position combined with a short futures position.

Cox-Ross-Rubinstein Option Pricing model   An option pricing model developed by John Cox, Stephen Ross, and Mark Rubinstein that can be adopted to include effects not included in the Black and Scholes

Model (for example, early exercise and price supports).

CPO See commodity pool operator.

credit spread option An option whose payoff is based on the credit spread between the debt of a particular borrower and similar maturity Treasury debt.

crop year The time period from one harvest to the next, varying according to the commodity (for example, July 1 to June 30 for wheat; September 1 to August 31 for soybeans).

cross-hedge Hedging a cash market position in a futures or option contract for a different but price-related commodity.

crush spread In the soybean futures market, the simultaneous purchase of soybean futures and the sale of soybean meal and soybean oil futures. See reverse crush spread.

CTA See Commodity Trading Advisor.

D

daily price limit The maximum price advance or decline from the previous day's settlement price permitted during one trading session, as fixed by the rules of an exchange.

day order An order that expires automatically at the end of each day's trading session. There may be a day order with time contingency. For example, an "off at a specific time" order is an order that remains in force until the specified time during the session is reached. At such time, the order is automatically canceled.

day trader A trader, often a person with exchange trading privileges, who takes positions and then offsets them during the same trading session prior to the close of trading.

deck The orders for purchase or sale of futures and option contracts held by a floor broker. Also referred to as an order book.

declaration date See expiration date.

declaration (of options) See exercise price.

default Failure to perform on a futures contract as required by exchange rules, such as failure to meet a margin call, or to make or take delivery.

deferred futures See back months.

deliverable stocks Stocks of commodities located in exchange-approved storage for which receipts may be used in making delivery on futures contracts. In the cotton trade, the term refers to cotton certified for delivery. Also see certificated or certified stocks.

deliverable supply   The total supply of a commodity that meets the delivery specifications of a futures contract.

delivery   The tender and receipt of the actual commodity, the cash value of the commodity, or of a delivery instrument covering the commodity (for example, warehouse receipts or shipping certificates), used to settle a futures contract. See notice of intent to deliver, delivery notice.

delivery date   The date on which the commodity or instrument of delivery must be delivered to fulfill the terms of a contract.

delivery instrument   A document used to effect delivery on a futures contract, such as a warehouse receipt or shipping certificate.

delivery month   The specified month within which a futures contract matures and can be settled by delivery or the specified month in which the delivery period begins.

delivery, nearby   The nearest traded month, the front month. In plural form, one of the nearer trading months.

delivery notice   The written notice given by the seller of his intention to make delivery against an open short futures position on a particular date. This notice, delivered through the clearing organization, is separate and distinct from the warehouse receipt or other instrument that will be used to transfer title. Also called notice of intent to deliver or notice of delivery.

delivery option   A provision of a futures contract that provides the short with flexibility in regard to timing, location, quantity, or quality in the delivery process.

delivery point   A location designated by a commodity exchange where stocks of a commodity represented by a futures contract may be delivered in fulfillment of the contract. Also called location.

delivery price   The price fixed by the clearing organization at which deliveries on futures are invoiced—generally the price at which the futures contract is settled when deliveries are made. Also called invoice price.

delta   The expected change in an option's price given a one-unit change in the price of the underlying futures contract or physical commodity. For example, an option with a delta of 0.5 would change $.50 when the underlying commodity moves $1.00.

delta neutral   Refers to a position involving options that is designed to have an overall delta of zero.

deposit   See initial margin.

derivative   A financial instrument, traded on or off an exchange, the price of which is directly dependent on (that is, "derived from") the value of one or more underlying securities, equity indices, debt instruments, commodities, other derivative instruments, or any agreed on pricing index or arrangement (for example, the movement over time of the Consumer Price Index or freight rates). Derivatives involve the trading of rights or obligations based on the underlying product, but do not directly transfer property. They are used to hedge risk or to exchange a floating rate of return for fixed rate of return. Derivatives include futures, options, and swaps. For example, futures contracts are derivatives of the physical contract, and options on futures are derivatives of futures contracts.

derivatives clearing organization A clearing organization or similar entity that, in respect to a contract (1) enables each party to the contract to substitute, through novation or otherwise, the credit of the derivatives clearing organization for the credit of the parties; (2) arranges or provides, on a multilateral basis, for the settlement or netting of obligations resulting from such contracts; or (3) otherwise provides clearing services or arrangements that mutualize or transfer among participants in the derivatives clearing organization the credit risk arising from such contracts.

designated contract market See contract market.

diagonal spread A spread between two call options or two put options with different strike prices and different expiration dates. See horizontal spread, vertical spread.

differentials The discount (premium) allowed for grades or locations of a commodity lower (higher) than the par of basis grade or location specified in the futures contact.

directional trading Trading strategies designed to speculate on the direction of the underlying market, especially in contrast to volatility trading.

disclosure document A statement that must be provided to prospective customers that describes trading strategy, potential risk, commissions, fees, performance, and other relevant information.

discount (1) The amount a price would be reduced to purchase a commodity of lesser grade; (2) sometimes used to refer to the price differences between futures of different delivery months, as in the phrase "July at a discount to May," indicating that the price for the July futures is lower than that of May.

discretionary account An arrangement by which the holder of an account gives written power of attorney to someone else, often a commodity trading advisor, to buy and sell without prior approval of the holder; often referred to as a managed account or controlled account.

distant or deferred months See back months.

dominant future That future having the largest amount of open interest.

E

ease off A minor and/or slow decline in the price of a market.

ECN Electronic Communications Network, frequently used for creating electronic stock or futures markets.

efficient market In economic theory, an efficient market is one in which market prices adjust rapidly to reflect new information. The degree to which the market is efficient depends on the quality of information reflected in market prices. In an efficient market, profitable arbitrage opportunities do not exist and traders cannot expect to consistently outperform the market unless they have lower-cost access to information that is reflected in market prices or unless they have access to information before it is reflected in market prices.

EFP See exchange for physicals.

electronic trading facility A trading facility that operates by an electronic or telecommunications network instead of a trading floor and maintains an automated audit trail of transactions.

E-Local A person with trading privileges at an exchange with an electronic trading facility who trades electronically (rather than in a pit or ring) for his or her own account, often at a trading arcade.

E-Mini A mini contract that is traded exclusively on an electronic trading facility. E-Mini is a trademark of the Chicago Mercantile Exchange.

equity As used on a trading account statement, refers to the residual dollar value of a futures or option trading account, assuming it was liquidated at current prices.

European option An option that may be exercised only on the expiration date. See American option.

even lot A unit of trading in a commodity established by an exchange to which official price quotations apply.

exchange A central marketplace with established rules and regulations where buyers and sellers meet to trade futures and options contracts or securities. Exchanges include designated contract markets and derivatives transaction execution facilities.

exchange for physicals (EFP) A transaction in which the buyer of a cash commodity transfers to the seller a corresponding amount of long futures contracts, or receives from the seller a corresponding amount of short futures, at a price difference mutually agreed on. In this way, the opposite hedges in futures of both parties are closed out simultaneously. Also called exchange of futures for cash, AA (against actuals), or Ex-Pit transactions.

exchange of futures for cash See exchange for physicals.

exchange rate The price of one currency stated in terms of another currency.

exchange risk factor The delta of an option as computed daily by the exchange on which it is traded.

exercise price (strike price) The price, specified in the option contract, at which the underlying futures contract, security, or commodity will move from seller to buyer.

expiration date The date on which an option contract automatically expires; the last day an option may be exercised.

extrinsic value See time value.

F

fast market Transactions in the pit or ring take place in such volume and with such rapidity that price reporters behind with price quotations insert "FAST" and show a range of prices. Also called a fast tape.

feed ratio The relationship of the cost of feed, expressed as a ratio to the sale price of animals, such as the corn-hog ratio. These serve as indicators of the profit margin or lack of profit in feeding animals to market weight.

Fibonacci numbers A number sequence discovered by a thirteenth century Italian mathematician Leonardo Fibonacci (circa 1170-1250), who introduced Arabic numbers to Europe, in which the sum of any two consecutive numbers equals the next highest number—that is, following this sequence: 1, 1, 2, 3, 5, 8, 13, 21, 34, 55, and so on. The ratio of any number to its next highest number approaches 0.618 after the first four numbers. These numbers are used by technical analysts to determine price objectives from percentage retracements.

fill The execution of an order.

final settlement price The price at which a cash-settled futures contract is settled at maturity, pursuant to a procedure specified by the exchange.

financial instruments As used by the CFTC, this term generally refers to any futures or option contract that is not based on an agricultural commodity or a natural resource. It includes currencies, equity securities, fixed income securities, and indexes of various kinds.

financial settlement Cash settlement, especially for energy derivatives.

first notice day The first day on which notices of intent to deliver actual commodities against futures market positions can be received. First notice day may vary with each commodity and exchange.

floor broker A person with exchange trading privileges who, in any pit, ring, post, or other place provided by an exchange for the meeting of persons similarly engaged, executes for another person any orders for the purchase or sale of any commodity for future delivery.

floor trader A person with exchange trading privileges who executes his own trades by being personally present in the pit or ring for futures trading. See local.

forced liquidation The situation in which a customer's account is liquidated (open positions are offset) by the brokerage firm holding the account, usually after notification that the account is undermargined due to adverse price

movements and failure to meet margin calls.

forwardation See contango.

forward contract A cash transaction common in many industries, including commodity merchandising, in which a commercial buyer and seller agree on delivery of a specified quality and quantity of goods at a specified future date. Terms may be more "personalized" than is the case with standardized futures contracts (that is, delivery time and amount are as determined between seller and buyer). A price may be agreed on in advance, or there may be agreement that the price will be determined at the time of delivery.

forward market The over-the-counter market for forward contracts.

forward months Futures contracts, currently trading, calling for later or distant delivery. See deferred futures, back months.

front month The spot or nearby delivery month, the nearest traded contract month. See back months.

front spread A delta-neutral ratio spread in which more options are sold than bought. Also called ratio vertical spread. A front spread will increase in value if volatility decreases.

full carrying charge, full carry See carrying charges.

fundamental analysis Study of basic, underlying factors that will affect the supply and demand of the commodity being traded in futures contracts. See technical analysis.

fungibility The characteristic of interchangeability. Futures contracts for the same commodity and delivery month traded on the same exchange are fungible due to their standardized specifications for quality, quantity, delivery date, and delivery locations.

futures See futures contract.

futures commission merchant (FCM) Individuals, associations, partnerships, corporations, and trusts that solicit or accept orders for the purchase or sale of any commodity for future delivery on or subject to the rules of any exchange and that accept payment from or extend credit to those whose orders are accepted.

futures contract An agreement to purchase or sell a commodity for delivery in the future: (1) at a price that is determined at initiation of the contract; (2) that obligates each party to the contract to fulfill the contract at the specified price; (3) that is used to assume or shift price risk; and (4) that may be satisfied by delivery or offset.

futures-equivalent A term frequently used with reference to speculative position limits for options on futures contracts. The futures-equivalent of an option position is the number of options multiplied by the previous day's risk factor or delta for the option series. For example, ten deep out-of-money options with a delta of 0.20 would be considered two futures-equivalent contracts. The delta or risk factor used for this purpose is the same as that used in delta-based margining and risk analysis systems.

futures option An option on a futures contract.

futures price (1) Commonly held to mean the price of a commodity for future delivery that is traded on a futures exchange; (2) the price of any futures contract.

G

gamma A measurement of how fast the delta of an option changes, given a unit change in the underlying futures price; the "delta of the delta."

give up A contract executed by one broker for the client of another broker that the client orders to be turned over to the second broker. The broker accepting the order from the customer collects a fee from the carrying broker for the use of the facilities. Often used to consolidate many small orders or to disperse large ones.

Good 'Til Canceled order (GTC)
An order that is valid until canceled by the customer. Unless specified GTC, unfilled orders expire at the end of the trading day. See open order.

grades Various qualities of a commodity.

Grain Futures Act Federal statute that provided for the regulation of trading in grain futures, effective June 22, 1923; administered by the U.S. Department of Agriculture; amended in 1936 by the Commodity Exchange Act.

grantor The maker, writer, or issuer of an option contract who, in return for the premium paid for the option, stands ready to purchase the underlying commodity (or futures contract) in the case of a put option or to sell the underlying commodity (or futures contract) in the case of a call option.

GTC See Good 'Til Canceled order.

guaranteed introducing broker An introducing broker who has entered into a guarantee agreement with a futures commission merchant (FCM), whereby the FCM agrees to be jointly and severally liable for all of the introducing broker's obligations under the Commodity Exchange Act. By entering into the agreement, the introducing broker is relieved from the necessity of raising its own capital to satisfy minimum financial requirements. In contrast, an independent introducing broker must raise its own capital to meet minimum financial requirements.

H

hand-held terminal A small computer terminal used by floor brokers or floor traders on an exchange to record trade information and transmit that information to the clearing organization.

head and shoulders In technical analysis, a chart formation that resembles a human head and shoulders and is generally considered to be predictive of a price reversal. A head and shoulders top (which is considered predictive of a price decline) consists of a high price, a decline to a support level, a rally to a higher price than the previous high price, a second decline to the support level, and a weaker rally to about the level of the first high price. The reverse (upside-down) formation is called a head and shoulders bottom (which is considered predictive of a price rally).

hedge exemption An exemption from speculative position limits for bona fide hedgers and certain other persons who meet the requirements of exchange and CFTC rules.

hedge fund A private investment fund or pool that trades and invests in various assets such as securities, commodities, currency, and derivatives on behalf of its clients, typically wealthy individuals. Some commodity pool operators operate hedge funds.

hedge ratio Ratio of the value of futures contracts purchased or sold to the value of the cash commodity being hedged, a computation necessary to minimize basis risk.

hedging Taking a position in a futures market opposite to a position held in the cash market to minimize the risk of financial loss from an adverse price change; or a purchase or sale of futures as a temporary substitute for a cash transaction that will occur later. One can hedge either a long cash market position (for example, one owns the cash commodity) or a short cash market position (for example, one plans on buying the cash commodity in the future).

historical volatility A statistical measure of the volatility of a futures contract, security, or other instrument over a specified number of past trading days.

horizontal spread (also called time spread or calendar spread) An option spread involving the simultaneous purchase and sale of options of the same class and strike prices but different expiration dates. See diagonal spread, vertical spread.

IJK

IB See introducing broker.

implied volatility The volatility of a futures contract, security, or other instrument as implied by the prices of an option on that instrument, calculated using an options pricing model.

index arbitrage The simultaneous purchase (sale) of stock index futures and the sale (purchase) of some or all of the component stocks that make up the particular stock index to profit from sufficiently large intermarket spreads between the futures contract and the index itself. Also see arbitrage.

initial deposit See initial margin.

initial margin Customers' funds put up as security for a guarantee of contract fulfillment at the time a futures market position is established. See original margin.

instrument A tradable asset such as a commodity, security, or derivative, or an index or value that underlies a derivative or could underlie a derivative.

intercommodity spread A spread in which the long and short legs are in two different but generally related commodity markets. Also called an intermarket spread. See spread.

interdelivery spread   A spread involving two different months of the same commodity. Also called an intracommodity spread. See spread.

intermarket spread   See spread and intercommodity spread.

in-the-money   A term used to describe an option contract that has a positive value if exercised. A call with a strike price of $390 on gold trading at $400 is in-the-money 10 dollars. See intrinsic value.

intracommodity spread   See spread and interdelivery spread.

intrinsic value   A measure of the value of an option or a warrant if immediately exercised—that is, the extent to which it is in-the-money. The amount by which the current price for the underlying commodity or futures contract is above the strike price of a call option or below the strike price of a put option for the commodity or futures contract.

introducing broker (IB)   A person (other than a person registered as an associated person of a futures commission merchant) who is engaged in soliciting or in accepting orders for the purchase or sale of any commodity for future delivery on an exchange who does not accept any money, securities, or property to margin, guarantee, or secure any trades or contracts that result therefrom.

inverted market   A futures market in which the nearer months are selling at prices higher than the more distant months; a market displaying "inverse carrying charges," characteristic of markets with supply shortages. See backwardation.

invisible supply   Uncounted stocks of a commodity in the hands of wholesalers, manufacturers, and producers that cannot be identified accurately; stocks outside commercial channels but theoretically available to the market. See visible supply.

iron condor   The simultaneous holding of a bear call spread and a bull put spread. See bear call spread and bull put spread.

L

large traders   One who holds or controls a position in any one future or in any one option expiration series of a commodity on any one exchange equaling or exceeding the exchange or CFTC-specified reporting level.

last notice day   The final day on which notices of intent to deliver on futures contracts may be issued.

last trading day   Day on which trading ceases for the maturing (current) delivery month.

leverage The ability to control large dollar amounts of a commodity or security with a comparatively small amount of capital.

life of contract Period between the beginning of trading in a particular futures contract and the expiration of trading. In some cases, this phrase denotes the period already passed in which trading has already occurred. For example, "The life-of-contract high so far is $2.50." Same as life of delivery or life of the future.

limit (up or down) The maximum price advance or decline from the previous day's settlement price permit-ted during one trading session, as fixed by the rules of an exchange. In some futures contracts, the limit may be expanded or removed during a trading session a specified period of time after the contract is locked limit. See daily price limit.

limit move See locked limit.

limit only The definite price stated by a customer to a broker re-stricting the execution of an order to buy for not more than, or to sell for not less than, the stated price.

limit order An order in which the customer specifies a minimum sale price or maximum purchase price, as contrasted with a market order, which implies that the order should be filled as soon as possible at the market price.

liquidation The closing out of a long position. The term is sometimes used to denote closing out a short position, but this is more often referred to as covering. See cover, offset.

liquid market A market in which selling and buying can be accomplished with minimal effect on price.

local An individual with exchange trading privileges who trades for his own account, traditionally on an exchange floor, and whose activities provide market liquidity. See floor trader, E-Local.

location A delivery point for a futures contract.

locked limit A price that has advanced or declined the permissible limit during one trading session, as fixed by the rules of an exchange. Also called limit move.

long (1) One who has bought a futures contract to establish a market position; (2) a market position that obligates the holder to take delivery; (3) one who owns an inventory of commodities. See short.

long hedge See buying hedge.

long the basis A person or firm that has bought the spot commodity and hedged with a sale of futures is said to be long the basis.

lot A unit of trading. See even lot.

M

maintenance margin   See margin.

managed account   See discretionary account.

manipulation   Any planned operation, transaction, or practice that causes or maintains an artificial price. Specific types include corners and squeezes as well as unusually large purchases or sales of a commodity or security in a short period of time to distort prices, and putting out false information to distort prices.

margin   The amount of money or collateral deposited by a customer with his broker, by a broker with a clearing member, or by a clearing member with a clearing organization. The margin is not partial payment on a purchase. Also called performance bond. (1) Initial margin is the amount of margin required by the broker when a futures position is opened; (2) maintenance margin is an amount that must be maintained on deposit at all times. If the equity in a customer's account drops to or below the level of maintenance margin because of adverse price movement, the broker must issue a margin call to restore the customer's equity to the initial level. Exchanges specify levels of initial margin and maintenance margin for each futures contract, but futures commission merchants may require their customers to post margin at higher levels than those specified by the exchange. Futures margin is determined by the SPAN margining system, which takes into account all positions in a customer's portfolio.

margin call   (1) A request from a brokerage firm to a customer to bring margin deposits up to initial levels; (2) a request by the clearing organization to a clearing member to make a deposit of original margin, or a daily or intraday variation margin payment because of adverse price movement, based on positions carried by the clearing member.

market maker   A professional securities dealer or person with trading privileges on an exchange who has an obligation to buy when there is an excess of sell orders and to sell when there is an excess of buy orders. By maintaining an offering price sufficiently higher than their buying price, these firms are compensated for the risk involved in allowing their inventory of securities to act as a buffer against temporary order imbalances. In the futures industry, this term is sometimes loosely used to refer to a floor trader or local who, in speculating for his own account, provides a market for commercial users of the market. Occasionally a futures exchange will compensate a person with exchange trading privileges to take on the obligations of a market maker to enhance liquidity in a newly listed or lightly traded futures contract.

market-on-close An order to buy or sell at the end of the trading session at a price within the closing range of prices.

market-on-opening An order to buy or sell at the beginning of the trading session at a price within the opening range of prices.

market order An order to buy or sell a futures contract at whatever price is obtainable at the time it is entered in the ring, pit, or other trading platform.

mark-to-market Part of the daily cash flow system used by U.S. futures exchanges to maintain a minimum level of margin equity for a given futures or option contract position by calculating the gain or loss in each contract position resulting from changes in the price of the futures or option contracts at the end of each trading session. These amounts are added or subtracted to each account balance.

maturity Period within which a futures contract can be settled by delivery of the actual commodity.

maximum price fluctuation See limit (up or down) and daily price limit.

member rate Commission charged for the execution of an order for a person who is a member of or has trading privileges at the exchange.

mini Refers to a futures contract that has a smaller contract size than an otherwise identical futures contract.

minimum price fluctuation (minimum tick) Smallest increment of price movement possible in trading a given contract.

minimum tick See minimum price fluctuation.

momentum In technical analysis, the relative change in price over a specific time interval. Often equated with speed or velocity and considered in terms of relative strength.

money market The market for short-term debt instruments.

multilateral clearing organization See clearing organization.

N

naked option The sale of a call or put option without holding an equal and opposite position in the underlying instrument. Also referred to as an uncovered option, naked call, or naked put.

National Futures Association (NFA) A self-regulatory organization, whose members include futures commission merchants, commodity pool operators, commodity trading advisors, introducing brokers, commodity exchanges, commercial firms, and banks, that is responsible—under CFTC oversight—for certain aspects of the regulation of FCMs, CPOs, CTAs, IBs, and their associated persons, focusing primarily on the qualifications and proficiency, financial condition, retail sales practices, and business conduct of these futures professionals. NFA also performs arbitration and dispute resolution functions for industry participants.

nearby delivery month The month of the futures contract closest to maturity; the front month or lead month.

nearbys The nearest delivery months of a commodity futures market.

negative carry The cost of financing a financial instrument (the short-term rate of interest), when the cost is above the current return of the financial instrument. See carrying charges and positive carry.

net asset value (NAV) The value of each unit of participation in a commodity pool.

net position The difference between the open long contracts and the open short contracts held by a trader in any one commodity.

NFA See National Futures Association.

notice day Any day on which notices of intent to deliver on futures contracts may be issued.

notice of intent to deliver A notice that must be presented by the seller of a futures contract to the clearing organization prior to delivery. The clearing organization then assigns the notice and subsequent delivery instrument to a buyer. Also called notice of delivery.

O

offer An indication of willingness to sell at a given price; opposite of bid, the price level of the offer may be referred to as the ask.

offset Liquidating a purchase of futures contracts through the sale of an equal number of contracts of the same delivery month, or liquidating a short sale of futures through the purchase of an equal number of contracts of the same delivery month. See closing-out and cover.

opening price (or range) The price (or price range) recorded during the period designated by the exchange as the official opening.

opening The period at the beginning of the trading session officially designated by the exchange during which all transactions are considered made "at the opening."

open interest The total number of futures contracts long or short in a delivery month or market that has been entered into and not yet liquidated by an offsetting transaction or fulfilled by delivery. Also called open contracts or open commitments.

open order (or orders) An order that remains in force until it is canceled or until the futures contracts expire. See Good 'Til Canceled and Good This Week orders.

open outcry A method of public auction, common to most U.S. commodity exchanges, where trading occurs on a trading floor and traders may bid and offer simultaneously either for their own accounts or for the accounts of customers. Transactions may take place simultaneously at different places in the trading pit or ring. At most exchanges outside the U.S., open outcry has been replaced by electronic trading platforms.

open trade equity The unrealized gain or loss on open futures positions.

option A contract that gives the buyer the right, but not the obligation, to buy or sell a specified quantity of a commodity or other instrument at a specific price within a specified period of time, regardless of the market price of that instrument. Also see put and call.

option buyer The person who buys calls, puts, or any combination of calls and puts.

option pricing model A mathematical model used to calculate the theoretical value of an option. Inputs to option pricing models typically include the price of the underlying instrument, the option strike price, the time remaining till the expiration date, the volatility of the underlying instrument, and the risk-free interest rate (for example, the Treasury bill interest rate). Examples of option pricing models include Black and Scholes and Cox-Ross-Rubinstein.

option writer The person who originates an option contract by promising to perform a certain obligation in return for the price or premium of the option. Also known as option grantor or option seller.

original margin Term applied to the initial deposit of margin money each clearing member firm is required to make according to clearing organization rules based on positions carried, determined separately for customer and proprietary positions; similar in concept to the initial margin or security deposit required of customers by exchange rules. See initial margin.

OTC See over-the-counter.

out-of-the-money   A term used to describe an option that has no intrinsic value. For example, a call with a strike price of $400 on gold trading at $390 is out-of-the-money 10 dollars.

outright   An order to buy or sell only one specific type of futures contract; an order that is not a spread order.

out trade   A trade that cannot be cleared by a clearing organization because the trade data submitted by the two clearing members or two traders involved in the trade differs in some respect (for example, price and/or quantity). In such cases, the two clearing members or traders involved must reconcile the discrepancy, if possible, and resubmit the trade for clearing. If an agreement cannot be reached by the two clearing members or traders involved, the dispute would be settled by an appropriate exchange committee.

overbought   A technical opinion that the market price has risen too steeply and too fast in relation to underlying fundamental factors. Rank and file traders who were bullish and long have turned bearish.

overnight trade   A trade that is not liquidated during the same trading session during which it was established.

oversold   A technical opinion that the market price has declined too steeply and too fast in relation to underlying fundamental factors; rank and file traders who were bearish and short have turned bullish.

over-the-counter (OTC)   The trading of commodities, contracts, or other instruments not listed on any exchange. OTC transactions can occur electronically or over the telephone. Also referred to as off-exchange.

P

P&S (purchase and sale statement)   A statement sent by a futures commission merchant to a customer when any part of a futures position is offset, showing the number of contracts involved, the prices at which the contracts were bought or sold, the gross profit or loss, the commission charges, the net profit or loss on the transactions, and the balance. FCMs also send P&S statements whenever any other event occurs that alters the account balance including when the customer deposits or withdraws margin and when the FCM places excess margin in interest-bearing instruments for the customer's benefit.

paper profit or loss The profit or loss that would be realized if open contracts were liquidated as of a certain time or at a certain price.

par (1) Refers to the standard delivery point(s) and/or quality of a commodity that is deliverable on a futures contract at contract price. Serves as a benchmark on which to base discounts or premiums for varying quality and delivery locations; (2) in bond markets, an index (usually 100) representing the face value of a bond.

pegged price The price at which a commodity has been fixed by agreement.

performance bond See margin.

pit A specially constructed area on the trading floor of some exchanges where trading in a futures contract or option is conducted. On other exchanges, the term ring designates the trading area for commodity contract.

pit brokers See floor broker.

position An interest in the market, either long or short, in the form of one or more open contracts.

position accountability A rule adopted by an exchange requiring persons holding a certain number of outstanding contracts to report the nature of the position, trading strategy, and hedging information of the position to the exchange,

upon request of the exchange. See speculative position limit.

position limit See speculative position limit.

position trader A commodity trader who either buys or sells contracts and holds them for an extended period of time, as distinguished from a day trader, who will normally initiate and offset a futures position within a single trading session.

positive carry The cost of financing a financial instrument (the short-term rate of interest), where the cost is less than the current return of the financial instrument. See carrying charges and negative carry.

premium (1) The payment an option buyer makes to the option writer for granting an option contract; (2) the amount a price would be increased to purchase a better quality commodity; (3) refers to a futures delivery month selling at a higher price than another, as "July is at a premium over May."

price movement limit See limit (up or down).

primary market (1) For producers, their major purchaser of commodities; (2) to processors, the market that is the major supplier of their commodity needs; and (3) in commercial marketing channels, an important center at which spot commodities are concentrated for shipment to terminal markets.

public In trade parlance, nonprofessional speculators as distinguished from hedgers and professional speculators or traders.

purchase and sale statement See P&S.

put An option contract that gives the holder the right but not the obligation to sell a specified quantity of a particular commodity or other interest at a given price (the "strike price") prior to or on a future date.

Q

quotation The actual price or the bid or ask price of either cash commodities or futures contracts.

R

rally An upward movement of prices.

random walk Financial theory claiming that market prices evolve according to a random walk as opposed to a predictable pattern.

range The difference between the high and low price of a commodity, futures, or option contract during a given period.

ratio spread This strategy, which applies to both puts and calls, involves buying or selling options at one strike price in greater number than those bought or sold at another strike price. Ratio spreads are typically designed to be delta neutral. Back spreads and front spreads are types of ratio spreads.

ratio vertical spread See front spread.

reaction A downward price movement after a price advance.

recovery An upward price movement after a decline.

reporting level Sizes of positions set by the exchanges and/or the CFTC at or above which commodity traders or brokers who carry these accounts must make daily reports about the size of the position by commodity, by delivery month, and whether the position is controlled by a commercial or noncommercial trader.

resistance In technical analysis, a price area where new selling will emerge to dampen a continued rise. See support.

retail customer A customer who does not qualify as an eligible contract participant under Section 1a(12) of the Commodity Exchange Act, 7 USC 1a(12). An individual with total assets that do not exceed $10 million, or $5 million if the individual is entering into an agreement, contract, or transaction to manage risk, would be considered a retail customer.

retender In specific circumstances, some exchanges permit holders of futures contracts who have received a delivery notice through the clearing organization to sell a futures contract and return the notice to the clearing organization to be reissued to another long; others permit transfer of notices to another buyer. In either case, the trader is said to have retendered the notice.

retracement A reversal within a major price trend.

reversal A change of direction in prices.

reverse-break-even (RBE) The point at which a short option or option spread executed at a credit monetarily breaks even at expiration. Beyond this point the trade becomes a loser at expiration.

reverse crush spread The sale of soybean futures and the simultaneous purchase of soybean oil and meal futures. See crush spread.

ring A circular area on the trading floor of an exchange where traders and brokers stand while executing futures trades. Some exchanges use pits rather than rings.

risk factor See delta.

risk/reward ratio The relationship between the probability of loss and profit. This ratio is often used as a basis for trade selection or comparison.

roll-over A trading procedure involving the shift of one month of a straddle into another future month while holding the other contract month. The shift can take place in either the long or short straddle month. The term also applies to lifting a near futures position and re-establishing it in a more deferred delivery month.

round trip trading See wash trading.

round turn A completed transaction involving both a purchase and a liquidating sale, or a sale followed by a covering purchase.

rules The principles for governing an exchange. In some exchanges, rules are adopted by a vote of the membership; while in others, they can be imposed by the governing board.

runners Messengers or clerks who deliver orders received by phone clerks to brokers for execution in the pit.

S

scale down (or up) To purchase or sell a scale down means to buy or sell at regular price intervals in a declining market. To buy or sell on scale up means to buy or sell at regular price intervals as the market advances.

scalper A speculator on the trading floor of an exchange who buys and sells rapidly, with small profits or losses, holding his positions for only a short time during a trading session. Typically, a scalper will stand ready to buy at a fraction below the last transaction price and to sell at a fraction above—for example, to buy at the bid and sell at the offer or ask price, with the intent of capturing the spread between the two, thus creating market liquidity. See day trader, position trader.

seasonality claims Misleading sales pitches that one can earn large profits with little risk based on predictable seasonal changes in supply or demand, published reports, or other well-known events.

seat An instrument granting trading privileges on an exchange. A seat may also represent an ownership interest in the exchange.

security deposit See margin.

seller's call Also referred to as call purchase, is the same as the buyer's call except that the seller has the right to determine the time to fix the price. See buyer's call.

seller's market A condition of the market in which there is a scarcity of goods available and hence sellers can obtain better conditions of sale or higher prices. See buyer's market.

seller's option The right of a seller to select, within the limits prescribed by a contract, the quality of the commodity delivered and the time and place of delivery.

selling hedge (or short hedge) Selling futures contracts to protect against possible decreased prices of commodities. See hedging.

settlement The act of fulfilling the delivery requirements of the futures contract.

settlement price The daily price at which the clearing organization clears all trades and settles all accounts between clearing members of each contract month. Settlement prices are used to determine both margin calls and invoice prices for deliveries. The term also refers to a price established by the exchange to even up positions which may not be able to be liquidated in regular trading.

shock absorber A temporary restriction in the trading of certain stock index futures contracts that becomes effective following a significant intraday decrease in stock index futures prices. Designed to provide an adjustment period to digest new market information, the restriction bars trading below a specified price level. Shock absorbers are generally market specific and at tighter levels than circuit breakers.

short   (1) The selling side of an open futures contract; (2) a trader whose net position in the futures market shows an excess of open sales over open purchases. See long.

short covering   See cover.

short hedge   See selling hedge.

short selling   Selling a futures contract or other instrument with the idea of delivering on it or offsetting it at a later date.

short squeeze   See squeeze.

short the basis   The purchase of futures as a hedge against a commitment to sell in the cash or spot markets. See hedging.

small traders   Traders who hold or control positions in futures or options that are below the reporting level specified by the exchange or the CFTC.

soft   (1) A description of a price that is gradually weakening; or (2) this term also refers to certain "soft" commodities such as sugar, cocoa, and coffee.

SPAN (Standard Portfolio Analysis of Risk)   As developed by the Chicago Mercantile Exchange, the industry standard for calculating performance bond requirements (margins) on the basis of overall portfolio risk. SPAN calculates risk for all enterprise levels on derivative and nonderivative instruments at numerous exchanges and clearing organizations worldwide.

speculative limit   See speculative position limit.

speculative position limit   The maximum position, either net long or net short, in one commodity future (or option) or in all futures (or options) of one commodity combined that may be held or controlled by one person (other than a person eligible for a hedge exemption) as prescribed by an exchange and/or by the CFTC.

speculator   In commodity futures, an individual who does not hedge, but who trades with the objective of achieving profits through the successful anticipation of price movements.

spot   Market of immediate delivery of and payment for the product.

spot commodity   (1) The actual commodity as distinguished from a futures contract; (2) sometimes used to refer to cash commodities available for immediate delivery. See actuals or cash commodity.

spot month   The futures contract that matures and becomes deliverable during the present month. Also called current delivery month.

spot price   The price at which a physical commodity for immediate delivery is selling at a given time and place. See cash price.

spread (or straddle) The purchase of one futures delivery month against the sale of another futures delivery month of the same commodity; the purchase of one delivery month of one commodity against the sale of that same delivery month of a different commodity; or the purchase of one commodity in one market against the sale of the commodity in another market, to take advantage of a profit from a change in price relationships. The term spread is also used to refer to the difference between the price of a futures month and the price of another month of the same commodity. A spread can also apply to options. See arbitrage.

squeeze A market situation in which the lack of supplies tends to force shorts to cover their positions by offset at higher prices. Also see congestion, corner.

stop loss order See stop order.

stop order An order that becomes a market order when a particular price level is reached. A sell stop is placed below the market, a buy stop is placed above the market. Sometimes referred to as stop loss order. Compare to market-if-touched order.

straddle (1) See spread; (2) an option position consisting of the purchase of put and call options having the same expiration date and strike price.

strangle An option position consisting of the purchase of put and call options having the same expiration date, but different strike prices.

strike price (exercise price) The price, specified in the option contract, at which the underlying futures contract, security, or commodity will move from seller to buyer.

support In technical analysis, a price area where new buying is likely to come in and stem any decline. See resistance.

synthetic futures A position created by combining call and put options. A synthetic long futures position is created by combining a long call option and a short put option for the same expiration date and the same strike price. A synthetic short futures contract is created by combining a long put and a short call with the same expiration date and the same strike price.

synthetic swing trading A strategy that involves the creation of positions with high deltas by combining long and short options, or long options and long and short futures contracts.

T

taker The buyer of an option contract.

T-bond See Treasury bond.

technical analysis An approach to forecasting commodity prices that examines patterns of price change, rates of change, and changes in volume of trading and open interest, without regard to underlying fundamental market factors. Technical analysis can work consistently only if the theory that price movements are a random walk is incorrect. See fundamental analysis.

tender To give notice to the clearing organization of the intention to initiate delivery of the physical commodity in satisfaction of a short futures contract. Also see retender.

tenderable grades See contract grades.

tick Refers to a minimum change in price up or down. An up-tick means that the last trade was at a higher price than the one preceding it. A down-tick means that the last price was lower than the one preceding it. See minimum price fluctuation.

time decay The tendency of an option to decline in value as the expiration date approaches, especially if the price of the underlying instrument is exhibiting low volatility. See time value.

time spread The selling of a nearby option and buying of a more deferred option with the same strike price. Also called horizontal spread.

time value That portion of an option's premium that exceeds the intrinsic value. The time value of an option reflects the probability that the option will move into-the-money. Therefore, the longer the time remaining until expiration of the option, the greater its time value. Also called extrinsic value.

trade option A commodity option transaction in which the purchaser is reasonably believed by the writer to be engaged in business involving use of that commodity or a related commodity.

trader (1) A merchant involved in cash commodities; (2) a professional speculator who trades for his own account and who typically holds exchange trading privileges.

trading facility A person or group of persons that provides a physical or electronic facility or system in which multiple participants have the ability to execute or trade agreements, contracts, or transactions by accepting bids and offers made by other participants in the facility or system.

trading floor A physical trading facility where traders make bids and offers via open outcry or the specialist system.

transaction The entry or liquidation of a trade.

transfer notice A term used on some exchanges to describe a notice of delivery. See retender.

Treasury bond (or T-bond) Long-term (more than ten years) obligation of the U.S. government that pay interest semiannually until it matures, at which time the principal and the final interest payment are paid to the investor.

trend The general direction, either upward or downward, in which prices have been moving.

trendline In charting, a line drawn across the bottom or top of a price chart indicating the direction or trend of price movement. If up, the trendline is called bullish; if down, it is called bearish.

U

unable All orders not filled by the end of a trading day are deemed "unable" and void, unless they are designated GTC (Good 'Til Canceled) or open.

uncovered option See naked option.

underlying commodity The cash commodity underlying a futures contract. Also, the commodity or futures contract on which a commodity option is based, and which must be accepted or delivered if the option is exercised.

V

variable price limit A price limit schedule, determined by an exchange, that permits variations above or below the normally allowable price movement for any one trading day.

vega Coefficient measuring the sensitivity of an option value to a change in volatility.

vertical spread Any of several types of option spread involving the simultaneous purchase and sale of options of the same class and expiration date but different strike prices, including bull vertical spreads, bear vertical spreads, back spreads, and front spreads. See horizontal spread and diagonal spread.

visible supply Usually refers to supplies of a commodity in licensed warehouses. Often includes floats and all other supplies "in sight" in producing areas. See invisible supply.

volatility A statistical measurement of the rate of price change of a futures contract, security, or other instrument underlying an option. See historical volatility, implied volatility.

volatility spread A delta-neutral option spread designed to speculate on changes in the volatility of the market rather than the direction of the market.

volatility trading Strategies designed to speculate on changes in the volatility of the market rather than the direction of the market.

volume of trade The number of contracts traded during a specified period of time. It may be quoted as the number of contracts traded or as the total of physical units, such as bales or bushels, pounds or dozens.

WXYZ

warrant An issuer-based product that gives the buyer the right, but not the obligation, to buy (in the case of a call) or to sell (in the case of a put) a stock or a commodity at a set price during a specified period.

wash sale See wash trading.

wash trading Entering into, or purporting to enter into, transactions to give the appearance that purchases and sales have been made, without incurring market risk or changing the trader's market position. The Commodity Exchange Act prohibits wash trading. Also called round trip trading, wash sales.

writer The issuer, grantor, or seller of an option contract.

**Most definitions were provided by the CFTC (U.S. Commodity Futures Trading Commission) and were obtained from www.CFTC.gov. There are a limited number of definitions that were not available from the CFTC.gov which we added.

Index

Press
FINANCIAL TIMES

In an increasingly competitive world, it is quality of thinking that gives an edge—an idea that opens new doors, a technique that solves a problem, or an insight that simply helps make sense of it all.

We work with leading authors in the various arenas of business and finance to bring cutting-edge thinking and best-learning practices to a global market.

It is our goal to create world-class print publications and electronic products that give readers knowledge and understanding that can then be applied, whether studying or at work.

To find out more about our business products, you can visit us at www.ftpress.com.